LEARNING DISABILITIES AND ADHD

A Family Guide to Living and Learning Together

Betty B. Osman, Ph.D.

A ROBERT L. BERNSTEIN BOOK

John Wiley & Sons, Inc.

New York • Chichester • Weinheim • Brisbane • Singapore • Toronto

To the children and their families who
have taught me the meaning of courage.

Author's Note: The names of the children and other subjects in this book, as well as the names of family members, have been changed to protect their privacy.

Library of Congress Cataloging-in-Publication Data

Osman, Betty B.
    Learning disabilities and ADHD: a family guide to
living and learning together / Betty Osman.
       p. cm.
    Rev. ed. of: Learning disabilities. c1979.
    Includes bibliographical references (p.) and index.
    ISBN 0-471-15510-1 (pbk. : alk. paper)
    1. Learning disabilities. 2. Attention-deficit hyperactivity
disorder. 3. Learning disabled children—Education. 4. Attention-
deficit-disordered children—Education. I. Osman, Betty B.
Learning disabilities. II. Title.
LC4704.086   1997
371.92'6—dc21   97-1211

CONTENTS

LEARNING
DISABILITIES
AND ADHD

INTRODUCTION

I wrote this book primarily for parents who are concerned about their children and their children's learning. The priority placed on education today, and the competitiveness for success, have made parents more aware than ever of their children's development and progress in school. Yet too often, a mother's or father's expressed concerns are taken too lightly by professionals, dismissed as the "anxious parent" syndrome. But as parents, you are, after all, your children's first teachers, and you should trust your intuitions. You know your child and know what you see. It is the responsibility of educators to listen to you and provide you with the support and know-how to help your children survive in school and thrive at home. At the same time, it is your responsibility to learn enough to know if your child is receiving the appropriate help. In this book, I hope to provide you with the information you need to evaluate that.

But school is not the only area of concern. From the moment a parent becomes aware of his or her child's possible "developmental lag," attention deficit disorder, or learning disability, another dimension is added to the family system. While a youngster's problems may appear to be centered in school, they quickly become a family affair, with widespread repercussions. All family members must make many practical adjustments, including emotional ones, that reflect the goals and values of the family as a unit as well as the needs of its individual members.

My mission for this book is to help you as parents recognize when and where your child may have difficulty and suggest ways to make their lives easier at home and at school. When your child is content and functioning well, you (and your children's teachers) reap the rewards. Life at home should be more harmonious, and you will know you have been successful in your effort to help. The premise of this book, then, is

1

that with information and insight, you'll gain understanding, acceptance, and the ability to help your child.

I wrote the original edition of this book fifteen years ago, and my mission remains the same today. However, more information about learning disabilities and attention deficit disorders is now available. Parents are also better informed and perhaps even more involved with their children's education than they were a decade ago. And recent research techniques have produced advanced educational, medical, and psychological treatment methods. This edition will reflect the progress and advances made in these fields.

In writing this new edition, I have had the continued support of both family and colleagues, for which I am deeply grateful. My husband, Al, encouraged me to tell this story, often at the sacrifice of time spent with him and our family. To him and our children, I owe a debt of gratitude that cannot be measured.

This book could not have been written without my close friend and colleague, Henriette Blinder, who gave so generously of her time, expertise, and encouragement. I am more appreciative of her ideas, her editing, and her assistance than can possibly be expressed. I also give special thanks to Judith McCarthy, my editor, for her patience, wisdom, and guidance, and to all the families and children with whom I have worked for providing me with their stories and the material for this book.

1

EARLY SIGNS AND SYMPTOMS OF LEARNING DISABILITIES

Though almost a year old, Jimmy doesn't sleep through the night and seems restless and more active than his sister was at that age. Five-year-old Betsy doesn't like kindergarten and can't seem to remember the names of her teacher or her classmates. Billy is four and hasn't learned to name colors or to count past five. Johnny's second grade teacher complains that he can't sit still long enough to listen to instructions or complete an assigned task. Michael, eleven years old, never reads unless forced to, and fourteen-year-old Sarah is barely passing ninth grade. Are these children of normal ability merely "immature," or are they showing symptoms of Attention Deficit Disorder or learning disabilities?

How do we as parents handle a child like Richard when, at ten years of age, any denial of his wants can trigger a temper tantrum? And how do we answer when the family asks why, at age eight, Jennifer is having such trouble learning to read? These and many more questions might occur to you as your children grow and develop. Frequently, I find that parents don't know whom to ask, and, more important, they lack confidence in their own judgment, particularly when it comes to evaluating their children's development and learning.

We hear so much these days about the importance of early diagnosis and treatment of learning disabilities, and yet Billy's preschool teacher suggests that his parents "wait and see" when she mentions his "immaturity" and "poor memory." And you might receive a similar wait and see from your family physician: "There's nothing wrong with Billy, and after all, he *is* only four. He'll catch up. Just give him time."

As Billy's parents, though, you are not so sure. You may have

3

many more questions but feel foolish asking them. You remember that Billy seemed cranky as an infant, he didn't babble as much or as early as his sisters, and he spoke later and with less clarity. He still can't play alone and demands constant attention. On the other hand, maybe he's just like his uncle, a bit absent-minded and not too good with words. So you are reassured for a while. After all, he can catch and throw a ball better than Evan next door, and his temper tantrums do seem to be diminishing.

However, in the fall, Billy's kindergarten teacher notes that he is easily distracted and has trouble expressing himself. He can't seem to think of the right words when he tries to relate an event, and he gets frustrated when his classmates interrupt him. Is Billy simply immature, or does he have a learning disability? What should you do?

WHAT IS A LEARNING DISABILITY?

"Learning disability," or LD, has become a familiar term for parents, as has Attention Deficit Disorder, or ADD.* But children with problems in school have been with us for centuries. Some eminent people have found learning difficult: Thomas Alva Edison, Albert Einstein, and Hans Christian Andersen, to name only a few. In the past several years, some prominent men and women have candidly discussed their learning problems in the media: actors Cher and Tom Cruise, car racer Jackie Stewart, and stockbroker Charles Schwab are a few who have shared their stories. How they were treated, however, depended on when and where they lived and upon who pronounced their diagnosis.

Even today, a classroom teacher, psychologist, neurologist, or concerned grandparent may each have a different view of the same child. Each will see the child from the perspective of his or her own experience and expertise. Many parents know this all too well, having sought opinions and advice from many along the diagnostic trail. As an example, you might recall the class clown in your eighth grade homeroom. He was also, incidentally, the poorest reader in the class, but you never made the connection. Looking back on it, perhaps he had a learning disability or an attention deficit disorder. Teachers might have called

---

*Although Attention-Deficit/Hyperactivity Disorder (ADHD) is now the official designation, ADD is still accepted. Therefore, both terms will be used in this book.

him lazy, unmotivated, emotionally disturbed, dyslexic, or perceptually handicapped, while a classmate might have said that he was just plain "dumb" or "hyper." Sometimes, when learning is hard and a child feels unsuccessful and stupid, he'll do anything for attention and peer acceptance. As one boy expressed it many years later, "It was worth getting kicked out of class to be noticed. I hated school anyway and I had to do something to get friends."

But what exactly *is* a learning disability? Although the definition and criteria continue to be debated, the term is currently used to describe a handicapping condition that interferes with the ability to store, process, or produce desired information. The federal government defines learning disabilities in Public Law 94–142, as amended by Public Law 101–476 (Individuals with Disabilities Education Act—IDEA), as follows:

> Specific learning disability means a disorder in one or more of the basic psychological processes involved in understanding or in using language, spoken or written, which may manifest itself in an imperfect ability to listen, think, speak, read, write, spell, or to do mathematical calculations. The term includes such conditions as perceptual handicaps, brain injury, minimal brain dysfunction, dyslexia, and developmental aphasia. The term does not include children who have problems that are primarily the result of visual, hearing, or motor disabilities, or mental retardation, emotional disturbance, or of environmental, cultural, or economic disadvantage. (United States Office of Education, 1977, Federal Register, 42:250 p. 65083. Washington, D.C.: U.S. Government Printing Office.)

A child unable to learn in a poor or restrictive educational situation, for example, does not necessarily have a learning disability; rather, that youngster has an "environmental disadvantage." The same might be said of a child living in substandard conditions who is malnourished and lacks educational support.

In a more recent report (1987) to Congress, the Interagency Committee on Learning Disabilities defined learning disabilities as

> a heterogeneous group of disorders manifested by significant difficulties in acquisition and use of listening, speaking, reading, writing, reasoning, or mathematical abilities, or of social

skills. These disorders are intrinsic to the individual and presumed to be due to central nervous dysfunction. Even though a learning disability may occur concomitantly with other handicapping conditions (e.g., sensory impairment, mental retardation, social and emotional disturbance), with socioenvironmental influences (e.g., cultural differences, insufficient or inappropriate instruction, psychogenic factors), and especially attention deficit disorder, all of which may cause learning problems, a learning disability is not the direct result of those conditions or influences. (*Learning Disabilities: A Report to the U.S. Congress.* Bethesda, MD: National Institutes of Health, p. 222.)

As defined today, then, learning disabilities typically affect one or more of five general areas:

1. Spoken language—difficulty in listening, comprehending, or speaking
2. Written language—difficulty in reading, writing, or spelling
3. Arithmetic—difficulty in understanding numbers concepts or performing mathematical operations
4. Reasoning—difficulty in organizing and integrating thoughts
5. Memory—difficulty in recalling information

Several years ago, a federal interagency committee appointed to study current research and future needs in the field of learning disabilities recommended that social disabilities should also be included in the definition. This was not actually accomplished, but the prevalence of social difficulties in association with learning disabilities has become widely accepted.

ATTENTION-DEFICIT/HYPERACTIVITY DISORDER

Attention Deficit Disorder (ADD), or Attention-Deficit/Hyperactivity Disorder (ADHD) as it is called today, is quickly becoming the most frequently diagnosed problem of childhood. According to the DSM-IV, the *Diagnostic and Statistical Manual of Mental Disorders*, 4th Ed., published by the American Psychiatric Association (1994), the criteria for the designation of ADHD include symptoms associated with inattention and hyperactivity–impulsivity. Like learning disabilities, ADD is considered to have a neurophysiological basis. Unlike learning disabilities, ADD reflects an inability to selectively focus and maintain attention, rather than deficiencies in information processing. While attentional problems frequently interfere with a child's learning in school, they do not necessarily signify a learning disability, according to the criteria. Many children do have both LD and ADD, but not necessarily. The overlap is high, though, with estimates ranging from 30 to 80 percent.

To be considered ADHD, the symptoms must be present before the age of seven years, persist for at least six months, and be inconsistent with a child's developmental level. They also must be observable in at least two settings (e.g., at school and at home), with "evidence of significant impairment in social, academic, or occupational functioning." Lastly, the symptoms are not better accounted for by another mental disorder (e.g., mood disorder or anxiety disorder).

Three types of Attention-Deficit/Hyperactivity Disorder are specified in the manual:

1. Attention-Deficit/Hyperactivity Disorder, Combined Type
2. Attention-Deficit/Hyperactivity Disorder, Predominantly Inattentive Type
3. Attention-Deficit/Hyperactivity Disorder, Predominantly Hyperactive–Impulsive Type

The diagnostic criteria as specified in the manual are reprinted in Appendix C, pages 201–202.

Children with the first type of ADHD, Combined Type, are the easiest to spot. They have difficulty paying attention to tasks or play activities, are easily distracted, and tend to lose not only their favorite possessions but important school assignments and books. In addition, they are volatile, impulsive, and "always on the go," unable to engage quietly in leisure activities such as puzzles or reading books.

Children with the second type of ADHD, Predominantly Inattentive Type, are viewed as "space cadets" in the classroom and/or on the ball field. They may not be noticed by their teachers because they are quiet and unobtrusive, but they simply "aren't there." They watch the butterflies on the soccer field instead of the ball and frequently appear to be lost in thought. They don't listen when spoken to, and they can't seem to follow through on instructions or projects. Complaints about their disorganization and forgetfulness are myriad.

Youngsters of the third type, the Predominantly Hyperactive–Impulsive Type, tend to be overly energetic, racing everywhere and "leaping before they look." In spite of this, though, and to everyone's surprise, they frequently are able to pay attention in class and do seem to learn, even when they don't appear to be listening.

Parents may detect signs of an attention disorder in their toddler long before the child enters school. For example, as a four-year-old, John's son already displayed signs of hyperactivity. He darted off during a meal or a game and couldn't seem to focus on anything for more than a second. Because children mature at different rates and are different in temperament, personality, and energy level, it is sometimes difficult to determine whether a child has an attention deficit, is simply immature, or is just exuberant.

Adults as well as children may suffer from these disorders, which cut across all socioeconomic levels and cultures. In fact, many parents, undiagnosed as children, recognize their own attention deficits only when their children are diagnosed. Perhaps the defining characteristic of both ADHD and learning differences, though, is a significant difference between one's overall ability and one's day-to-day performance, at home, at school, or at work.

Of course, it is important to remember that few children or adults learn or behave in precisely the same way or at the same chronological age. We all have strengths and weaknesses that are reflected in our ability to learn and process information. As Howard Gardner pointed out in his book *Multiple Intelligences*, we have several intelligences rather than just one level of intellectual functioning. Gardner listed seven types: linguistic, logical–mathematical, spatial, musical, bodily kinesthetic, interpersonal, and intrapersonal. For example, a child may perform well in music and athletics but have difficulty learning logical–mathematical skills. It is our abilities—skills that we *do* have—that determine whether we can successfully complete a task.

"Learning disability," then, may be an unfortunate term because it places too much emphasis on what a person *cannot* do. It might be more productive to focus our attention on those areas in which a child *is* ready to learn. With the recognition that most children can indeed learn, albeit more slowly or differently from their classmates, we might more aptly think of learning *differences* rather than disabilities. So, in this book I will be using the term "learning difference" in addition to "learning disability," the official term recognized by the federal government, which provides the funding for diagnosis and treatment.

HOW CAN I TELL IF MY CHILD HAS A LEARNING DIFFERENCE AND/OR ADHD?

Just as one swallow doesn't make a summer, no single pattern of behavior identifies a child as having a learning difficulty. In fact, there is no easily identifiable group of characteristics that identify a learning difference. If we speak of children with LD or ADHD, we must be aware of the vast differences that exist among them. What these children tend to have in common is the effect that their problems have on themselves and their families. Although the focus of a learning difference is usually in school, its consequences are rarely confined to the classroom. Many areas of a child's life are affected, including his role in the family, his relationship with friends, his ability to excel in sports, and surely his self-image and confidence in his ability to handle situations.

The diversity of children with learning problems can make it hard for parents and teachers to recognize them. For the sake of convenience, however, we can look at three general areas that encompass some of the symptoms of what might signify a learning difference:

1. Language and concept development
2. Perceptual skills
3. Attentional and behavioral problems

Of course, few, if any, children fit neatly into any one group. Also, problems in these areas may simply indicate that a child is immature or has a unique developmental style. Looking at the symptoms in each category is like reading a Chinese menu, where you take one from column A and one from column B. For the moment, though, let's look at some of the signs and symptoms you might see in your young child at risk for LD and/or ADHD.

Language Problems

Difficulties in the area of what professionals call "linguistic intelligence," in other words, language skills, are an early indicator of a "child at risk" (a term you might hear from your pediatrician or family doctor). When language is significantly delayed or remains immature for a prolonged period, it may signify that the child is having difficulty understanding, processing, or expressing spoken language. In a child of school age this is sometimes referred to as a "specific language disability."

Children with language problems frequently seem less mature than their peers. They may not comprehend much of what is said to them and may even appear deaf to their worried parents. Many a parent has come to me thinking that his or her child might be retarded because the child always asked, "What?", particularly when told to do something. This may mean "I don't want to" or it may have to do with a "receptive language problem," that is, a difficulty in understanding and processing what is said.

Other children who hear and understand adequately may have trouble expressing their ideas. Still others may have trouble recalling names of objects such as toys and even names of colors, although they can recognize them. In trying to tell me how the popcorn burned at school, Peter, age five, said, "When my . . . you know, the lady at school [teacher] put the . . . thing [pot] on the . . . that thing you cook on [stove] the . . . corn pop got . . . black."

Prepositions are also likely to be confused, and ideas sometimes get turned around. Jill, a seven-year-old, used to say, "Mommy, I want to sit with you in the back seat when you drive" and "I'm hot. I want my sweater on." A boy I treated looked bewildered when we read that beavers build their homes "near a bank." He knew the bank where his money was deposited after his birthday, but he didn't think beavers went there. He could not associate another meaning of the word "bank" until it was explained to him. Jeff, at thirteen, couldn't pronounce the word "magnification"; it kept coming out "magnicifation," no matter how hard he tried to say it correctly. He also told me proudly that his science class was "getting into disintegration" of a frog on Monday. Of course, I understood that he meant "dissection," but had he said that to a peer, he might have been ridiculed. Difficulties with language, then, may affect a child's speech and later reading, spelling, and written expression, such important skills in school.

Of course, inadequate language development may not signify a learning difference at all. It can mean many other things, ranging from simple immaturity to retardation or emotional problems. Often, even an experienced clinician cannot determine whether a preschooler's behavior can be attributed to immaturity, a learning difference, or an emotional disorder. Then, too, a chronic ear infection (otitis media) is known to affect language development. Fluid in the ear causes a temporary hearing loss at an age when the child is learning to associate sounds with meaning. This can result in a delay in the onset of speech or an articulation problem.

It is not always possible to answer the broader question "Does my preschooler have a language problem that will persist in the future?" This is not always predictable. Although you are understandably concerned about the future, you might better focus on where your child is now in terms of her development. Observe her language carefully. It may be hard to acknowledge that she is immature in some areas, but once you recognize any difficulty, you can try to enrich her environment and help her along. If her concepts or use of language don't seem up to par, for example, you might seek a consultation with a language specialist or you may be able to help her on your own. Try reading and talking frequently to your young child to help her build an understanding of language and the idea that words are used to communicate. Encourage her to ask questions and express her thoughts. This will build a sense of competence as well as verbal fluency.

Two children with early indications of language difficulties come to mind. One was Jeremy, the youngest of five children. His language problems were reflected in the way he pronounced words and expressed his ideas. He was not quite five when I first saw him, but he had attended day care for two years. He was an independent little boy, very advanced in manipulating objects. He could dress himself, write his name, copy geometric shapes, and do puzzles with ease. Jeremy's mother told me that he had started to speak at approximately two years of age, but his speech remained indistinct and rather garbled. He was hard to understand, with babyish articulation and misuse of words. He said "big" when he meant "little" and "her" for "she" as the subject of a sentence, as in "Her was reading a book." He also had difficulty naming objects, although his concepts seemed appropriate for his age. He said once that windowpanes were made of "ice," which indicated to me that he grasped the concept. But it often seemed to require too much effort for Jeremy to express his thoughts verbally. At such moments, he'd try to say what was on his mind, then give up in frustration, saying, "Oh, nebber mind." Perhaps related to the difficulties he had communicating, he seemed immature socially. The children in his group tended to refer to him as a "baby," which invariably brought tears and howls of frustration from Jeremy.

Jeremy's mother wondered if perhaps he "didn't have to speak" because of his position in the family. His older brothers and sisters, who adored him, gave him whatever he wanted, but at the same time never gave him a chance to talk. His mother was aware of Jeremy's need to express himself and asked his siblings to give him that opportunity—at his own pace. I supported that idea, but I also suggested that the family not wait too long for Jeremy to struggle to find a word, but rather to supply it, so he wouldn't be so frustrated. It was painful to see him so angry when he couldn't think of a word. Although he sometimes resisted their help, their patience and occasional contributions made his conversation seem more natural, fluent, and surely more functional. I also recommended that Jeremy remain in a preschool program for an additional year before going on to kindergarten. His parents and I met with his teacher, who agreed that the emphasis should be on language development and social learning in preparation for his going to the "big school" the following year. In accordance with current legislation, Jeremy would qualify for the services of a language therapist provided by the district.

Danny, another four-year-old, showed early symptoms of language problems that were very different from Jeremy's. He came for an appointment with me after his mother had a conference with his nursery school teacher. She was an astute young woman who reported that Danny was having trouble following directions and keeping up with the class. "He can't seem to remember anything I tell him. He echoes what is said, but seems to be on another planet. He gets into trouble because he's so impulsive and unfocused."

His parents described Danny, the younger of two boys in his family, as a "loving and lovable child," but very hard to be with. His mother said, "He can't seem to entertain himself, even for five minutes, and always demands our time and attention." She remembered that Danny started talking much later than his brother Robert, but then, she had had less time to spend "doing constructive things" with him and "perhaps he watched too much TV." Both parents agreed that Danny talked constantly, but often rambled, losing his train of thought. A few additional observations were the following:

- "Sometimes he ignores you or doesn't seem to hear. Maybe he's just being obstinate."
- "He has a tendency to say 'chickendary' for 'dictionary.' " His mother said she thought this was cute, though, and didn't correct it.
- "He sometimes tunes you out . . . particularly when watching TV. He can sit for hours in front of the 'tube,' but otherwise has the attention span of a flea."

- "He hates loud noises and puts his hands over his ears when he hears the vacuum cleaner or his brother singing in the car."

Danny's selective tuning out, his short attention span, his absorption in TV, and his hypersensitivity to noise are fairly common symptoms associated with ADHD, which often accompanies developmental learning problems. (Some youngsters are also hypersensitive to texture and touch.) Whereas Jeremy seemed the prototype of a young child at risk for learning disabilities, Danny's behavior was more like an ADHD child, but both had specific language disabilities. Jeremy's and Danny's stories are typical, not only because of some of the early signs and symptoms but also because of their parents' responses to those signs. I don't know what eventually happened to Jeremy or Danny, but without the early interventions they had, it is probable that they would have had difficulty when they entered school. Studies have shown that addressing children's needs early, particularly in the area of language, can prevent or at least ameliorate school problems.

Perceptual Skills

In contrast to children like Jeremy and Danny, who have trouble early on, are those talkative, highly verbal children whom everyone expects to be star performers. Their sophistication with words might mask learning differences involving perception, that is, how they understand and process information coming in through their senses. We see with our eyes, but we process and understand what we see with our minds. We are all familiar with the sight of parallel railroad tracks that appear to meet in the distance. No one would venture to board a train if our brains didn't assure us that our eyes were playing tricks on us; those rails really don't come together—it's just perspective, an optical illusion. If we were not able to perceive what we hear, see, taste, smell, and touch, and to learn from our perceptions, each experience would be a first. We would have to learn that a chair is a chair each time we see one, and we'd be hard put to get through a day's activities.

A child's first point of reference in the world around him is his own body. He learns "up," "down," "big," "tall," and "front" and "back" in terms of himself. We've all seen babies who back away from a toy they are trying to reach when they first learn to crawl. They have misperceived the direction in which they should move. It is also hard for a toddler to catch a ball because his hands and eyes don't coordinate and he can't judge precisely where the ball is in relation to himself.

Some young children seem particularly clumsy. They trip over their own feet more than others, spill their milk too often, and fall off chairs. In addition to immature physical coordination, this may be a sign of poor spatial judgment. While such difficulties will not necessarily affect reading later on, they may lead to weaker math and geometry skills, as well as poor athletic performance. The school years can be a long struggle for these children. Barry, who is nine, has problems judging space and direction. His mother told me that with much practice and effort, Barry finally learned to hit a baseball, but then he asked innocently, "Where are the bases and which way is first?" He simply didn't know which way to run. His mother was laughing, but with tears of empathy for her son, who mirrored some of her own early perceptual problems.

I have actually taken children outside and practiced catching, hitting, and throwing a ball. Youngsters who might be embarrassed to get up to bat in front of their classmates at school often feel more comfortable with someone who will not stand in judgment or be in a position to reject them for a team. Several self-proclaimed nonathletes in my practice have found sports enjoyable in the safe environment of my office. Jake, a lovely but poorly coordinated fourteen-year-old, even purchased his first mitt and asked his father to put up a basketball hoop.

The old adage about "Which do we see, the doughnut or the hole?" may be an apt description of how some youngsters with problems see things. They have trouble seeing the bird on the grass or the teddy bear on the shelf. Parents may report, "He can't find his favorite toy even if it's right under his nose." The print on a page may also be confusing; words tend to "move" when a child reads or may "look different" from sentence to sentence. Kenny, age eleven, used to say that the pages "glared" and the words "jumped all over the place." Robert, his classmate, looked totally confused working on a subtraction problem, commenting, "That's weird, a minute ago, the eight was on top!"

Even if perceived accurately, a word that some children learn on one page may be unrecognizable to them just a moment later. Older children may have trouble remembering over time, and this may be reflected in their misspelling of common words. "Uv" (of), "sed," and "cum" are good indicators of poor visual memory. Roger, a bright twelve-year-old, could "hear" the way words should be spelled, but he could not see in his mind how they should look. After spending a weekend on a farm in Long Island, he wrote the following for a school assignment:

I whent to Longe Isind and got to rid on a bot and fede hourses
and shas rabits. it was vere fun

We can decipher what Roger meant, but he'll never win any
spelling bees. He also has to cope with his teacher's reaction to his
"carelessness"—and to the low grade he'll probably receive.

Some educators have hypothesized that spelling difficulties are
increasing, because of the abandonment of phonics in the reading curriculum. In recent years, the Whole Language approach, which emphasizes literary content over word analysis, has been favored in many
school districts throughout the country. Some children need one teaching technique while others thrive on another. As I write this, there
seems to be a developing rapprochement between the two methods and
a better balance in reading programs, with the recognition that phonics
is important, particularly in the early stages of reading.

Many children who perceive visual stimuli accurately and whose
hearing is within the normal range on a hearing test cannot make sense
out of what they hear. Roland, in third grade, heard a car honk outside.
He looked puzzled and asked, "What was that, a firecracker?" Most of
us wouldn't hesitate a moment before recognizing that sound and moving out of the car's path if one were heading toward us. With his difficulties, though, what would Roland do? On the other hand, some
children have such acute hearing that they are distracted by the sound
of a bicycle going by or even a leaf falling. This can seriously affect
their concentration in school.

Related to a child's ability to listen attentively are background
noises and other distractions. Many children complain that they can't
concentrate in class because "it's too noisy" and "the other kids bother
me." If you have ever tried to hold a serious conversation in a crowded
restaurant or at a large party, you can probably sympathize.

Some LD children seem to catch only small pieces of what is said,
although they do comprehend the literal meaning of the words. They
process language so slowly that they miss much of the message. A
tourist trying to understand a foreign language, or a moviegoer seeing a
foreign film, might have a similar problem. Although a few words or
phrases might be heard, most cannot be translated amid the barrage of
unintelligible sounds. For instance, you might ask your eight-year-old
daughter to "go upstairs, get dressed, and bring down a sweater to take
to school." She may have heard only the phrases "go upstairs" and "to
school," returning after a while still in her pajamas and empty-handed,
looking utterly confused. She is not being deliberately disobedient; she

simply cannot listen well enough. Incidentally, this is a skill that can develop with age and some careful handling by adults. Before accusing a child of being purposely deaf or ignoring you, it might help to speak more slowly and give fewer instructions at once.

Words that sound alike may also be easily confused by children who hear speech sounds imprecisely. Carrie thought her father said, "Your goat is dead," when in reality he had shouted, "You go to bed!" Only her horrified expression told her father he clearly had been misunderstood. "Deaf" and "death" also tend to be frequently interchanged in a child's communication, to the consternation of an adult listener.

Most young children associate some words incorrectly at one time or another, as my daughter Meg did, at age three, when she begged me to take her swimming in the "noise." After a great deal of frustration caused by my inability to understand her, I finally realized that Meg was referring to Long Island Sound, a body of water nearby. Another child assured me he had seen the "Monsters" play football at the Meadowlands the previous week. Of course, he was referring to the Giants football team.

To effectively retell a story or the essence of a TV sitcom, we have to recall it in sequence or order, which can sometimes be difficult to remember. Ordering sounds also presents problems for some children, who may continue to pronounce "aminal," "pisgetti," and "hopsital" long after this kind of reversal is usually outgrown. Some common effects of sequencing problems include difficulty with learning to tell time, naming the days of the week and months in order, reciting the alphabet, and counting numbers.

When a child in preschool or kindergarten avoids drawing, coloring, and cutting activities, it may indicate that she is having trouble working with her hands. This may show up again when she can't learn to tie shoes or to write legibly in school. I've received many referrals from observant teachers who have recognized that a fourth grader who participates actively in class discussions becomes immobilized when she has to put pencil to paper. Anthony, an eighth grader, had this kind of difficulty. He gave me an insightful oral review of *The Chariots of the Gods,* but he couldn't begin to write about it coherently. He never asked how to spell words and struggled to write each word as he heard it. When I was unable to decipher his report, which is reprinted here, I was embarrassed, but asked him to read it to me. What was worse, he couldn't make any sense of it either. He said "Wow! What I think and what I write are two different things."

Some children accurately perceive information that they see, hear, or feel, but become confused when they have to integrate the information that comes to them through separate senses. As parents, we're often puzzled by a child who can say the alphabet and recognize a "Q" when he sees one but can't remember how to write it. Dr. Martha Denckla, a prominent neurologist, called this the George Washington Bridge Syndrome. "Everything's fine in New York and all is well in New Jersey, but it's the George Washington connection that's awry."

Attention and Behavior Problems

Problems with attention and concentration may be present with or without learning disabilities, although they often occur together. Parents of children diagnosed with LD have reported that, even as infants, their children were "moody," "active," "restless," and "stubborn." As they grew, they were "always running," "exhausting but never exhausted," "impulsive," and "lacking in caution." Certainly there are inborn temperamental differences among children in their attention spans and degree of physical activity as well as in their timetable of maturation and development of self-control.

Many preschoolers can be quite wild, constantly exploring their surroundings rather than engaging in quieter activities. If their parents consult family friends, relatives, or physicians, they may be told to be patient; the child will grow out of it. About half the time this advice is correct—the difficult behaviors are transient and developmental. However, a large percentage of "difficult preschoolers" continue to display symptoms of inattention, hyperactivity, and impulsivity that today, after careful evaluation, would be diagnosed as ADHD, that is, Attention-Deficit/Hyperactivity Disorder.

Frequently, ADHD children have problems in school as well, attributable to their behavioral symptoms. Research has shown a significant overlap between ADHD and other disabilities, particularly learning disabilities, although learning disabilities may not be present. Two children come to mind: one a first grader, the other a child in kindergarten. Both are bright and good learners in their respective classrooms. But both have managed to alienate their classmates as well as frustrate their teachers. They lack inner controls, running wildly around the school and ignoring their teachers' directives. Even at their young ages, the boys are well known throughout the school as "problem children" because of their behavior.

The character of The Greeks

The Greek Theory is people once mourned The theory overaed Them will be 100 yrs from now.

They brought up alot of different things as you argu with alot The Pyramats with slash weigh a minum of a ton and They are Zngitalle as the whole thing there so many of Them mathmaticly over the years and no. of slaves They couldn't do This and The achive of Then was frantic

One of the main characteristics of ADHD is difficulty with concentration. A person may make careless mistakes in school or at work, lose things, and be easily distracted from a lesson or the task at hand. People with ADHD do not lack the intelligence to carry out tasks; rather, they have difficulty applying what they know, and their performance suffers. As indicated earlier, some, but not all, children with ADHD are hyperactive and impulsive. They fidget in class and are excessively restless; they may also be impatient and unable to wait, and they may interrupt others when they are speaking.

In addition to the variety of symptoms associated with ADHD, there are also gender differences. Boys tend to be more hyperactive, aggressive, and disruptive in class, undoubtedly accounting for the predominance of males identified as ADHD. Only recently have we begun to recognize more girls as ADHD, because they are generally not "acter-outers" but rather tend to internalize their difficulties. They withdraw and are more likely to be anxious than boys, who tend to be more aggressive and prone to conduct disorders.

When the possibility of an attention deficit disorder is mentioned to parents, they frequently reply, "That can't be the problem because he can watch TV by the hour." My antennae go up when I hear that. Children with ADHD can, indeed, focus on activities of interest to them, particularly if the tasks are not difficult. What they have trouble sustaining their attention on are intellectually challenging activities or chores they don't want to do, such as homework or the dishes.

Another complaint of parents is that their youngster is afraid of change and reluctant to try anything new. One child even cried when his father took a different route to my office. The child walked in complaining bitterly. After much discussion, he finally admitted that he was sure his father was lost, and he was frightened. With little confidence and security in his perception of the world, it is no wonder that he needed to rely on the familiar, the tried and true.

Transitions and unstructured periods in school are also known to be difficult for these youngsters. Lunchtime, recess, and free time may be their least favorite periods of the school day. That's when their social problems become most apparent and they get into trouble. Chris, a fourth grader, told me that he hates recess "cause there's nothing to do outside and all the kids are mean." He tends to pick on the younger children, and any friendships he makes are never smooth but are short lived, usually ending in a fight. His teacher attributed his social problems to his being "disruptive and annoying the other children." When I discussed this with Chris, he insisted, "But I don't do anything; they just don't like me."

Psychologists tend to think of these socially maladaptive behaviors as "emotional," to differentiate them from "learning" problems, but they often are part of the same underlying LD/ADD syndrome. Every aspect of a child's world can be unsteady when learning is hard.

Seth, the oldest child in his family, was born while his father, a pediatrician, was in the navy and away much of the time. His mother felt isolated in their new home away from relatives and friends, particularly since Seth had not been an easy baby since birth. He was high-strung, demanding, and exceptionally active. Eventually the family returned to their home state, where Seth started school.

Seth's behavior in kindergarten was a problem from the start, and he continued to be a challenge to his parents. By the time he was in second grade, his mother and father realized that most of the family tension stemmed from him. He was cranky, had increasingly severe temper tantrums, and was mean and aggressive toward his younger sisters. At school his teacher was frustrated, too. She told his parents that although Seth was obviously intelligent, he certainly was not learning what she was trying to teach. He was so fidgety and disruptive in class that the other children were beginning to reject him as well.

It seemed to Seth's parents that their son had emotional problems and this was the reason for his poor schoolwork. His father, realizing that the family needed help, called me for an appointment. In consultation, we decided that a psychoeducational evaluation was warranted for Seth. To begin the process, I interviewed Seth's parents to hear about the family and the boy's early history. Then I observed Seth in my office and in his school, and asked his parents and teachers to complete behavior rating scales. Assessment techniques followed, spread over a few sessions in my office.

My evaluation revealed that Seth was indeed a bright child, testing in the superior range on a standardized IQ test. His difficulties were not solely emotional, however. He was reading at a mid-first-grade level, approximately one year below his actual grade in school, but far below his native abilities. To add to his problems, most of his classmates were reading at third-grade level. They recognized words at sight that Seth was laboriously trying to sound out. And Seth also had problems with writing. His handwriting resembled the uneven scratches of a lame chicken limping across a page, and it was painful to watch him form even one shaky letter.

In contrast to his difficulties with reading and writing, Seth's fund of information and his ability to contribute to class discussions were superior—when he could pay attention. Usually, he found himself thinking of other things until his teacher yelled at him. All in all, school was not a happy or rewarding place for Seth—or for his teacher. Is it surprising that he was cranky and irritable when he came home?

Seth surely had a volatile temperament, typical of ADHD children, but perhaps his family's lack of understanding and impatience added to his unhappiness. Nevertheless, he did have a learning difference that undoubtedly contributed to his frustration and poor self-image. When he was helped to focus, with the aid of medication (Ritalin, in this case), and learned to read and write, his disposition improved, along with his social interactions.

WHAT CAUSES LEARNING DISABILITIES?

It is difficult to determine just what combination of factors causes LD. It is not uncommon for parents to assume responsibility for their children's every failure, and certainly for their problems in school. ("I must have done something wrong.") At the same time, parents may try to make excuses for children. ("Maybe he's been watching too much TV.") We tend to look for someone or something to blame and feel less anxious if we can identify the source of the trouble, even if it's ourselves. In most cases, though, a youngster's learning differences are no one's fault, and we are unable to pinpoint a precise cause. There may be numerous sources of difficulty. Usually there are many causal factors, biological and psychosocial, with a cluster of symptoms present. Sometimes we may just have to treat what we see, even without knowing the cause. This is difficult for parents and teachers to accept, but it is hard to be absolutely scientific when dealing with human behavior. Although newer technologies are being explored with promising results, we still don't have all the answers. With LD and ADHD, there are no bacteria to immunize against, and we can't remove the problem as if it were an inflamed appendix.

A rather irreverent story was told by a colleague of mine, an authority on learning disabilities who had attended a three-day conference. Many prominent people in the field were there. According to the agenda, the first day was to be spent defining terms such as "learning disabilities" and "ADHD." The second day's topic was diagnosis, and the third day was to be devoted to methods of treatment. "The first day," this man reported, "we were unable to agree on a single definition or term. We fared no better with diagnosis on the second day, but that didn't prevent us from arriving at appropriate modes of treatment on the third day."

Professionals have tried for years to identify specific causes of learning differences. Current research is focusing on anatomical differences in the brain, genetic factors, and biochemical deficiencies. All of these are yielding promising findings. For the present, though, the many factors that contribute to learning difficulties seem to interact and interrelate in the living, breathing child and cannot be specifically identified. However, I will mention some of the presumed causes that may, singly or in combination, contribute to learning differences.

1. *Intelligence.* Learning differences occur in all segments of the population, from the gifted to the retarded, but professionals tend to speak of learning disabilities only for children of average or above-average ability. Learning differences are not actually limited to this group, however. Children of all ranges of intelligence can have learning problems, even though the criteria are not met for an LD classification. If a child is mentally retarded, for example, his problems in school are not considered to be a learning disability. However, IQ per se is perhaps not as significant as once thought in contributing to specific learning disabilities.

   On the other hand, youngsters of superior ability who are just passing in school are showing evidence of underachievement and perhaps even a learning difference. They should be doing better. I have seen youngsters whose learning disabilities mask their giftedness, and vice versa. Tom, a ninth grader, was considered an "average student" who was "lazy." He rarely participated in class and never handed in written assignments on time. A diagnostic evaluation revealed that Tom was a highly gifted young man who was both bored and frustrated in school. He had a learning disability that made writing almost impossible for him—except on the computer. When we arranged for him to use a laptop computer in school and to work on projects that related to his interests and hobbies, his academic life changed. And so, too, did his parents' appreciation of their son.

According to many researchers, the most that intelligence does is to possibly limit the depth of understanding or the rate at which a person might learn. It does *not* predict how well or how much a child will or will not learn. Motivation, the quality of teaching, and family goals, among other factors, play a determining role. The way parents and teachers view a child also has an impact on his ability. I'll never forget the twenty-five-year-old man who told me so poignantly, "If my father had only told me I was smart instead of calling me stupid when I was growing up, who knows what I might have aspired to. . . ." We know from earlier studies that teachers' expectations can affect children's achievement in school. When supervisors in one study told teachers that children in their classes were capable and should do well during the year, the children achieved beyond anyone's expectations. However, when teachers were told that students in another class were "below average" and not much could be expected, the youngsters accomplished little. This occurred despite the fact that the makeup of the classes was similar. The implications for teaching, particularly in urban or economically deprived areas, are enormous. If we lower our expectations for students because of the environment in which they live, we may be encouraging failure through a self-fulfilling prophecy. Children need standards and expectations to fulfill their promise as learners.

2. *Sensory Deficits.* For children with learning disabilities, sensory deficits refer to deficiencies in the working of the child's eyes and ears, or in the central nervous system's connections to or from those organs. To hear music or see a beautiful sunrise, one must have healthy eyes and ears, but some people with 20/20 vision and perfect hearing might misinterpret sensory impressions because of a central nervous system dysfunction. In short, their brains give them the wrong messages. So-called perceptual training programs, popular years ago, were meant to address this but have not been found to improve learning. With some exceptions, there is little faith today that retraining sensory pathways will affect academic learning. Still, teaching young children to perceive and appreciate their surroundings is important. Little children need auditory and visual stimulation to prepare them for learning in school.

Just as each of us has his or her own learning style, so too does the youngster for whom learning is difficult. One child will remember a word on a page by picturing it in her mind, while another will mentally hear the sounds to form a meaningful association. Eventually, most of us learn, albeit unconsciously, to live with and compensate for our weaker areas. We use lists, date books, and memory hooks such as mnemonic devices to function in daily life. And if puzzles are frustrating for us, we can usually avoid them. Just as we can provide children with glasses to help them compensate for inadequate visual acuity, so too should we look for appropriate ways to help children compensate for their learning deficits.

3. *Activity Level and Attention Span.* The ability to focus and concentrate on a task, including sitting still when necessary, is an important prerequisite for learning: A child must attend to a lesson in order to learn the material. The much-discussed symptoms of attention deficit disorder—inattentiveness, impulsivity, and distractibility—clearly preclude this. However, to say that a youngster "can't pay attention" may not be an accurate description. More likely, he may be noticing *everything* in the environment—all at the same time. With the influx of stimuli, he is unable to disregard the irrelevant, so everything captures his attention, albeit briefly. However, not all children with ADHD have learning disabilities, even if they have problems in school.

The hyperactive child is usually easy to notice. He can sit for only a few minutes at a time and wiggles and fidgets even while sitting. I once saw a tiny tot, not more than a year and a half old, running barefoot a mile a minute through a department store, her exasperated father in tow. Her parents were trying in vain to buy shoes for her. I smiled sympathetically, commenting, "She's really quite active, isn't she?" The little girl's mother retorted, without hesitation, "*Hyperactive,* you mean!" She obviously knew whereof she spoke.

Young children are known to be active and impulsive and to have short attention spans. No one would expect a three- or four-year-old to sit quietly to listen to a discussion. However, a large percentage of difficult-to-manage preschoolers continue to display distractibility, overactivity, and impulsivity and eventually are labeled ADHD. Regardless of whether he is diagnosed, a preschooler who is constantly "on the go," rushing headlong into possibly dangerous situations, failing to listen to instructions, and demanding constant supervision, is stressful and exhausting for parents. And it doesn't necessarily get easier as the hyperactive child grows older.

Teachers, parents, and friends of the family tend to use the term hyperactive quite freely these days to describe a person's activity level. Actually, the term may be misleading. A child might be hyperactive but, then again, he might just be restless when he has to sit in school or merely "all boy." (Girls are rarely quite as "hyper" or disruptive as boys.)

In some situations, hyperactivity may reflect the judgment of the beholder even more than the child's behavior. It may be a question of "hyperactivity as compared with what?" Harry's mother complained that her son was hyperactive. To his preschool teachers, though, Harry did not seem overly active; he was simply more energetic and perhaps more curious than his older brother had been. The danger exists that some children may be perceived as ADHD by teachers who have a need for order and tranquility in their classrooms. Other teachers who are less structured might not view them this way. Charlie, who was considered disruptive in a "law and order" classroom, had no trouble when he was moved to a more open and less structured class. His new teacher didn't mind if he stood up to work, and she expected him to move from one station to another in the classroom to complete assignments.

4. *Genetic Factors.* A family history of learning disabilities and/or ADHD, including those of grandparents, aunts, uncles, and cousins, is sometimes a clue to a youngster's problems in school. I wish I had a nickel for every father of a child with learning differences who remembers having been a poor student or a troublemaker when he was young. Just as artistic talent and athletic ability seem to run in families, so do learning problems. Some researchers have attributed learning problems to specific genes, but these theories have not been substantiated to date.

5. *Prenatal, Birth, or Postnatal Trauma.* Prematurity, low birth weight for gestational age, anoxia (a lack of oxygen supply to the brain, either during or after birth), or a serious physical injury may significantly affect a child's ability to learn. In most cases, we can only speculate about the precise cause. It is important to remember, though, that many children with recognizable neurological impairment, such as cerebral palsy and seizure disorders, do learn extremely well. The relationship between organic impairment and

learning is far from clear. Why do some children with physical disabilities perform well academically, while others struggle in school? Multidisciplinary studies are currently being carried out in an effort to provide the answers.

6. *Immaturity or Maturational Lag.* Learning differences in the early years are most frequently attributed to a child's immaturity. Most often this is probably true. A youngster may just be developing more slowly than his peers *in some areas.* It is not the number of candles on a child's birthday cake, after all, that determines his readiness to learn, but rather his rate of development and level of maturity. If a child is physically small, is late to lose his baby teeth, and perhaps walks and talks somewhat later than his peers, we might well expect his learning to follow suit. But his problems are compounded if he enters school before he is ready to learn.

Parents and teachers respect individual differences among children, but only up to a point. No one worries if Johnny doesn't learn to swim at the same age as the boy next door or if he gets his permanent teeth after everyone else on the block, but we do expect Johnny to learn to read in first grade, and we tend to look for problems if he doesn't.

Some experts have suggested that a child's apparent learning differences are often the result of his being "overplaced" in school. In the early days of special education, theorists such as Arnold Gesell and Louise Ames, for example, recommended that the first course of treatment for a child should be an additional year in a grade. This is now considered a more complicated issue, which I'll discuss later in more detail. But, in short, the idea of retention is not met with much favor in many school districts. It is true, though, that fewer reading problems have been found to exist in Sweden, where children don't begin elementary school until the age of seven.

7. *Emotional Factors.* People have debated for years the significance of emotional factors in learning. Under what conditions do emotional problems cause learning difficulties? We all know many troubled children who are highly motivated to learn and succeed in school. Perhaps one of the most important reasons for others who fail in school lies in the key word *fear*—fear of trying and failing, fear of competing with an exceptional brother or sister, or even fear of growing up. An anxious child with a lot on her mind might not be able to concentrate on schoolwork. Lizzie, in third grade, told

me she was "too sad and scared" about her parents' fighting to worry about school. She also had no one to play with at recess and frequently walked around in tears. Lizzie's teacher had noticed her "depression" and inability to pay attention in school, but when she talked to Lizzie's parents it was clear that they were too preoccupied with their own problems to do much to help their daughter.

Too much emphasis on school and pressure on a child to achieve might have a negative effect. I'm reminded of Larry, who at fourteen complained that his parents thought only intellectual pursuits mattered. They were consumed with his education and insisted that his leisure time be spent "productively." That, in essence, meant reading. Larry's interest in and talent for sports earned no recognition at home, only jibes about his being "a jock." In his anger and sadness at not being accepted for himself, he tuned out at school and eventually failed most of his subjects.

A learning difference itself is likely to cause depression for a child who is failing in school. It would be an unusual young person who could withstand frustration and failure in school every day without feeling terrible. How could he possibly maintain his equanimity and good feeling about himself?

8. *Environmental Factors.* Negative environmental factors include neglect, abuse, malnutrition, and cultural deprivation. Children who are chronically mistreated or deprived at home cannot possibly perform well in school. When youngsters in urban areas are given a hot breakfast every day, their school achievement rises. Several researchers have demonstrated that intelligence, as measured by IQ tests, does too. Unfortunately, problems of homelessness and inadequate caregiving are painfully visible in many classrooms today.

Cultural deprivation is not confined to areas of poverty. Just because a child is well dressed or lives in the suburbs does not mean she is necessarily immune to neglect or cultural deprivation. Children who are left in the care of uneducated and perhaps disinterested guardians may suffer from a lack of experience with language as well as concepts. Lisa, age ten, tried hard not to care when she realized that her mother had to work while Lisa was on vacation from school. "At least I can watch TV all day," she said with a smile. Lisa's day might have been relaxing and carefree, but in all probability, this electronic "mother substitute" would not do much to promote learning.

9. *Educational Factors.* Inappropriate or inadequate teaching may also be a consideration in some children's learning problems, although this is obviously an unpopular idea with educators. Youngsters often seem to learn by osmosis, regardless of curriculum and teaching methods. But for some children, the quality and consistency of teaching are crucial. In addition to teaching style, materials accommodating cultural diversity are still lacking in many schools, and some children have a hard time relating to a curriculum that has little relationship to their lives. Educators are increasingly taking this into account, and newer curricula include materials more relevant to students from different cultures.

We expect teachers to know a great deal about the education of children with a variety of school problems. Under the guidelines of IDEA, the federal law mandating an appropriate education for all children "in the least restrictive environment," youngsters with a variety of handicapping conditions are increasingly placed in regular classes. Yet, in many states, prospective teachers are not required during their preservice training to take even one course in the teaching of children with special needs. Recently, more than thirty states have recommended such courses for teacher preparation programs, but their inclusion in the curriculum is voluntary.

Teachers may not fully understand how a child learns or how he may be helped to compensate for his learning problems. I counseled one teenager who reported that even with a huge file documenting his inability to spell and write throughout his school career, his tenth-grade English teacher still gave him an F on a paper written in class, with the following note written in red pencil: "Spelling is careless and your handwriting sloppy. This is unacceptable. Please rewrite." When Michael discussed this with her, she told him that she had deliberately *not* read his old school records so as "not to become prejudiced" in her judgment of him. While this is understandable, we do students no favor when we judge them in a vacuum. As important as it is to know their cultural and academic environments, so is it helpful for teachers to understand their special needs. Incidentally, if Michael had rewritten his paper, he probably would have made errors that hadn't appeared the first time. I tried to help his teacher understand that, whenever feasible, Michael needed to use a word processor for writing assignments.

Sometimes teachers may inadvertently espouse learning programs that complicate learning for some children with more than their share of problems. The popular Whole Language approach to reading, which works well for many students, may be an inappropriate choice for a child who can't remember what a word looks like, even after repeated exposures. Some children might lack the prerequisite skills for the instruction or concepts offered at a particular time. It may well be the child who is out of step, not the teacher, but this must be taken into account by the teacher. Individualized programs can be created to reinforce and strengthen skills. In addition, a child may need other resources such as tutoring or a compensatory program.

WHAT YOU CAN DO

Teachers, pediatricians, and parents may be reluctant to identify a learning problem in a young child because they fear the ramifications of labeling. Surely no one wants to categorize or pigeonhole a three- or four-year-old as having a learning disability or any other problem that might later show up as a blot on her school record or affect her self-esteem. We need to try to understand *why* a young child acts as he does, not for the purpose of labeling, but to facilitate change and improvement. Parents and teachers usually can do much to help a young child in areas of development in which she lags behind—without labels or stigmas.

None of the causes of learning differences or ADHD stands alone; several usually interact, affecting each child differently. No two young people are alike; each responds in a different way to similar conditions, and in turn invites very different reactions from parents and teachers.

As I mentioned before, we can't always know the origins of the problem. Professionals and parents need to communicate and collaborate to find a positive approach to helping a child who is struggling. A youngster with a learning difference needs special understanding from the supportive people in his life.

If you suspect that your young child might be at risk for learning or attentional difficulties, you might consider the following:

1. Discuss your concerns with your pediatrician or family physician. Some pediatricians may do an assessment for ADHD themselves, while others will refer you to a specialist they know and trust.

2. Obtain as accurate a family history as you can. Did other relatives have similar problems when they were young?

3. Ask day-care personnel or preschool teachers for their observations of your young child. If your child is already enrolled in elementary school, the teacher and/or school psychologist should be asked for their observations. Public schools are obligated to do a complete evaluation if you request it.

4. Make sure your expectations for your child are appropriate. Speak to professionals. You might find books in the library about child development and the changes to expect as a child grows.

5. Include members of your family in discussion and educational planning for your child.

6. Join a parent training class, where you can get support from the group while learning strategies for behavior management.

7. Seek professional advice if your child's problems persist and don't seem to be merely developmental in nature.

2

THE EFFECT ON THE FAMILY

Chances are that you're reading this book because your child has a learning disability, attention deficit disorder, or other problem, and you want to find out as much as you can about these subjects to improve your family life. Your memory of the fateful conference at which you heard this news may be very dim. Perhaps you weren't even sure what the professional was talking about. He might have said something like "Billy's having difficulty learning to read. . . . We might think about retaining him in first grade next year," or "Billy is so disruptive in class; I always see him sitting in the principal's office. . . ." You probably felt as if you had been kicked in the solar plexus, and the rest of the conference remains a blur. You may recall wanting to ask questions but were afraid you'd burst into tears. At the time, you had even forgotten about the vague worries you had about Billy when he was a preschooler, but now that others have observed his problems, you have to confront them. It is a painful time and hardly what you had envisioned when Billy started school in September.

THE LEARNING PROCESS FOR PARENTS

All too frequently, parents become aware of a child's problems only after he or she begins elementary school. You may have had some earlier suspicion that something was not quite right, but no one really talked about it until the difficulties at school became obvious. Many preschool teachers and pediatricians tend to be reluctant to talk with parents about a young child's problems because they feel that the child is merely "immature" and will do better next year. Why alarm parents needlessly?

Sometimes a child may even have reached third grade before parents are finally called to school. As an extreme example, I recently saw a girl whose learning problems weren't noticed until she was in seventh grade. She had great difficulty reading but had been fooling most of the people most of the time, and she had undoubtedly survived by her wits. She was a bright young girl who absorbed a great deal of information by listening attentively. She participated actively in class discussions and even wrote book reports on books she had never read. It is uncommon today, however, that difficulties in school are recognized so late. Indications of her reading problems—and the potential for remediation—were probably there long before her middle school years, but the earlier signs must have been ignored.

Many parents have described to me their initial reactions to hearing about their children's learning differences. Sometimes the feeling is one of relief because their suspicions are finally confirmed. But more often, the response to the news is amazement, shock, disbelief, and especially anger—at the teacher, the school, and particularly the child. In retrospect, many parents realize that this first "professional diagnosis" has even made them see their child differently. Suddenly the child appears less mature, less competent, and surely less successful than they had previously thought. Some parents have even said that their children "looked different," resembling for the first time that black sheep brother or other unsuccessful relative.

Accepting the idea of a child's special needs or school-related problem is an ongoing process and a painful learning experience for parents. It doesn't happen all at once during one conference at school or in a physician's office. Indeed, complete acceptance or understanding may not be possible at all. The feelings that emerge along the way are many and ever-changing, and they may be very different for each member of the family.

While feelings are quite varied and as individual as fingerprints, I have noticed that most parents go through similar emotional stages after being told of a child's learning difference. The feelings may even parallel the emotions experienced after a painful loss or the death of someone close. Maybe, in a sense, there *is* a loss—the loss of the ideal child for whom parents might have hoped.

THE EMOTIONAL RESPONSE

When a professional (physician, psychologist, teacher, or social worker) expresses concern about your child's learning or behavior, you may respond initially with disbelief or denial. "He always seemed so bright" or "She must be wrong" may be your thoughts. You might even shop around, hoping to find a professional who agrees with you. Then, later on, there is anger: "What does she know about my child?" or "It must be the way she's teaching her." At this time, parents may look with annoyance or even envy at Susie's friends who are more success-ful in school. "Why Susie?" or "Why is this happening to us?" are questions frequently asked. Typically, you might place the blame on your spouse, on the school, or even on Susie, for "not trying hard enough" or perhaps for being "lazy."

In time, as happens after a loss or separation, the anger gives way to feelings of resignation and finally acceptance. Now you and your spouse might say, "Susie does have a problem. What should we do?" Although you might have stormed out of that first conference, angry and upset with the authority who confronted you, you are now, weeks or months later, ready to accept advice and offers of help. That is when effective treatment can begin. Too often, a psychologist or educator ex-plains the problem to parents, senses their anger, and decides that they are "difficult people, impossible to work with." Having thus dismissed the parents, these professionals have, in effect, closed the door to future contacts.

You should not be intimidated by a professional who becomes impatient or critical of your feelings. It may not be easy, but don't hes-itate to ask more questions in an attempt to clarify your concerns. If you continue to feel frustrated, say, by a professional at your child's school, you may want to request a meeting with someone else in the school or seek a second opinion privately. You also have the right to ask that a report from the school be sent to an outside professional for interpretation. I have been a backup consultant for many parents who misunderstood or were confused by their initial contacts with a profes-sional.

Just as understanding learning differences is an ongoing process for parents, professionals must understand that parents may not "hear" the first explanation. It is our responsibility as professionals, then, to keep the lines of communication open so parents can return when they feel ready to hear the diagnosis, ask questions, and be helped to support their child.

The director of a clinic for children with learning disabilities told a professional audience that in a situation where the staff could not work successfully with parents, the clinic was reluctant to treat the child. She had apparently forgotten that the parents had voluntarily sought help in the first place. While it is certainly important to work with parents and caregivers in treating a child, it is not always possible. They may be un-available, fearful, or resistant, that is true. But sometimes what comes across to professionals as hostility or antagonism is really an expres-sion of the parents' frustration and anxiety. In time, this may abate and they will be more cooperative.

Your feelings about your child also influence the child's feelings about herself. Some of the loudest messages that children receive from their parents remain unspoken. Many children seem particularly tuned-in to moods or feelings around them. They know when their parents are upset and, conversely, when they can be depended upon for support and reassurance. Learning-disabled and ADHD children appear to be particularly vulnerable to family problems and stresses. They are also acutely aware of parental disappointment and frustration with them. Because it is not easy to live in a family with a child who requires enor-mous doses of time and attention, sisters and brothers also feel the ten-sion and react accordingly. Children's learning differences and other problems are, indeed, a family affair. Whether a family discusses the problems openly or keeps them a secret, everyone in the family re-sponds in some way to a child's difficulties.

BLAME AND RESENTMENT

Parents tend to blame themselves for their children's problems. A mother or father may think, "Maybe it's my fault. It must come from my side of the family" or "I don't spend enough time at home; I'm al-ways working." One young mother recalled her disappointment in her son. "He was clumsy, he didn't talk much, and he clung to me all the time. I felt that I had failed as a mother."

There also may be resentment between parents. One may feel that the other is responsible for the child's dysfunctions, particularly if the spouse being blamed also had problems as a child. I've often heard,

"He's just like his dad and his grandfather. Their sense of direction is pathetic. They couldn't find their way home from next door." While these feelings are not uncommon, personal attacks really don't solve much. Your spouse may be feeling guilty enough and doesn't need to be put down even more. In fact, if one parent has had similar problems, he or she may become the child's best ally.

I remember being on an airplane when a man sitting next to me asked about the book I was reading, which was about learning disabilities. He inquired as to my interest in the field, and then told me the story of his child. Robbie was the youngest of his three sons and a concern to his mother almost from birth, the man said. Robbie wasn't developing the way the others did, according to his mother, and "just didn't seem quite right." Robbie's father thought his wife was needlessly anxious and didn't hesitate to tell her so. He thought Robbie was simply spoiled and needed more discipline. By the time Robbie was in kindergarten, his parents were arguing about him, with mutual frustration and anger.

Finally, in November of Robbie's first-grade year, his teacher called. She told Robbie's parents that she was concerned about his "lack of readiness skills," and said that "the only thing he has finished since September is his lunch." She was recommending that he be evaluated at school to determine the nature of the problem. Results of the testing indicated that Robbie did have a learning disability, probably dyslexia. Remediation was subsequently implemented at school, and Robbie's father became his son's strongest ally and supporter. He realized that he had been too hard on the boy prior to understanding the problem.

This story illustrates that just as children need time to learn to walk and adjust to new situations, so, too, do fathers frequently need time to understand and accept a child's learning disability or difference. Perhaps it also suggests that a child's problems may, more frequently than we like to think, affect a parent's self-esteem. We know from studies that a child's imperfect physical or mental condition may threaten parents' feelings of competence and self-worth. Parents' frustration and sense of helplessness may trigger anger, which is then unwittingly expressed toward the child.

When parents struggle with guilt or anger, they often find it hard to talk about their feelings. I had seen eight-year-old Stefania for six months before I realized that her father didn't know she was coming for help. (I almost always meet both parents before seeing a young child, but this time was different.) Stefania's mother was unwilling to discuss her child's problem with anyone, even her husband. Stefania had been adopted in spite of some strong family opposition, and her mother could not admit that something might be wrong with her. Perhaps some part of her, too, felt that the adoption was a mistake. Weeks later, after a great deal of encouragement from me, she phoned, much relieved that she had told Stefania's father everything. To her surprise, he seemed to understand and was very willing to help.

DENIAL

Some parents don't feel any guilt or anger about a child's problems. They just don't seem to feel anything at all—or at least they think they don't. They dismiss problems as unimportant, if they ever acknowledge them at all. "So long as James is a good boy and gets along well with his friends on the ball field, we are satisfied." Sometimes this can actually work to a child's advantage. When he goes home after school, no one judges him by his reading. Because he is not constantly confronted with failure, home truly becomes a refuge and a haven. Although this sounds ideal, it may also mean that his difficulties are disregarded and therefore go untreated. Everyone takes the cue from his parents' denial; even the school may be afraid to rock the boat by mentioning any problems.

Two children come to mind: Klaus, an eight-year-old, had identified learning problems as well as ADHD. In fact, he was in a special education class and was taking Ritalin, which helped him focus in school. Nonetheless, he rarely interacted with other children and his solitary play was often violent. He "hung" toy figures, destroyed them, and on occasion could be heard talking to himself about death. When counselors and teachers mentioned these incidents to his mother, it was apparent that she did not want to hear about them. She brushed them off lightly or made excuses for his behavior. Finally, everyone seemed to get the hint, and Klaus's actions were no longer mentioned—until the day when he almost carried out his destructive fantasies by attacking another child. Suddenly everyone was mobilized, and appropriate action was taken.

Max was in sixth grade by the time his parents brought him to me for help, and then it was only because the school had insisted. In our initial meeting, Max's parents said they weren't sure if Max had a problem worthy of my attention, but the school apparently felt strongly that he did. Mr. and Mrs. J. described a well-functioning boy with perhaps "a few problems" in some academic areas. I began to feel that Max's teacher had exaggerated. When I finally met Max, I was more than surprised to find that although he could read, he could not write or spell even the words required of a fourth grader. His writing was almost illegible, and his math seemed below the level expected of a boy of his intelligence.

From the moment Max entered my office, it was evident that he would rather be anywhere else than with me. He looked sullen and unhappy. When I asked him why he had come for the appointment (often a revealing question), he replied that he had "no idea." I believed him, although I have met some young people who do know why they've come but refuse to admit it. Max did not seem to feel that he had a problem, and he certainly was less than enthusiastic about coming for help. He claimed to not care about schoolwork, anyway, and just wanted to be "left alone." I suggested that we meet three or four times, then we'd compare notes, telling each other what we thought about his need for help and whether I was the right person for the job.

That was three years ago, and Max and I still meet. I don't think Max's parents have fully accepted his difficulties, but they have come a long way. They are now reconciled to the fact that Max should enroll in a modified or slower math program in high school, and they are providing outside tutoring. As his parents have faced Max's problems, he, too, has accepted the reality. Recently, he told me that his counselor at school had asked him his view of learning disabilities. Max's answer was the following: "You can be a genius, but there are some areas you have trouble with. You should take the things that you are good at and excel in those to work around your disabilities. It takes work, but it's worth it."

DISAPPOINTMENT

Following the initial feelings of guilt and anger, disappointment and anxiety are perhaps the most universal feelings that parents have about their children's learning differences. Typically, they wonder whether their son or daughter will ever go to college or even complete the requirements for a high school diploma. This may be a particularly difficult time for an ambitious and successful father of a son. Accepting the fact that Jimmy may not be either "Harvard material" or first string on the football team may be more of a blow to Dad's pride than he realizes. How many thousands of Saturday-afternoon hours fathers spend trying to create young athletic stars from unable and unwilling candidates. Parents have wishes and fantasies about their children, and it is hard for them to accept their unrealized dreams when youngsters don't live up to those expectations.

NEIGHBORS

Acceptance by the family is hard enough, but the hurt may grow when the neighbors learn not only that Jimmy will not go to Harvard but also that he might even need special education services. The special treatment itself can become a stigma in the neighborhood. I have known children who have been discouraged from playing with a child because "he goes to a special school." The implication is that something must be really wrong with the child who has learning differences, and perhaps it's even contagious.

We profess to respect individual differences today, but our society rewards similarities. We expect our children to conform to community norms and to develop just like everyone else on the block. I've been told that in other countries, the extended family and neighbors provide more of a support system for special-needs children than we do in the United States. This means that the immediate family does not have to face the disappointment and pressures of raising a challenging child alone.

TOO-INVOLVED PARENTS

Some parents don't feel shame or resentment about their child's problems. They tend, instead, to focus their energies and optimism on their child's needs. Some, though, may go to extremes, making the child's learning difference a full-time career. A father I know made his son's problems the focal point of his life. He spent more time lobbying for programs in the school district and fund-raising for the special school John attended than he did at the office or at home with his family.

John's mother, too, not only spoke in public at every invitation and devised daily lessons for her son but also eventually became a tutor for other children when John no longer needed her services. While constructive for the cause and supportive for John, such efforts seemed to be out of proportion and detrimental to the marriage and the other children in the family, who clearly felt left out.

SIBLINGS

Siblings have very real problems when a brother or sister has ADHD, learning disabilities, and/or other disorders. All sorts of thoughts and emotions come into play. They may fear that their brother's problems are contagious and they'll "catch" them. They are also likely to hear arguments at home about their sibling's poor grades, current treatment, or being coddled too much. And if younger brothers and sisters are witness to their older sibling's resistance to reading and school, they may become frightened in anticipation of entering school or the next grade. One kindergartner, brought into my office for an evaluation because of "school reluctance," the new term for school phobia, had refused to go to school after the first week, saying that he hated school "because of the homework." When he was questioned, he admitted that he had not had any homework assigned yet but expected the boom to lower any day.

Occasionally, a sister or brother may feel guilty about her or his success in school. Achievement can then become both a responsibility and a burden. Such a child may sense the extent of his parents' investment in him and feel that their approval depends on the number of A's on his report card. And he may be almost right. Some parents rely too heavily on the successes of their other children to assuage their own feelings of inadequacy and their disappointment with the child who doesn't learn easily. On the other hand, parents may hardly mention the excellent report card to protect the LD child from the pain of comparison. You are best off trying to find a middle road. While you don't have to make a child's A's the big news of the week, neither should they be ignored. You might even say to your LD child, "It doesn't seem quite fair, does it? Some people are lucky—school is just easier for them."

On a deeper level, all siblings at times exhibit their dislike of a sister or brother. When that individual turns out to have a problem, the other may feel an enormous amount of guilt and anxiety. In a child's mind, wishes can create fact. That accounts for some of their fears, too. Many young children are convinced that they (or others) will be punished for their "bad" thoughts and angry feelings. They are unable to distinguish between fantasy and logical events. A seven-year-old girl, angry with her mother, knew exactly why she was afraid to go to sleep at night: "Because if a robber comes in and I'm awake, he'll tip-toe away, out of the house. But if I'm asleep, he'll go into my mother's room and kill her." I had to reassure her that nothing would happen to her mother simply because of her anger, no matter how angry she was.

Another poignant example of primitive thinking occurred during a blackout. A six-year-old was in big trouble with his mother for picking on his little brother. She had insisted that he be home at five o'clock as a form of punishment for his fraternal hostility. As he arrived at his front gate, he angrily kicked the telephone pole. At the same instant, the lights went out all over town. It was learned later that he felt personally responsible for having caused the darkness that had engulfed his neighborhood that evening, and he was waiting for his punishment to be meted out. When his mother became aware of this, she was able to reassure him that he was not being punished for his "angry feelings," only for his actions toward his brother. She made it clear that anger is a perfectly natural human emotion that is neither good nor bad. It is only how it is acted out that may be destructive and therefore forbidden.

A fifteen-year-old boy confessed to me that he did not want to grow up. He didn't look forward to birthdays and even forgot how old he was at times, claiming to be a year younger than his actual age. He was particularly worried about graduating from high school and going to work. The prospect of independence and a job terrified him. I understood his feelings more easily when I learned that his older brother had had severe problems in school, had been through a drug rehabilitation program, and was still living at home, unable to get a job. Little wonder my young friend was afraid to assume the responsibilities inherent in growing up.

OTHER RELATIVES

A young person's difficulties are likely to affect other relatives in a family, too. For grandparents living with or even near the family, the generation gap may seem to be ever-widening. One grandmother told me she felt like a fifth wheel, left out of any discussions about her grandson's problems in school. She never did understand why no one talked about them when she was there. Her grandson seemed all right to her, if somewhat overindulged, and she couldn't quite see the cause for all the concern. Her husband, a proud grandfather, had been the fourth generation in his family to go to a fine school in the West. He refused to believe that his grandson would, in all probability, not follow suit. Whenever he brought up the subject, the rest of the family cringed, but were unable (and perhaps unwilling) to tell him the truth and help him accept it.

THE LD CHILD

How does the child feel about his own problems and the response of others to him? In a word, different! If he's above the age of a toddler, he usually knows something is wrong long before anyone discusses it with his parents. He is likely to apply the vernacular of today's youth and call himself a "retard." He probably can't imagine why he can do some things, such as drawing and puzzles, while he struggles at school. Following a visit to the psychologist for an evaluation, one child said, "No one told me why they were giving me all those tests. I was scared she'd find out I was retarded."

Scared or not, a child knows when she can't read or spell; there-fore, she "knows" she's dumb. Other kids in her class agree and don't hesitate to tell her so. They call her "stupid" or "baby" and she believes them. She may feel isolated and alone with her problems. And she dismisses her parents' reassuring claims that she is *not* dumb. She knows all too well how she feels, and besides, "they're my parents." Occasionally, I have made a friendly wager with a child whom I know will eventually be a good student. I tell her that, impossible as it now seems, her teachers and classmates will one day recognize her abilities. I stand to lose a good deal of trust if I'm wrong, but I only bet when I'm sure.

Kevin was a nonreader when he moved from Tennessee and en-tered second grade. He was bright and inquisitive, and he excelled in math. As the year progressed, he became disenchanted with his new school and discouraged about his inability to read. Finally, he con-fessed that he hated school and *never* wanted to learn to read. I made a bet that someday he would even like to read when he didn't have to struggle so hard to do so. He didn't believe me at first; he was sure his dislike of school was forever. It takes a big man to admit he's wrong, but six months later, Kevin came into my office, saying in his lovely Tennessee drawl, "Dr. Osman, would you believe I'm beginnin' to like readin'?" I would indeed!

Incidentally, the more intelligent the child, the more intensely she is likely to feel the frustration of a learning difference. She can't understand why she can't perform as she knows she should. At six years old, Amy couldn't write her name or recall how to draw a triangle, although she could recognize and name both when she saw them. She used to stamp her foot in anger, crying, "I always forget it and I knowed it before." She needed a great deal of help to understand that remembering was hard, but that she could, with good instruction and a lot of effort on her part, learn how to learn and even master the things that seemed so challenging.

"No one understands me" must be the feeling many children have, particularly when no one talks to them about their problems. Children who have difficulty in school probably feel much the same as we would if traveling in a foreign country whose language was unfamiliar to us. We couldn't read the street signs or make sense of the words we hear or express ourselves easily to others. It is important for us to put ourselves in our children's shoes. Imagine trying to accomplish the tasks of everyday life without the skills we so easily take for granted.

THE IMPORTANCE OF COMMUNICATION

A child's feelings of isolation and inadequacy can only be dealt with if the lines of communication in the family are kept open. Openness is the key. Many families do not share their feelings or thoughts easily. Each individual keeps his feelings to himself, exchanging few words with the others in the course of a day. People talk only when things have to be done. "Do your homework." "Go to bed." "Hurry up, I'm leaving!" These kinds of remarks may be the only communication in the family. One father professed that he and his wife did not "know" his son at all. A special class placement in another school was under consideration, and when I asked the parents how their son felt about it, the father said, "I don't know. He keeps to himself and we never know what he's thinking." The parents acknowledged that they, too, were uncomfortable discussing feelings, particularly unpleasant ones, and probably had never encouraged their son to share his feelings with them. It was apparent that the adults in this child's world had failed to convey the idea that feelings are valid and that words exist to express them.

In other families, few subjects are taboo; almost nothing is off limits. There is a great deal of open discussion. Feelings are freely dispensed, and even the subject of death can be discussed. But a child's learning differences frequently remain under wraps, classified information. The parents may acknowledge this, saying that they don't want to call attention to their child's problems because "it will make her feel different." Again, I suspect this is more self-protection for parents than real help for the child. In all probability, the child feels different anyway, and her fantasies about her "difference" may be far worse than the reality.

I can usually tell quite early when a child's learning difference or attention deficit is a secret in the family. It's not unusual for me to extend an open invitation to a child to bring a sibling or friend to an occasional session. Many children love this and proudly show their buddies around the office, commenting, "This is the game I told you about, and here's where she keeps the snacks." Sometimes, though, a child will recoil at the idea of bringing someone along. She doesn't even want her friends to know where she goes on Wednesday afternoons, and she ducks if someone walks by. Some children desire secrecy even more than their parents, but in most instances, their attitudes reflect their parents' feelings about it and perhaps their sense of shame.

PARENTAL ROLES

All too often, parents' reactions to a child with problems reflect a house divided. From the start, parental roles and participation are likely to be different. First, a mother gives birth to an infant and seems almost clairvoyant about her child's early development. Although fathers today are assuming more caretaking responsibilities for children than in past generations, mothers still tend to be more "in charge" during the day, even if they work full time. Scheduling school conferences can be problematic for two working parents, and sometimes only one can attend. If the results can't be shared until late that night after the children are in bed, the impact may be lost. Both parents are tired by then and in no mood to discuss problems, so the matter may be dropped until it is forgotten.

One father I knew had unrealistic expectations for his son, refusing to believe that he couldn't achieve like everyone else. "He's smart; I know he could do it if he tried harder," he would say. He had convinced himself that Roger would catch up in high school, as he had. After all, he had had similar problems when he was young. The father had little patience with his wife's more realistic appraisal of their son and disparaged her efforts to help him. He accused her of "spoiling" Roger and being "overprotective." In fact, he resented the time she spent on Roger's homework and even suspected that she was contributing to his dependency and, therefore, to his disability as well. The resentment put an additional strain on the marital relationship and drove the father even further away from his son. It's possible that Roger's experiences reminded him of his own painful school years, and it was hard to relive them.

It is not unusual for fathers, in particular, to exclude themselves from their children's lives at school, particularly when there's a problem. They maintain the attitude that "Mother is in charge of school matters." Then Mother may have no choice but to assume the full responsibility for the child's education, even to the point of making all decisions—whether he should be evaluated, tutored, or placed in a special school or camp. She helps with homework and soon becomes his advocate and chief supporter. The mother/child alliance becomes stronger, and Father is excluded.

This doesn't have to happen. I have found that when a mother and the professionals involved take the time to include the child's father in the planning and carrying out of programs, he can be a most effective member of the team. And it is important to do so, not only to prevent early burnout for the mother but also because fathers' interventions often carry more weight at school. And when it comes to the legal aspects of procuring special services and programs, many fathers become instant lawyers for their children. Unfortunately, many school systems still tend to be chauvinistic, and men's opinions may be thought of as more objective, that is, less emotional, than their wives'. This is a bias that needs to be addressed.

Fathers do have a special role for their children with problems. First, they are important role models. A boy admires his father, whether or not his father is a good athlete and/or successful in his job. Similarly, a daughter is influenced by her father's interest in her, his attentions, and perhaps his career as well. Children need to know that they can become healthy adults in spite of their problems. A father's tacit acceptance makes this growth process easier and more comfortable for everyone. Conversely, fathers can all too easily make healthy growth impossible if they convey the message that their children are incompetent and unable to measure up to their expectations.

Fathers can also be involved directly with their children's education. Many fathers have a talent for helping with homework, while a mother may not. She may be tired and harassed by homework time or simply not have the skill. If a father can take a fresh look at his daughter's needs and be objective in his approach, there is much to be gained for both of them. However, fathers are apt to teach children more than they need or want to know, which can be hazardous. In general, the parent of choice for homework duty is the one who can be patient, realistic, and sensitive to the child's needs. My best advice is to look at who does what best and divide the educational chores accordingly.

Even when parents are divorced, the involvement of both parents in their child's schooling is important. If it's not comfortable to attend conferences at school together, a request can be made for separate meetings with teachers. I have known many families where, despite different lifestyles, both parents have taken an interest and active role in their child's education.

Recently, I invited some high school students to speak to a class of graduate students in special education. The teenage panelists were asked how they felt about their learning differences and what had been most helpful to them during their difficult years. One boy told the group how supportive his father had been while he struggled through school. He said he couldn't have made it without his father's understanding. A member of the audience later recalled how far this father had come in coping with his son's learning problems. When first told of the difficulty his son was having, when the child was in second grade, the father responded with denial and violent anger. Through the years, the boy's psychologist had helped him see how effective he could be in helping his son. He became an ardent supporter of the rights and programs for the learning-disabled children in his community and deeply involved with his own son. Their relationship went far beyond school and became mutually very rewarding.

Once parents recognize their child's problems and can acknowledge how they feel about them, they can alleviate a significant amount of the child's anxiety by talking to her as honestly as possible. Children need to know the truth in language they can understand. Try to relieve your child's guilt that arises from not feeling "smart" or not being the kind of person others would want her to be. With acceptance and support at home, your child can better face what may often appear to be a teasing or hostile world. She'll be reassured that her troubles can't be so terrible if they can be discussed, and she'll be less likely to invent frightening reasons for her differences. Young imaginations can run wild, and half-understood concepts can create demons. A child may also find unexpected allies in his brothers and sisters if they understand the true nature of their sibling's difficulties. The whole family will benefit from talking about this formerly taboo subject.

You must also tell your child what is *right* with her. There must always be something to praise. One part of a child's life—student, athlete, or artist—should not become all-important to anyone. After all, she is more than the sum of her weakest parts. To develop trust in others and faith in herself, she needs to know that someone cares about *all* of her, not just her learning or her actions in school.

3

IMPROVING LIFE AT HOME

"Jimmy, what is *taking* you so long? You're going to be late for the school bus again. I give up! Why can't you ever be on time?"

The time is eight o'clock on Tuesday morning, and everyone at the Millers' is angry at Jimmy. He woke up in a bad mood and nothing has gone right since. He's complaining that his pants don't fit right and he refuses to wear them. His mother was supposed to leave for work ten minutes ago, but now she has to take Jimmy and his older sister, Susan, to school on her way to work—and Jennie to day care. Susan is also angry with Jimmy. It's not her turn to walk the dog, but Jimmy hasn't done it. Mrs. Miller has been through this chaotic scene every weekday morning since school began in September, and nothing seems to change. Why is Jimmy always so irritable and irritating? Her frustration with him rises when she remembers that she didn't sleep last night because of him. He had come into her room again in the middle of the night, complaining that he was scared. He'd been doing that more often since the divorce, but "he should be over that by now," she thought. "Why does my ten-year-old demand so much time and attention—so much more than the other two?"

Upstairs, Jimmy is oblivious to the tension he's created below. He's still in his pajamas, but he did get out of bed. He's watching his goldfish chase each other around the bowl. He comes to with a start when he hears the urgency in his mother's voice, and he remembers unhappily that this is yet another school day. Where did his shoes go? They were here last night. And one leg of his pants is turned inside out, and he can't straighten it out. Now Mother is angry again. Why does this always happen to him? It's not fair!

Later that afternoon, Mrs. Miller is fixing dinner in the kitchen and Susan is trying to talk to a friend on the telephone. It's not easy when Jimmy screams at his little sister, Jennie, for merely entering his room.

Mother has a tense, grim expression on her face. She had a hard day at the office, and Jimmy hasn't made it any easier. He raided the refrigerator before she came home from work, spilling the orange juice, and then left the fridge open. A little while later, Mrs. Miller had to rescue the puppy from Jimmy's tight clutches. She had known from the moment he woke up this morning that this was going to be another of his bad days. Why do his difficult times affect the mood of the entire household? Susan put the situation in perspective when she said, "It sure is different around here when the brat is out of the house!"

Why is it that in so many homes, children with ADHD and/or learning differences seem to be the catalysts for tension and chaos? Some of the reasons undoubtedly lie within the children themselves. Their anxieties and unpredictable outbursts seem impossible to control. They dawdle, they're disorganized, and they often seem completely unaware of the consequences of their actions. They don't mean to squeeze the puppy too tightly or to push the glass pane out of the door. But these are all behaviors associated with their impulsivity. There's a children's book entitled *Alexander and the Terrible, Horrible, No Good, Very Bad Day,* and all too often this seems to be the story of these children's lives. I am also convinced that the hyperactive-impulsive ADHD child needs—and finds—stimulation. He isn't content when life around him is calm and, in the absence of chaos, he manages to create it.

Specialists have argued, and some research has shown, that the families of these children tend to be more chaotic and disorganized than other families—perhaps even before the child with the problem arrived on the scene. Some have said that the child only adds to family patterns already in existence. Which comes first is a moot point. In any case, the problems create a vicious cycle, with the youngster contributing to the tension in the family. The atmosphere at home augments the frustration with the child, who may, in fact, be held responsible for more chaos than even he could create.

At the Miller house, Jimmy's very presence seemed to charge the atmosphere in his family. Much of the arguing, teasing, and screaming revolved around him. His sisters resented him for it and let him know it. Jimmy became so accustomed to his role as family troublemaker that he accepted it and never expected anything to change. He was shocked when his mother suggested that they all come to me for family therapy to try to create a more harmonious atmosphere at home. She requested that his father be included as well, even though he lives apart.

THE NEED FOR CHANGE

Life at the Millers may seem all too familiar to many of you. But is this chaotic scenario really necessary? Can nothing be done to alleviate the tension and aggravation that exist? Perhaps aggravating behaviors are taken for granted, or maybe the status quo is so ingrained that the family fails to recognize the possibilities for improvement and change.

Admittedly, it is difficult to change habits of long-standing. Today, with two working parents in many families, single parents, and divorced families, it's even hard to find the time to plan and implement the desired changes. Too often, contact between family members is limited to passing one another in the kitchen on the way to and from work or school. And except for psychological counseling, which may be inaccessible because of scheduling or expense, parents receive little guidance in parenting their challenging children. They are expected to "do what comes naturally," but under the best of circumstances, this isn't easy. It's certainly more difficult when youngsters have problems.

ORGANIZATION

When the Millers came as a family for the first time, we talked about the situations that were most troubling to each of them. Everyone, including Jimmy, had issues of their own. From that discussion, we decided that perhaps the first priority for change had to do with the morning routine. Jimmy conceded that he sometimes needed more time to get dressed, eat breakfast, and get organized for school, much less complete his chores. Rather than his mother awakening him, we decided that Jimmy would have his own alarm clock, and he would get up a half hour earlier. Mother, of course, would be on hand to keep him moving. He would also lay out his own clothes the night before to prevent the indecisiveness in the morning that wasted so much time. And breakfast could be toast and a banana or some other finger food to eat on the way to school if he was rushed. His sister thought of a storage box near the door for their boots and schoolbooks, to be grabbed quickly on the way out.

In other words, if we know that Jimmy has a hard time organizing his belongings and his time, we have to structure his life from the outside. Realistically, his mother could not depend on him to get up, dress himself, feed his goldfish, make his bed, eat breakfast, and gather his belongings in time to leave for school. Therefore, she had to provide the order in his world until he could learn to manage it himself. Eventually, a checklist of tasks to be accomplished before school helped Jimmy become more independent, and he was thrilled not to have to be reminded every morning to wash his face and make his bed. Jimmy's job list is included here, but it could be changed to suit the needs of your family.

Parents sometimes refuse to help their children with organization, feeling that they must learn to be independent, to function on their own. "We mustn't baby him or he'll never dress himself," they say, or "He could do it if he tried." However, children with learning and/or behavioral problems can learn more efficiently from a good example than from criticism and/or punishment for what they did wrong. Psychologists of the behavioral school claim that punishment can actually serve to reinforce undesirable behavior. Establishing the habit of good organization by example and help will teach a child more than a string of verbal directives.

Many adults also need help with organizational skills. I knew a man with ADHD for whom organization was a major problem. His job after dinner was to empty the dishwasher, which he usually did, but not to his wife's liking. Bowls weren't stacked according to size, and sometimes she couldn't find the things he had put away. When she asked him to straighten a cupboard, in hopes that he would learn to organize, the project was doomed to failure. He procrastinated, knowing he couldn't do it the way his wife would want, and then he would be criticized. Finally, she did it with him to show him how. He may not have been a quick study, but he eventually caught on.

THE FAMILY SCAPEGOAT

The scientific axiom "For every action there is a reaction" applies to human beings as well as to physics. I am reminded of Henry, who at the age of eleven got attention at home and at school by being irritating and annoying. He interrupted every conversation, made peculiar noises when people were trying to read, and was a "hands-on" boy, always touching and bothering other children. No one took notice of him when

MY JOB LIST

	S	M	T	W	T	F	S
TAKING CARE OF MYSELF							
I brushed my teeth.							
I took my bath/shower.							
I dressed myself.							
I brushed my hair.							
I left for school on time.							
TAKING CARE OF MY ROOM							
I made my bed.							
I put away my clothes.							
I picked up my toys and other things.							
My room is neat.							
I HELP MY FAMILY							
I set the table.							
I emptied the dishwasher.							
I took out the garbage.							
I put my dishes in the sink.							
I did all my assigned chores.							
ABOUT SCHOOL							
I finished my work in school.							
I did my homework without arguing.							
I remembered my books and lunch money.							
I practiced my musical instrument.							

he was good—at least that's the way it seemed to him—so he made sure he was noticed. His need for recognition and attention seemed insatiable. His mother in turn became angry, then felt guilty because of her hostile feelings toward him, and the vicious cycle went on and on. Henry knew when his mother was upset with him, although he denied that it affected him. "It doesn't bother me when my mother cries," he said. "It just makes me yell at her more."

Finally, I helped Henry's mother see that she need not feel guilty; her anger was a natural reaction to an irritating situation. But Henry had to reconstruct his role in the family, learning that negative behavior would not pay off and that acceptable behavior could be more rewarding.

Henry happened to be the only child in his family with behavioral difficulties, but when more than one child has problems—and we know that learning disabilities as well as ADD seem to be inherited—the family situation is different. On the one hand, misery loves company, and mutual understanding and bonds may develop among the learning-disabled or ADHD children. No child stands out in the family as being different or "weird," and parents may be able to enforce a more uniform standard of expectations. Parents in one family with five learning-disabled children geared the pace and activities of family life to the capabilities of their children, so no one felt out of step.

I have no doubt that it requires a great deal of stamina and patience for parents to provide the support and guidance for one, let alone several, children with special needs. Parents can run out of steam and become less patient as additional children show signs of having problems. As one father groaned when his third child was diagnosed in kindergarten, "I'm too old to go through this again." He managed, however, and that daughter is now a teacher of LD children.

It can be another story when only one of several children in a family has a learning difference. In some families, the child with special needs unwillingly becomes the scapegoat, the target of everyone's frustration and hostility. A mother told me, "The other children in the family pick on Russell, but there isn't anything we can do about it. We tell them to stop, but nothing seems to work."

Russell was almost eleven, the middle child in his family and the only boy. His older sister admitted she thought he was "stupid" and told him so at every opportunity. Her parents agreed that she was hard on her brother, but they didn't know how to stop it. Russell's younger sister, who was only six, was a tease. She'd take his precious possessions and wouldn't give them back. Then, after Russell hit her, she'd yell and run to tell their mother. She knew very well what would happen. "You should know better," his parents would say as they meted out Russell's punishment. "She's just a baby."

Russell knew he was picked on more than his sisters, but told me it was because he always did "bad things." He had begun to accept the fact that he couldn't do anything right, and that when his sister called him "a retard," she wasn't far wrong. He used to deprecate himself aggressively, as if to beat her to the punch, saying "I'm dumb" or "I should be dead," which upset his family even more. Wistfully, Russell recalled that his happiest time at home was when his father woke him late at night to praise him for having such a good day.

Dinnertime wasn't fun for Russell either. He never seemed to know what anyone in the family was talking about, and when he asked a question, he was either ignored or scorned. Russell's dad confessed that his son annoyed him at the table because his remarks were "usually irrelevant or two topics behind." During one meal, his older sister complained about his table manners and the mess he made with his food. Then his mother chimed in, saying that his room was a wreck and she couldn't get in to clean it. Russell finally left the table, too upset to eat.

When a child is the scapegoat in a family, it is often with the unconscious consent of the parents. When this was brought up in a family session, Russell's parents were surprised to hear that he had become the full-fledged scapegoat, the foil for everyone's frustrations. Only Russell's father seemed slightly aware of the difficult time his son was having at home. Unconsciously, everyone in the family had chosen the weakest link in the chain—namely, Russell—to bear the brunt of their poorly understood anger. Unfortunately, persons with learning differences often seem to be particularly vulnerable to scapegoating as a consequence of their deficient coping skills and their weak self-image. It is a well-known tenet in family therapy, however, that the "identified patient" may not actually be the root of the problem. It was learned that there were other issues within Russell's family, that is, financial pressures and marital conflicts, that contributed to their anger.

Nonetheless, there can't be a victim without acquiescence and silent consent. Russell had to understand that he, too, had some responsibility for his role. His feeling of "I get what I deserve" had to change. His parents also had to take a fresh look at their relationship with Russell, because awareness is the beginning of change. I tried to help Russell's mother see that when she expected him to "act his age" in the face of his little sister's teasing, she was demanding more maturity than he was capable of. She was critical of him for getting down to his sister's level, but maybe that is really where he was. A child's learning difference frequently reflects a maturational lag in behavior as well as in learning, and Russell was probably close to the same maturity level, educationally and emotionally, as his six-year-old sister.

In our sessions together, Russell's parents began to gain a better understanding of the family dynamics and realized that their son needed more than just their understanding and passive acceptance. He needed their active support. We agreed on two strategies. First, the children would try to work out their own problems without interference—unless, of course, someone was about to get hurt. That precluded "tattling" designed to get each other in trouble. Second, Russell's mother or father would come to his defense only in battles where he might be overwhelmed or unable to contain himself.

We began to see—and talk about—progress. When Russell's mother scolded his sister for using Russell's Walkman without his permission, everyone was shocked. Russell told me he couldn't believe his ears. But even that wasn't enough. Part of the change had to come from Russell. He needed to learn to assert himself in a positive way rather than to strike back at his sisters. This was the most difficult change to accomplish. As I have said, a child's destructive patterns can become his way of gaining recognition and attention, even if it is the wrong kind. "It's better to be yelled at than never noticed at all" seems to be the philosophy of many children.

Actions speak louder than words. Merely explaining to children that they are behaving inappropriately at home probably will not promote change. Chances are they won't even know what their parents are talking about. On the other hand, rewarding honest effort with recognition and praise is a far better way to effect change. Occasionally, when this technique is suggested, a parent will say, "I tried that once, but it didn't work." Granted, it will take more than one try for a child to unlearn inappropriate behavior. It took years to learn it, and there's no shortcut to changing old ways. We can't expect magic, but if we begin with small expectations and see one small change in behavior, the child will see that success is attainable. For example, if he comes home on time for dinner four out of five nights, there might be a small reward waiting for him at the end of the week. Gradually, we can increase our expectations.

I also taught eight-year-old Alex to accept that he could make a mistake and to take responsibility for it. We attempted to play Ping-Pong one day and he kept insisting that everything was his point, even when it clearly wasn't. I, on the other hand, said "my fault" whenever I hit a bad shot. Eventually, Alex began to say that, too, and when he did, I congratulated him, noting that it's not easy to accept blame. This seemed to be the start of his becoming more aware of his actions, and his awareness has continued to grow in our sessions.

Role-playing between parent and child or professional and child is another way to help the child understand concretely that what he is doing may not be acceptable and that there are alternatives. In essence, an adult and a child create a story or play script to illustrate the undesirable behavior as well as the hoped-for changes. If your child has difficulty thinking conceptually, such a graphic illustration might be helpful in transforming the most firmly entrenched of inappropriate habits. I recall Julien, who came home from school in an angry mood. He told his mother that a boy in class had said, "You can't sit at our table. It's full; you have to sit on the floor," when, in fact, there were two empty seats. In response, Julien had grabbed the boy and "floored" him, only to be sent to the principal and suspended for a day. Rather than either defending or blaming him, his mother suggested that they act out the scene, with Julien pretending to be the other boy; she would be Julien. They "rewrote" the event, so to speak, with Julien's mother responding verbally to the provocation rather than physically. In the "play," she said to the assaulter, "No problem; I wouldn't want to sit with *you* anyway." In responding that way, Julien might have saved face and would not have gotten in trouble. He got the message.

Timing is important. You can't teach a child alternative ways of acting in the heat of a dispute or conflict. Once the tension is over and the air has cleared, it may be possible for a child to recognize what provoked the argument or dispute in the first place. As parents, we sometimes want to handle an issue immediately, but for many ADHD youngsters, this is doomed to failure. Their tantrums or fireworks are so charged that no communication gets through. They may become violent, not from defiance but from fear. I can think of several children who acted like trapped animals when confronted by an angry authority figure. In general, confrontation doesn't work with ADD children. It is better to give them space until they can cool off and become rational enough to hear or discuss what went wrong.

Sometimes we blame a child for an argument or angry scene when our own mood or frustration may have caused the conflict. The way we respond to our children at any given time is likely to reflect the way we are feeling at the time. If we are emotionally stressed, we may have to step back to view more objectively what caused our vulnerability. And if we were at fault, an honest confession can be healing. When an adult assumes at least partial responsibility, some of the child's inevitable guilt will be alleviated. She'll recognize that her parents are human, too, which implies being imperfect. Parents can make mistakes and say some regrettable things that youngsters will tolerate, so long as there is honesty and basic good feeling between them.

I am reminded of the time a mother lost her temper at the end of a long day and gave her child a hard slap for a minor infraction. She felt great remorse and guilt, so she hugged her little boy and tearfully apologized. He began to jump up and down on the bed, shouting gleefully, "You're sorry, I'm sorry, we're both sorry!" Her frank expression of feeling undoubtedly cleared the air faster than any long-winded explanation or discussion would have.

OVERPROTECTION AND INDULGENCE

The flip side of being ignored or scapegoated is being overly indulged. In some families, everyone tries to compensate the child for his impairment by giving too much and overprotecting him. The child becomes the focus of everyone's attention and energy. To an observer, he would appear to be the favorite in the family. While his siblings grow up without being catered to, he is coddled and very little is asked of him.

One mother seemed to spend every waking moment attending to her son, chauffeuring him to swimming lessons, to tutors, and to the neighborhood toy store for presents. The rest of the family was lucky if they saw her over a take-out pizza. Tom's father accused his wife of spoiling Tom and admitted to me that he resented all the time and attention given to the child. Mother and son had, in effect, become a twosome, and he felt excluded—and even a bit jealous. Hearing that, his wife became annoyed, claiming that he was unsympathetic and insensitive to his son's difficulties. She argued that she had to be their son's protector because the father was not.

Tom's parents and I tried to assess the priorities in the family. How much energy did Tom's mother really have to expend, and how much of what she did was necessary for Tom's development and well-being?

Parents who overprotect their children certainly are not a homogeneous group, but they do have at least one thing in common—namely, that they do more for their children than the reality of the situation requires.

Parental overprotection has two aspects. One is the need to dominate and control the child; the other is to indulge the child's every wish. A parent may be domineering and permissive at the same time, although one behavior does not necessarily accompany the other. Some parents overprotect children because of their own insecurity or sense of inadequacy. By carefully paving the way, parents feel they will spare a youngster some of the discomfort and anxiety to which they themselves were vulnerable. If they lacked supportive parenting themselves, they may be attempting to compensate their children for what they missed in their youth.

It is also true that parents' anger or disappointment with a child may be more easily hidden or disguised when they are doing special favors for him. The attention and gifts become tangible evidence of their devotion and love. Related to this may be their guilt for having produced a youngster with real or imagined damage. Through selflessness and protection of the child above and beyond the call of duty, they attempt to assuage some of the guilt. However, protecting a child from all discomfort or pain is neither possible nor desirable. Children need to learn to cope with the age-appropriate stress inherent in the process of growing up. Without that, they will not be able to handle the pressures that adults inevitably face in their lives.

Barbara was a pretty and compliant twelve-year-old whose mother continued to assume most of the responsibility for her daily life. Having seen how ineptly Barbara planned her time, even for such simple tasks as bathing and dressing, her mother thought she was doing her a favor when she directed even those activities. Moreover, because she was Barbara's constant companion, she ensured that Barbara had little time in which to have to deal with the real world. She kept her daughter out of situations where she might have difficulty, thus making her disabilities appear less significant, hardly even noticeable.

With all this supervision, Barbara was not able to develop her capabilities, even in those areas in which she might have progressed. She passively accepted the identity her mother had created for her, becoming increasingly dependent on her parents. As time went on, she couldn't or wouldn't make a move without their guidance. Eventually, Barbara's parents began to worry about her future life without them. How could she possibly manage? She relied on them for everything. In effect, all three had become enslaved by the dependency they had helped to create.

Although it is important for parents to give support when needed, it is equally important to encourage a child to try his or her wings. Children with learning differences do tend to be more dependent than their siblings, but their parents need to be especially patient while they let their children try, fail, and try again. Children can only become independent, self-reliant, and well-functioning adults if they are encouraged and supported in their efforts to grow. Every parent knows it is easier and more efficient to make decisions and take over, but it is a disservice to the child, who needs to become autonomous.

This suggestion is often more easily given than followed. Fostering independence in a child for whom learning does not come easily would tax the patience of Job. It is twice as hard to teach a child with poor coordination to ride a two-wheeler or throw a baseball. And teaching an impulsive youngster to cross a busy thoroughfare only on the green light is undeniably frustrating. Even after having taught their children, parents may be nervous about giving them the freedom of independence. There is a fine line between protecting a child from a situation he clearly is not ready to handle and overprotecting him. I have worked with parents who, fearful for their children, claim they are just being cautious. Their anticipation of danger, however, is excessive and is conveyed to their children, who then become even more anxious and dependent. Parents, too, need to learn to take risks on behalf of their children—preferably safe ones, of course. They need insight, courage, a sense of humor, and patience to survive their children's trials and errors in the process of learning and living.

In thinking of overprotection and excessive indulgence, I remember Mike's mother and father. He was ten and, although he couldn't read or ride a bicycle yet, Mike surely had his parents under his thumb. Perhaps because they felt sorry for him, they couldn't do enough for him. His every wish was their command; rules of the house did not apply to him. He watched TV until all hours, ignored the established bedtime, and insisted that his parents keep him company far into the night. Mike managed to avoid assigned chores, too, by procrastinating or complaining so much that it was easier for his parents to do them.

As he grew older, Mike became more negative and demanding, until his parents adopted an attitude of peace at any price. It was simpler to appease him than to deal with his explosions and bad moods. At thirteen, Mike was a masterful manipulator at home, but he became unduly upset when confronted with the demands of the world outside. He saw the negative in every situation and was critical of everyone. There was no one he liked, and almost no one liked him. He had no friends, so his parents were his only companions, which they resented, too. They were an unhappy threesome until Mike's parents realized that they had to take charge but at the same time give their son some much-needed independence. Working with the parents was as important as my seeing Mike in an effort to establish realistic boundaries and goals for him.

THE SPECIAL PROBLEMS OF THE ADOLESCENT

To function adequately in the world, children need to feel some sense of autonomy, but they also need boundaries and limitations to feel safe. When they are given everything they want, they are robbed of this opportunity.

By the time a young person reaches adolescence, new and special problems arise, although many of the earlier symptoms may have disappeared. In all probability, a boy is no longer as overtly hyperactive as he was in earlier years, and he may even enjoy reading the sports page. But the discrepancy between his behavior and the expectations for someone of his age may appear wider than ever to those who know him well. Among the most conspicuous attributes of adolescents with ADHD or learning disabilities are their impulsivity and the need for immediate gratification. They tend to remain egocentric, concerned only with themselves and their problems. Many make little constructive use of their spare time and, consequently, appear both immature and uninteresting to their peers.

I knew a girl, indulged as a child, who lacked the skills essential for independence. She couldn't make decisions, relying on her parents or even her younger siblings to do so. Sally's developing womanly figure served to hide a little girl inside who shunned responsibility. However, like most adolescents, she resented the assistance and blamed her parents for the decisions they made. Thus, Sally could never be wrong; everything became her parents' problem and she was absolved of any responsibility.

To some degree, all adolescents are caught between the lures of adulthood and the irresponsibility and comfort of childhood, but this period also presents problems for parents. While it is true that adolescents need independence, those with learning differences, and perhaps poor judgment as well, require more support and guidance than many of their peers. Their immaturity pervades their social and sexual relationships, making them more suggestible to misguided leadership. Although some are afraid to get involved in boy-girl relationships, others may indulge too freely because of their need for acceptance. Some will require help in handling social interactions and even the telephone appropriately. Sally, in fact, used particularly poor judgment when she was convinced by a group of friends to pose for pictures in scant clothing. Her reputation spread and, for a time, she was persona non grata in her school. This was a terrible experience for Sally and her family, as well.

Many parents become weary of their teenager's problems and discouraged about the results of their teaching. While a child is young, parents feel there is time to remediate the disability and help him outgrow his differences. By the teen years, time is running out. Suddenly he's becoming a young adult—and he still has problems. He needs assistance with working papers, job applications, and even getting to a job on time. At this stage, it is more important than ever that parents don't let their anxieties interfere with their teenager's attempts to succeed. Parents need the courage to demand responsibility of their young adults while monitoring their progress. On the other hand, adolescents typically want to spend less time at home and more time with peers, and therefore they are less available—and less receptive—to parental guidance.

THE POSITIVES IN PARENTING

I don't want to overemphasize the negatives and the difficulties that parents have raising children with special needs. Moreover, I do not intend to convey the impression that a young person with a learning problem necessarily assumes a destructive or neurotic role in his family. In many homes, he is an integral, contributing member of the family, loved, respected, and admired by all. Indeed, he has much to teach others about the traits of perseverance, courage, and the determination to succeed.

On the other hand, many of the negative feelings discussed in this section—guilt, denial, frustration—occur in all families. These perfectly natural feelings, intrinsic to the growing process, are handled with equanimity and understanding in many families. Although I have observed such families with interest and admiration, trying to understand just what it is they do that works so well, I've found no standard formula or lifestyle. Some of the families live on farms, others in large cities or in the suburbs. They can be single-parent families or foster homes. Undoubtedly there is an element of luck, but some parents seem to be particularly sensitive and tuned in to the needs of their children. Whether or not their children have problems, these parents are able to provide an environment that is comfortable, accepting, and nurturing for all.

One such family, the Langs, seemed to pay little attention to their daughter's learning difference. They provided tutoring for Ashley after school, but they did not seem overly concerned about her academic progress, nor did they ever ask what occurred during her lessons. In contrast with many parents of youngsters who come for help, I had almost no contact with the Langs. They rarely phoned to relate behaviors of concern and almost never canceled appointments; they allowed Ashley to walk to my office alone, even in the rain. Usually I would take this behavior as indicative of parental disinterest or lack of involvement, but it became obvious that Ashley had her parents' love and respect and seemed to know just what she could expect of them. She relied on them for help when she needed to, but she was encouraged to be independent and to do for herself whenever possible. She was treated as a normal child with recognizable learning problems that could be coped with at home. Above all, her parents did not seem to need Ashley's successes for their own gratification or feelings of accomplishment.

Another family, the Brownells, had a boy of seven named Dan, for whom the diagnosis was Pervasive Developmental Disorders (PDD). These are considered to be neurologically based disorders with a range of problems that most often include difficulties in language and communication, social adaptability, and frequently cognitive functioning, as well. Dan was fairly high-functioning, to be sure, but he displayed many of the symptoms typical of PDD: repetitive and stereotypical speech patterns, little eye contact, and a refusal to try anything he perceived as challenging. He was also obsessed with trucks and could play with them by the hour without interacting with anyone.

Dan was in a special class in a public school with a teacher who worked hard to help him learn. I also saw Dan outside of school, to work on his social skills, his ability to communicate, and his self-esteem. His parents were incredibly patient and supportive of Dan.

They also welcomed any suggestions, providing stimulating experiences for Dan and following through with recommended learning activities and games. But Dan was also expected to adhere to the established standards of behavior of which he was capable. Within a few months, everyone noticed a different Dan. He seemed more mature, his conversation was more spontaneous and elaborate, and he was more receptive to new experiences. He was also beginning to learn to read and write.

Both the Langs and the Brownells understood that all children need standards and expectations. We do children no favor when we take pity on them and make no demands. They need to know that their parents and teachers will expect as much of them as they are capable of handling. We may, for example, not be able to insist on a neat, tidy room if organization is a problem for a child, but we can help him strive toward the goal. Help a child help himself, and he'll become his own master.

Most parents learn through experience how to manage their challenging children at home. Routines, demands of time, reward and punishment, and TV/computer scheduling are a few of the difficult areas with which they have to cope. A few suggestions culled from parents' experiences are offered here, in the interest of making daily living somewhat easier at home.

Give your child *time and attention.* These commodities are very much needed by children with learning differences, but often in busy families there aren't enough to go around. Children with learning problems usually require more parental time than their sisters and brothers. The basic rules of living may not come so easily, and there may be more difficult times and unhappy experiences to discuss.

A special time might be set aside for much-needed reading help and for sharing the day's happenings. One boy counted on special time with his father before bedtime to talk. This became known as their "life and stuff" time together. Of course, Mother or a sitter could take over on those nights when Father wasn't available or in the mood. But someone who cared was usually there for him. This ensured his parents a better night's sleep and a more contented child. It was worth it!

Help the child remember *instructions and directives.* These are often misunderstood or not heard at all. We can't assume that a child will know and understand directions after he's been told once, particularly if one eye is on the TV or if he is halfway out the door. Some youngsters with learning differences understand and process information slowly, and instructions spoken quickly get lost en route. Take your child's less efficient listening into account and be particularly precise and clear in your explanations.

Raymond had been told to meet his mother at the sporting goods store at four o'clock to select a new bicycle for his thirteenth birthday. He remembered his birthday and the bicycle, but he forgot where his mother said to meet her and when. She was angry and he was devastated when he missed the chance to choose his present. To avoid this scene, his mother might have written the instructions and clipped them to his notebook or tucked them in his pocket. Eventually, Raymond learned to walk around with a pocketful of notes and no longer missed so many important events in his life.

Merely telling a child to come home at six for dinner may not necessarily bring her home on time, particularly if she tends to be oblivious to the time. Providing her with a watch with an alarm might work, though. Or a phone call to the neighbors, if that's where she is playing, could serve as a reminder that she'd better start for home. Family life will be calmer and less fraught with tension if we can avoid a last-minute search for an absentminded child.

Establish—and stick to—*routines.* Routines are crucial for children with learning differences. They provide the stability and needed structure for youngsters who otherwise may seem lost in time and space. A special time for homework, TV, and dinner will take the guesswork out of living. While regularity may seem monotonous to many of us, it is reassuring for children who cannot handle change and uncertainty easily.

Be consistent. Consistency in handling is very desirable but rarely possible, as most parents know. The level of strictness or permissiveness at home will vary from family to family, but as long as a child knows the basic rules to rely on, he won't be confused. You might even think about three categories of rules, perhaps in descending order of parental control.

The first category would be the "have-to's" in the family, the few rules that are nonnegotiable and must be adhered to without discussion. Sometimes parents feel unsure of their stand on an issue, debating too long with a child who has all the talents of a trial lawyer, but it will give that child a sense of security when he knows that his parents are authority figures whose job it is to protect him. Children think they want unlimited power, but it scares them if they actually become omnipotent.

On the other hand, children also need to have some decision-making experience. That's where the second category, the "should-but-don't-have to's," come in. As parents, we know that children *should* wear coats on a cold day or boots when it rains. However, if they insist on not putting on the coat, we might let that be their choice, with the admonition, "at least take it with you in case you're cold." It reminds me of my grandmother's definition of a sweater: "something you put on when your mother is cold."

And, of course, there is the third category, those choices that are entirely the children's: with whom they play, the activities they select, and occasionally, but not always, what they want to eat. Parents certainly should not be "short-order cooks," catering to each child's preferences, but the choice of menu might be rotated to give everyone in the family a chance.

The flip side of consistency in handling children, then, is flexibility. Teaching a child that rules can be bent under special circumstances is important. Most people can remember those times when their parents threw caution to the wind and allowed something unexpected—and lovely—to occur.

Use effective *discipline* techniques. Discipline isn't easy. "Nothing works; we can't get through to him" is a comment heard frequently. A child with learning or attention problems is often hard to teach; no punishment seems to make an impression. Generally, the technique of anticipation and prevention is more effective than criticism or punishment after the fact, but parents can't always prevent the crime. A time-out or cooling-off period might not teach desired behavior, but it will give parents and family some temporary relief—after a warning, of course. Be careful, though, not to make a time-out too long. The rule of thumb is one minute for each year of the child's age. A three-year-old might be told to "sit right there" for three minutes, or five minutes in his room might work for a five-year-old. I've known young children who were banished to their rooms for a half hour or even the afternoon. That doesn't teach—it merely isolates the child. Sometimes, a parent's saying to a child, "We *both* need a time-out now," meaning a temporary separation, is enough to cool heated tempers, and the child doesn't feel as if he alone is being blamed.

An occasional spanking isn't the end of the world for a child, but as a form of punishment it doesn't accomplish much. It is just another negative expression, possibly even reinforcing an undesirable behavior. And, as I mentioned before, negative attention frequently seems more attractive to children than no attention at all.

Teasing and threatening are not just ineffectual disciplinary measures, they are also highly destructive, particularly for children who are sensitive to criticism. Teasing is really an expression of hostility conveyed with a smile, and most children quickly become aware of the underlying feelings. One father thought his son was a poor sport when he couldn't take the barbs thrown "jokingly" across the dinner table. He had not realized how much anger tipped each arrow until we talked about it.

When serious disciplinary action is required for a major infraction of a rule, parents need to make sure the punishment fits the crime. A punishment of long duration, such as "no TV for a month" or "you're grounded until school ends," will quickly lose its effect. By the end of the week, the child undoubtedly will remember the punishment, but not what it was for. Knowing your child and what pleasures he looks forward to most gives you some leverage. A warning that a sleepover will be canceled if the unacceptable behavior continues is often sufficient—if the child knows his parents mean what they say. Of course, we must assume that the child is able to control the behavior in question. Punishing an ADHD child for hopping around in a restaurant when he can't sit still at home or in school is clearly unfair.

Be fair, but that doesn't necessarily mean equal. Special privileges are not always earned. "Why can Jimmy watch TV and I can't?" "How come Tom doesn't have to stay at the table and I do? It's not fair!" Such comments are heard in every household, but they become more poignant in families where one child has a problem. "To each according to his need" might be more appropriate than "Tit for tat" as the family credo. When siblings ask why their sister or brother gets special treatment, an honest explanation is called for. Siblings need to know that Jimmy has some special needs, but in all probability they do, too, and their needs will also be met. Then the "fair treatment isn't necessarily equal" concept should be easier for them to understand.

Try to schedule limited amounts of *TV and computer time.* TV and computers are increasingly mentioned by parents as sources of conflict in the family. Not only is this issue a problem between parents and children, but it can be a source of friction between parents who are unsure how to deal with it. While some children enjoy a moderate amount of TV and computer games, others are completely addicted, losing themselves in "the tube." The admonition to "Turn off the boob tube and pick up a book for a change!" reflects a common parental attitude. However, if Billy has had a stressful day and reading is a chore, perhaps he needs to relax before tackling homework. An hour of a snack and TV on a rainy afternoon can provide a needed respite from the pressures of the day. However, for most children, I think TV viewing should be deferred until *after* homework is done. Tough on parents? You bet! Television time cannot be blanketly ordained, but should be a family decision. However, I don't believe that modern technology should replace human interaction, nor should it be unrestricted in its use.

Help your child stay *organized and on schedule.* This is often hard for adolescents in any family. Many seem to think they can accomplish more in ten minutes—after those long phone calls and their favorite TV show—than any human being can do in an hour. They somehow never get to that dreaded homework until almost midnight, and then Mom and Dad are too tired and too angry to be sympathetic. A fifteen-year-old girl came up with her own solution one day. In an attempt to get organized, she listed all the things she had to do after school—write a composition, shower, feed the dog and brush him, call Grandma and two friends, and "finish my math." Then she listed the tasks in the order in which she planned to do them and tried to "guestimate" the time allotted for each. She interspersed the phone calls among the chores, and her scheduling worked fairly well. The dog didn't get brushed and the shower was deferred until morning, but she was proud of her system and her ability to budget her time.

A few simple items can help with organization. Most can be made or used easily at home and should make life easier for children and parents.

1. *A bulletin board* with funny signs to remind a child of schedules or special appointments. These can be used to reinforce established routines. A section devoted to emergency telephone numbers, thoughts for the day, and household chores might be useful. One family even had a sign-out sheet for parents and children posted in the kitchen, with the message "I am at _____. Will be back at _____."

2. *Magnets* for notes on the refrigerator door or bathroom mirror. These hold brief messages and reminders of times and dates of activities. One family left all telephone messages on the refrigerator, the place everyone rushed to after school or work. In addition to the lure of food, it became the central clearinghouse for information,

where everyone checked in upon returning home. That way, no one forgot to pick up their messages.

3. *A key ring* on a string, and a special hook on which to hang it in a child's room. It won't get lost so quickly, and she'll be able to get into the house after school without bothering the neighbors—if she remembers to take it! It may be a good idea, too, to entrust neighbors with a key, just in case your child is locked out—unless, of course, they don't mind if she "boards" there until you come home.

4. *Name tapes* aren't babyish, even for adolescents, if they prevent weekly trips to the lost-and-found for misplaced jackets and sweaters left on the ball field. Parents will be spared the inevitable hunt for the missing items, as well as preserving cash in their pockets.

5. *Eyeglass cases and notebooks* that are indelibly marked with name, address, and phone number will accomplish the same as name tapes on clothing.

6. *Open shelves* to keep possessions off the floor. It is hard for some youngsters to put things away, but open shelves can be a reasonable alternative to under the bed. *Freaky Friday* by Mary Rodgers, a novel (and movie available on video) that presents a weird twist on parent-child relationships, gives an interesting perspective on how a teenager views her parents' comments about her room.

7. *Compartmentalized or divided drawers* are good for faster retrieval of articles needed for school in the morning.

There must be hundreds of other suggestions for more peaceful coexistence with children. You can add to the list those items and ideas that will make life easier for you and your family. Brainstorm with your child.

Remember to *take care of yourself*. This is perhaps most important of all. You need relief, too. It is not easy to be with people no higher than your waist all day, every day, and a child with problems can be even more active and infinitely more difficult than most. You cannot possibly be available to him at all times—and shouldn't be even if you could. If a child's parents are the only people he knows, he won't learn to relate to other adults. I suggest finding a willing grandmother, aunt, or local baby-sitter to relieve you at regular intervals. You'll come home refreshed and better able to care for your child. Parents of children with behavioral problems often feel guilty about leaving these challenging children with others. True, they may be hard to handle, but there must be someone who can cope. It's good for kids, too, to know they can't manipulate you into being there all the time.

To sum up, youngsters with learning differences and attention problems require what all children need, just more of it. They need to feel loved and accepted. However, it may not be as easy to have loving feelings all the time for a child whose moods, judgment, and sense of timing are out of kilter so often. At times, parents understandably feel anger, anxiety, frustration, fatigue, and even dislike. At such times it is hard, or even impossible, to be patient. Children with learning differences often seem the least lovable when they need to be loved the most. Therein lies the challenge for parents, brothers, sisters, and extended family. At the same time, as a parent, you should not be made to feel guilty or blame yourself for your children's problems. You, too, need understanding and support. Too often your plight evokes more criticism than compassion from professionals, relatives, and friends who hold parents responsible for their children's aberrant behavior. This criticism is unwarranted because outsiders may have little understanding of the pressures that exist in the families of LD and ADHD children.

I am convinced that most parents do the very best they can for their children, and they deserve support and help from others. It is not easy to be the parent of a child with problems. You need to treat yourself to some of the love and understanding you work so hard to provide for your children.

4

THE SOCIAL CONNECTION

When we think of learning differences, we tend to mean learning in an academic environment, namely, school. But learning encompasses much more than the three R's. From infancy on, most children begin to learn the important skills of living with others—that is, social perception and interpersonal behavior. A baby soon learns the sound of his mother's voice, "reads" her facial expression, and recognizes her touch. He senses when she is loving and when she feels angry or impatient. This awareness of himself as being distinct from others enables him to become his own person, capable of interacting with others. This is a milestone that influences his behavior throughout his life.

We know from the study of child development that children move from an egocentric existence toward socialization and companionship with others within the first three years of life, long before they enter school. Newborn infants have a selfish and narcissistic outlook on the world; other people matter only in relation to themselves. If babies' thoughts were expressed in language, those words might be "What can you do for me now?" Later, toddlers perceive others as things or objects to be used and pushed around at will. Then, as preschoolers, most begin to find that it pays to relate to other children. They gain a helper in building block towers or even in performing some mischief. The partnership is secondary to the activity and lasts only as long as it takes to complete the task. Finally, by the time they enter elementary school, most children have learned to view their peers as individuals with whom they can compete and share possessions, and whom they love and hate. It is only at this stage that enmities, friendships, and lasting relationships become possible.

Studies have shown that infants born prematurely not only are small in size but tend to remain immature longer than their full-term counterparts. They may speak later, walk later, and develop awareness

69

of social behavior at a later age, as well. Children with learning differences, even when born after a full-term pregnancy, may also be less mature than their peers. Their delay in social adaptation can match their lag in learning to read and write. They progress through the developmental stages, as do all children, but may always be a step or two behind others of their age group. I can recall a speaker years ago saying that, typically, young people with learning differences seem two to three years younger socially than their peers. I, too, frequently have to remind myself that a girl in my office is really eleven, rather than eight, as she appears. Her demeanor, her conversation, and even her interests suggest her immaturity. And even at twenty, many LD young adults act like typical teenagers.

To understand and truly help young people with learning differences, parents and teachers need to be aware that their social adjustment is simply part of the broader problem. While most children acquire social skills automatically by observation and imitation, those with learning differences and attention deficits may have to be carefully and explicitly taught.

THE THREE LEVELS OF SOCIAL PROBLEMS

There are three levels of social problems for children with learning differences and attention deficits. Some children may simply lack the knowledge about appropriate social behavior, others may have the knowledge but are unable to apply it, and still others may have the knowledge but can't see the effects of their behavior and so continue to behave inappropriately.

For children who don't understand appropriate social behavior, that is, how to act toward others in a given situation, we might introduce a "social lesson." This can take the form of a story designed to make a point. Role-playing can be very effective—for example, if the child has a fight with a classmate at school, you could take the role of your child and have your child enact the role of his classmate to see how the fight started and how it could have been avoided.

Many ADHD children, however, have social skills but can't apply them because their own needs get in the way of their intellect. As one boy said, "My mind knows what to do, but I can't control my body to do it." This is typical of children with attention deficits. They know, for example, that cheating isn't acceptable, but they need to win so badly that they cheat just to make sure. I also know children who preach honesty while lying to save face.

The third level of social problems is caused by the child's inability to monitor and evaluate his own behavior. Some children who understand appropriate behavior and can suppress their own needs when necessary seem totally unaware of the effect of their actions and how other people respond to them. They see each situation as a first-time event and, therefore, don't learn from experience. Social conventions and rules aren't generalized, so the inappropriate behaviors of the past persist. These are the hardest to address because the children don't understand what went wrong until after it happened.

HOW LEARNING PROBLEMS AFFECT SOCIAL ADJUSTMENT

It is not surprising that children with learning differences have social problems when we consider the factors that contribute to their academic difficulties in school. Many of the deficits that affect their learning have implications for their social adjustment, as well. Difficulty paying attention is a common trait among those with LD and ADHD. Children who can't focus on assignments in school are also likely to be inattentive in a game or even in conversation. They become confused because they cannot tune out what is unimportant and tune in to what *is* important, so they lose the context of the situation and respond inappropriately. What may seem to be an irrelevant response may, in fact, reflect thinking by association, indicative of immaturity. In addition, some children's impulsivity and lack of judgment make them overly sensitive, even to imagined slights, so they lash out, alienating would-be friends.

Because they tend to be less mature, more impulsive, and lacking in caution, young children at risk for learning and attention problems frequently can't be permitted the independence allowed other children. They need to be watched and guided more carefully in their social interactions, which may impede their social development.

I remember Jeffrey, who seemed particularly immature in his class of four-year-olds in a day care center. He was physically, cognitively, and socially young for his age. He didn't climb stairs one foot at a time (which is expected by age four), and color recognition was still tenuous. Jeffrey also had severe separation anxiety; he seemed frightened when his mother left him. Years ago, it was assumed that a child who reached the ripe old age of three and a half should be able to part from his mother on the first day of preschool, adapting easily to a teacher and new playmates. Now, although children tend to go to day care and preschool programs even earlier, we know that their readiness to leave their mothers is as individually and developmentally determined as learning to read. For Jeffrey, it came later rather than earlier.

In school, Jeffrey walked around hugging a stuffed dog, but he screamed in panic at a real one. He rarely played outside or participated in group activities. While the other children sang songs, built airports with blocks, and played house in the doll corner, Jeffrey remained alone, watching. The other children didn't dislike him; they just forgot he was there. Occasionally, a youngster would do something for Jeffrey in a protective, mothering way. It was evident that his classmates regarded him as the baby of the class. Actually, if Jeffrey's parents and teachers had thought of him as one or two years younger than his age, he probably would have seemed just fine.

Some children who seem young for their age might benefit from an additional year in the protective environment of home, perhaps in a small parent-run play group. If Jeffrey's mother hadn't been working outside of her home, she might have been his mentor and teacher until he was more prepared to leave her and join his peers in school. Or, an arranged play date twice a week with another child might have paved the way for his entering the larger environment. However, this isn't always practical or feasible in today's world and, for Jeffrey, day care was a necessity.

Joseph, too, seemed young, perhaps in part reflecting his language difficulties. He couldn't find the words with which to communicate with other children and tended to use his fists to express himself. Young children who cannot express their thoughts and feelings easily frequently become so frustrated that they strike out physically. These are the kids who are likely to be ignored or rejected because of their aggression.

By the time he entered kindergarten, Joseph's language problems, his impulsivity, and his quick temper affected his interpersonal relationships as well as his learning. He had trouble controlling his feelings and could only express them with his hands and feet. It was the only way he knew to try to connect with others, and of course it had a negative effect. Rather than risk being hit or kicked, children tried to stay away from him, so he was alone much of the time. That only increased Joseph's frustration, and he struck out even more. The cycle continued until the following year when his teacher referred him for language therapy and to the social worker in school for help with his anger.

Betsy, at six, was the opposite of Joseph in her approach to other children. Although she, too, had trouble understanding verbal communication and expressing herself, she kissed and hugged every prospective friend until they backed away. Betsy made connections with people and things by touching—much as younger children do. The children who were the objects of her affection were better able to convey their feelings by talking. They didn't need to touch someone they liked, and they thought Betsy was strange. Betsy, sensing the other children's disdain, became particularly possessive with one child at a time in her class. The more she was rebuffed, the more she tried to make a friend—in the wrong way. She would ask classmates, "Do you like me?" at inappropriate times, inevitably eliciting a negative answer. Then, feeling rejected, she provoked them even more. Eventually her claim that "Nobody likes me" seemed based more on reality than on Betsy's imagination.

Many lonely children do not have the faintest idea why they are being ignored or rejected. They don't understand that their behavior is inappropriate or socially unacceptable. Typically, they will acknowledge that they have no friends, but claim, "I don't do anything; they just don't like me," or find a lame excuse. When I asked a ten-year-old why he thought he had no friends, he looked puzzled and then said, "I guess it's because I have allergies and my nose runs. The kids call me Sniffles." He didn't see himself as the disruptive boy in class who constantly injected himself into other boys' games and conversations, much to their annoyance. A girl in the same class made up tall stories to make her feel important and ingratiate herself with her classmates. She seemed surprised to learn that few, if any, believed her tales and that the other children disliked her for "lying."

Most children love to feel smart. They may pretend they don't care and may even stay away from the "nerds" who are, but, deep down, they'd love to be among them. Roland was self-conscious about his learning problems and tended to blame his lack of friends on the fact that he couldn't read and wasn't a good athlete. Actually, fourth and fifth graders love to find a scapegoat, and a child's being dumb *and* a poor athlete provides as good a reason as any. To add to his problems,

Roland's parents were also disappointed in him. He didn't fit into the family any better than he did into his class at school. The rest of the family was outgoing and gregarious, while Roland was odd man out, shy and ill at ease. Although Roland withdrew from other children, hiding from the world behind his camera, he eventually became a good photographer, which brought him recognition. But until then, he was a loner.

HANDLING DIFFERENT PERSONALITIES

Children are born with their own temperaments and their own personalities. They are not, as Rousseau thought many years ago, blank slates on which parents write their futures. From the beginning, some children don't act in ways that parents can enjoy. It is not easy to adore a colicky or sleepless infant, or a toddler who cries too much and can't stop running long enough for a kiss. Both Joseph and Roland had been all this and more. They were difficult as babies and no easier as they grew. They were unhappy, lonely children who found little pleasure in life. Their parents couldn't enjoy doing things with them, because the children gave no indication that they were having fun. Instead, they usually became irritable and negative in response to anything new.

Frannie, too, was unpopular. She rarely went to anyone's house and never invited anyone to hers. Her parents were concerned about her isolation and tried to push her into as many activities as they could. She took music lessons, stayed for after-school activities, and went to birthday parties (to which she was invited by her parents' friends). She didn't like any of these activities, but had no choice. Frannie particularly disliked the birthday parties and used to dread opening the invitations, which she knew had not been issued voluntarily. When she went to the parties, she stood alone for the most part, not interacting with the other kids, who didn't even seem to notice. She complained vehemently to me, until her parents realized the futility of forcing her to go.

Many young children don't enjoy birthday parties, and the hosts may enjoy such parties least of all. Parties tend to be noisy and confusing, particularly for children who have trouble integrating too many stimuli simultaneously. They can easily become overwhelmed by too much going on at once. They may also be afraid to play competitive party games because they never win. Birthday parties seem to have been designed for very secure, assertive children who are confident and always at ease. I recommend Chapter 5 in Judy Blume's book *Tales of a Fourth-Grade Nothing* for a nine-year-old's humorous account of his younger brother's birthday party. It tells of the disasters and traumas suffered by each of the small guests at the party. One can only conclude by the end of this hilarious description that the only people who really enjoy a three-year-old's birthday party are the grandparents.

Parents of young children should attempt to understand their children's feelings and not push them into social situations for which they are not ready. Just as we don't expect children to be comfortable skipping a grade in school, we should not expect them to rush happily into unfamiliar social experiences. However, there are times in the life of a family when it is important for a child to participate in a social event in which he may feel challenged or ill at ease. Holidays and family gatherings are occasions that can be trying for parents as well as for children. A visit to relatives on Thanksgiving may be dreaded if is likely to be fraught with tension and tears. Countless parents have complained to me that their child "spoiled the day for everyone." They recount examples such as the following: "He didn't get along with his cousins," or "She tormented her brother until he was in tears," or "My son wouldn't leave my side and kept repeating that he wanted to go home. It was an awful day." One mother said she expected her son to act up whenever the family visited anyone. She realized that she became tense on each and every occasion, anticipating the worst. Perhaps because of her anxiety, her son rarely disappointed her.

If you have learned through experience that your child cannot manage an entire day in the company of friends, adults, or relatives, perhaps such visits can be abbreviated. A shorter stay may be easier for the whole family than a long stressful one, and it's better to quit while you're ahead—before things fall apart. Or, your child might even be happier at home with a baby-sitter. But if he does want to be with the family, it helps to prepare him in advance. Tell him who will be there, how long you plan to stay, and how he'll be expected to act. Packing a few of his favorite possessions and a familiar snack may also prevent the dreaded tantrum. And the useful technique of role-playing can smooth the adjustment to an unfamiliar situation. Acting out a scene together beforehand will make it seem more familiar when the child experiences it. Parents sometimes plan to surprise their children with an upcoming trip or outing, but the surprise is often the parents' when the children act up or fall apart.

Too much of a good thing can be worse than none at all. A frustrated mother described what should have been an ideal day for the family. In celebration of Ryan and his twin sister's birthday, the family spent the day in New York City, doing all the things both children loved. After lunch at McDonald's, they went to the zoo, which was Ryan's choice. Next came ice cream at Baskin-Robbins and a visit to their father's office, followed by a family dinner in Chinatown.

As Ryan's mother reported, all went well until after the ice cream. Suddenly, upon arriving at the office, Ryan had an unexplained temper tantrum and could not be reasoned with. The restaurant dinner was a nightmare, too, with Ryan running around and not eating. No one could understand what had happened; the day had started out so well, and Ryan had seemed so happy.

In retrospect, it was easy to see what had occurred. The perfectly planned day should have been divided into two or even three exciting days. The plans were just too ambitious for Ryan. He was reacting as any child would who had been exposed to too much stress—only Ryan's boiling point was quite a few degrees lower than his sister's.

THE SOCIAL IQ

A child's social intelligence has little to do with IQ. One of the boys I'll always remember was Steve. I met him when he was in first grade, and he was probably the most brilliant boy who ever came to my office. He broke all records on IQ tests, but in school he had great difficulty learning to read and write. He had even greater problems with friends. He was clumsy in his movements and, as he got older, was never a welcome addition on the ball field. He seemed to know that he'd probably drop the ball or make the first out, so he just stood on the sidelines. That would have been fine, except that he shouted curses at anyone who made an error. Perhaps it made him feel more powerful to be able to criticize someone else, but it certainly didn't ingratiate him with the boys on either team.

Once in a while Steve tried to have other children come to play at his house. He wanted to have friends, but he couldn't share his possessions easily and simply had to have his own way. It was a matter of "do it my way or not at all." Shortly after a new friend arrived, there would be fights and tears, and the boy would go home, never to be seen again. Steve was devastated each time this happened, but he never knew *why* it happened. He couldn't see how his own actions offended others because his own needs got in the way. Occasionally, Steve's mother or father would try to point out gently that perhaps he was being too bossy. However, this only led to further anguish because Steve felt they were just being "mean" and on the "other kid's side."

After a few meetings with Steve and his parents, we thought of some ways for him to get along better with friends who came to play. The first rule of thumb was for a parent to be on hand to supervise the boys fairly closely. It is certainly desirable for young people to handle their own social arrangements without parental involvement, but not until they are ready to take the responsibility. For Steve, activities had to be short and planned in advance, at least for a while. A backyard game of catch or a walk to the ice cream store might be as much of a social engagement as Steve could handle. A good short visit is worth many longer failures. In subsequent visits, his parents might be able to disappear for a while, and the length of the play date might be extended.

Steve became an outstanding student in school long before he mastered the social graces. He remained a loner for several years, only occasionally interacting with boys and girls of his own age. His inability to compete in athletics, his poor self-control, and his need to be boss made him less than appealing as a friend. Eventually, he became the best mathematician in his grade, and that gave him a certain status. He tutored younger children, and through them began to glean some insight into his own behavior.

While Steve probably won't ever be Mr. Gregarious, he has learned to be more tactful in his dealings with people. And there is a happy ending. He graduated from a small, academically challenging college, where he was able to find a few friends with similar interests. Now, as an adult, he is working in a field he likes and in which he is very successful. One advantage of being an adult is that one can avoid athletics, if that's a weakness, and concentrate instead on areas of strength without appearing strange.

Most of us learn to anticipate social situations and quickly interpret people's reactions to us. We know all too well when someone is displeased, even though the person may be speaking softly and the words are not harsh. Body language or other nonverbal communication gives us the essential clues to people's feelings. Many learning-disabled children have difficulty perceiving the subtleties of social interaction, however. They fail to observe facial expressions and body gestures, and the meaning of a tone of voice eludes them.

Lacking the ability to zero in and read those signals, such children may misinterpret humor as well as anger and may be at a loss as to how to respond to others. Upon running into a neighbor who casually asks, "How are you?" they may tell him more than he ever wanted to know—in great detail. Another child might chatter gaily on about his dog's newest trick, insensitive to the fact that his neighbor's dog has just died. One youngster innocently called loudly across the aisle on a bus: "Mom, why is that man so wrinkled?" We can accept this from a four-year-old, but it seems both inappropriate and insulting when the speaker is ten.

"He's so clumsy, and I don't mean physically." That is how one mother described her son's social behavior. It seems an apt description for many of the children who constantly embarrass their siblings and parents with untoward remarks and actions.

> "He tells the neighbors about each fight my husband and I have."

> "We can't discuss anything personal at dinner anymore because he will tell the world."

> "He doesn't know when to stop talking and let people go home. He seems to want to hang onto them, even on the telephone."

> "He always says the wrong thing at the wrong time. He didn't have to tell his uncle that I said he was lazy and irresponsible."

Most children want desperately to be accepted by their peers, but for many, the nature of their disorder seems to drive away the very people who mean the most to them. They may be like any of the children described thus far—immature and shy, overly aggressive and bossy, or selfish and tactless. And much more than others, young people with learning problems tend to be ingenuous, naive, even gullible. This gullibility makes them particularly vulnerable to innumerable hurts and humiliations. In this age of precocious and sophisticated children, gullibility is perhaps the quality most misunderstood by others. It would be easier for many young people if they truly did not care about having friends. But they want so much to belong, they may tend to believe and trust everyone, even a fickle or fair-weather friend. Their lack of broad social experience leaves them without the ability to discriminate wisely.

WHEN YOUR CHILD CHOOSES THE WRONG FRIENDS

As a consequence of being friendless, some children ally themselves with the losers in their class or in the neighborhood—anyone who likes them and is responsive receives their offer of friendship. A pecking order exists for choosing one's friends, as in the animal kingdom. We tend to select people who are like us in some way or who mirror what we are, or think we are. But for some children, it may come down to a matter of who is left. They may start at the top and go down the social ladder until they find someone with whom they can relate. For Michael, in third grade, it was a new boy from Sweden who couldn't speak a word of English. The others in the neighborhood were appropriately helpful to Sven, but Michael tried to devour him. It was great to have a constant companion who padded along behind you and never talked back. Once Sven learned English, though, he joined the other guys on the ball field, and that was the end of another friendship for Michael.

Parents may complain that their son or daughter is associating with the "worst child in the class, a bad influence." They will mention the undesirable language and the mischief the youngsters get into together. Although their child may not enjoy the trouble he gets into, it may well be that his choice of a friend is the result of having *no* choice.

Parents will undoubtedly find it difficult to watch a relationship in which their child is being led down the proverbial garden path, but this friendship may be a first step in the child's learning to handle a social interaction. With understanding and patience, she will be able to go on to bigger and better friendships when she is more secure. In the meantime, your child needs your help and support. Don't criticize or demean your child's choice of companion, because a first step is better than none at all. When your child is rejected by a friend, don't try to minimize the pain she is feeling with a reassuring "Don't worry. You'll find another friend." Home must be a bulwark of strength and empathy when a child is feeling weak. A simple "I know how much this must hurt" will help her live through the rejection or insult.

HOW GAMES CAN TEACH SOCIAL SKILLS

As I've said, some children with learning differences observe less in their environment, misperceive more, and may not learn easily from experience. Because of their immaturity and social clumsiness, they are excluded by peers. Like all children, they want acceptance, but their eagerness may cause them to try too hard in inappropriate ways. As a result, their social experiences become even more limited, giving them fewer opportunities to learn how to act with others. If this sounds like your child, you as parents need to work with teachers to teach the child social nuances. These children can learn, but they may have to be taught many of the social responses that other children pick up unconsciously.

An important aspect of a child's social adjustment is his skill in playing games. Most children of nine or ten know a dozen or more card games and board games. However, some children have trouble learning and remembering the rules of a game, and feel as inept in that arena as they do in the classroom. A child who has difficulty remembering the days of the week will probably find it hard to recall the steps of a game. In addition, it is hard for ADHD youngsters to wait their turn. Their much-discussed impulsivity and their need to win get in the way. They may even tell you they hate games and "won't play anymore." And if they do play, their interest can wane quickly, particularly when they're losing.

I spend a fair amount of time in my office teaching children to play games. The time is well spent, for game-playing accomplishes many skills. First, children master the rules and directions in sequence. They also gain a social learning experience. Children learn to share, to take turns, to trust their opponent, and eventually even to lose gracefully.

One young boy always wanted to play the card game War, the only game he had ever played successfully. But he usually forgot the name of the game and even how to play it. "I know how, but I forget," was his way of asking me to tell him again. It took many weeks for him to master more than one game, but it was worth the effort. It provided him with something to do when his brother deigned to play with him on a rainy day. Frequently a child will want to play the same game over and over until everyone is sick of it and wonders why he isn't, too. This may reflect his delight in having mastered a skill that didn't come easily. It feels good to feel competent rather than challenged.

On sunny days, most parents have but a single thought for their children's spare time: "Go play outside." For some children, this is the command they dread the most. They can't go out on the playground because no one will play with them—even though there may be an apartment building full of children out there. They claim the other boys won't let them in their games, and they return home a half hour later in tears, only to be sent out again by their frustrated parents.

For Mike, almost nine, this was a typical scene, one that happened week after week. He was rejected by the kids on the block but was sent out to battle again and again by his parents, who couldn't stand to see him alone in front of the TV all the time. Finally, after many bruises, physical and otherwise, Mike found a group of younger boys to play with. He liked kickball better than baseball anyway and at times even felt like a leader. The fact that the other boys were only six didn't bother Mike, but it made his parents unhappy. This was one problem they hadn't bargained for. They could accept the fact that Mike couldn't read well, but playing outside had nothing to do with that. They told him in no uncertain terms that he should play with boys more his own age, and then called me for confirmation.

While I could understand Mike's parents' concern, I felt it was important for them to acknowledge that he *was* less mature emotionally than the kids his age and less adept in sports. Under the circumstances, it seemed better for him to associate with younger children with whom he felt comfortable than to sit alone or rely on his parents for companionship. Practicing his social skills on the six-year-olds might eventually lead to more age-appropriate friendships.

Johnny used to stand alone on the school playground, sucking on one finger and twisting a lock of hair. Most of the sixth graders were too engrossed in their game to even notice that Johnny wasn't playing with them. And most of the time, Johnny wasn't even watching the game. He was standing too far away—where no one could see the occasional tear in his eye. Johnny rarely participated in any of the games at school. He didn't like being the last one chosen by the captain for the day and, as he put it, "If you don't play, you can't lose." He confessed, though, that since there was no one to be with during recess and nothing to do, he hated recess even more than reading or math. It was the loneliest and worst time of the day.

Inside the classroom, Johnny had his own way of getting even. Almost without realizing it, he used to annoy the other children. He pushed pencils off their desks, disturbed them when they were trying to work, and generally made a nuisance of himself. He complained that the other children bothered him, but he didn't seem to be aware that he played an active role in the teasing. He only knew that he was not happy in school, and given a choice, would much prefer to stay home. In fact, when Johnny didn't go to school in summer, he did much better. He went to a day camp for children with learning problems, where he was happy. He made new friends on the bus and received glowing reports from his counselors.

WHAT YOU CAN DO IN THE GOOD OLD SUMMERTIME

While summer vacations can be a great relief for many children, they frequently pose problems for their parents. I am often asked for advice on what a learning-disabled child should do in the summer. Should he stay home and be tutored in hopes of closing the educational gap, should he go away to camp for the social experience, or should he just relax at home? It all depends on the child's needs and the family situation. If the pressure on the child has been great during the school year, perhaps a relaxing summer at home without more schoolwork would be best, particularly if there are other children with whom to play. I knew a twelve-year-old who spent the summer painting the basement floor— and loved every minute of it. But if a boy has trouble organizing his time or would spend the summer lying on his bed watching TV, he obviously needs direction. In this case, a community recreation activity or structured program might be important. For older children, a camp away from home can foster independence and improve social ability as well as athletic skills. Although private camps are expensive, there are alternatives, such as 4-H, Pioneer, and scout camps. Some camps even have remediation as part of the program.

The choice of a camp again depends on the development and needs of the camper. If a boy or girl has a low threshold of tolerance for new situations and is anxious about leaving home, the protective environment of a special camp close by might be best. A highly competitive camp may impose the same level of stress that the child has had during the school year and should be avoided, unless of course he's a good athlete. If a child goes to a regular camp or recreation program, parents should be honest with the director about any problems or special needs their child has. Sometimes parents are reluctant to do this, hoping against hope, perhaps, that the difficulties won't be apparent in a camp setting. However, we usually do a child no favor when we try to hide problems that are evident every day.

While Nick was at a nature camp, his mother called me, sounding very upset. She said that her son's counselor had asked to meet with her to discuss Nick's behavior at the camp. Nick was "all over the place," he said, not paying attention and annoying the other children. As he put it, "He pushes kids on purpose, intruding on their space, and they get angry."

Nick and I spoke on the phone and I asked him to tell me about camp. His complaint, of course, was about the kids who were "mean" and his counselor, who "let a boy hit me." We talked about how he could have a better week at camp. I suggested that he try to spend time with the one boy he knew in the group and perhaps ask his counselor for help, too. He might ask to sit near the counselor during a nature demonstration or project to help him stay focused. I also wondered whether he would want me to talk to his counselor, as well. Nick liked the idea and his mother agreed. Then I learned that she had not said anything about Nick's history of ADHD, which had been an ongoing problem for years, at home as well as at school. When she realized she had not done her son a favor, she gave me permission to speak to Nick's counselor, who was most receptive and grateful for the suggestions I was able to offer. Had he known about Nick's history earlier, some of the problems might have been avoided.

HELPFUL HINTS FOR PARENTS

For many boys and girls like Nick, their social problems are possibly the saddest part of their lives and perhaps the most difficult to remediate. Most of the suggestions that I can give to parents are merely Band-Aids, not cures. Only a parent's understanding and patient support can help a child learn to live with others and handle the frustrations that come his way. This isn't easy for parents because their feelings are aroused, too. Memories of one's own hurts and unfulfilled childhood wishes make it especially hard to be objective. However, there are a few rules of thumb that might help the communication between you and your child during difficult times.

1. When your child talks about his troubles, don't blame him or say they don't exist. Acknowledge his pain and try to help him with the reality of the situation. Empathy, not judgment, may be all he is asking for. On the other hand, a little emotional distance is helpful. We can't help if we are so involved that his problems become ours.

2. "How could you try to be Jimmy's friend?" is a valid question to ask a boy or girl. I sometimes ask a child to name someone who is well-liked in class and tell me what the kids like about that person. I usually hear about a relatively cheerful boy or girl who can share and is a good sport. Getting children to look head-on at the requirements for a successful relationship may give them new insight and a fresh perspective.

3. Bribery might get you everywhere. Promising a reward for a successful social interchange or play date may encourage a child to exercise that extra bit of self-control. I frequently give a child who's a social isolate "homework," that is, an assignment to talk to or get together with another human being at least twice a week. Even when I forget to check, a child might remind me that he did his homework. Our mutual delight is usually a sufficient reward from me.

4. Setting standards for behavior (as discussed in Chapter 3) is important. As your child matures, temper tantrums should abate and greater self-control is expected. You may acknowledge to the child that you know self-restraint is difficult, but with effort and will power it can be exercised.

5. Patience and the gift of time help, too. The recognition that some children take longer to become ready for socialization may relieve the pressure for both parent and child. Just as some adults are not ready for marriage and a family in their twenties, some boys and girls are not able to handle a sleepover at eight or nine. It might help to remember that most shy children don't become reclusive adults, but eventually do find relationships that are comfortable for them.

WHAT YOU CAN DO AS YOUR CHILD GROWS OLDER

Parents and teachers tend to be more aware of children's social difficulties when they are in elementary school than when they are older. Younger children are more open about their problems, revealing their slights and hurts more readily. As they grow, they become more self-protective and secretive. Then, too, teachers in junior and senior high school usually see so many students in the course of a day that they don't know any of them well. It is the rare teacher who becomes a mentor for a teenager, particularly because the teacher's primary concern is with academic subjects. So, it is possible for the lonely high school student to suffer in silence, with no one able to comprehend why he is so "antisocial."

Sometimes parents do sense a teenager's isolation from the group, but they feel powerless to do much about it. Most adolescents do not take kindly to planned or guided social activities. They resent parental interference, even when it is well meant. They are cutting the ties at home, and the peer group takes over as all-important. At this age, they want most to conform and be like everyone else, even to the clothes and sneakers that might look ridiculous to parents but are in vogue. However, teenagers with learning problems may appear even more different than when they were younger. Their handicaps are more visible to others and more all-encompassing. They may talk too much, too loudly, and too repetitively. Their immaturity and weaker sense of identity make it harder to conform socially, and their lack of experience gives them a less than adequate repertoire of behaviors to use when the chips are down. When teenagers can't stay cool under fire and have no friend to come to their defense, scapegoating can be particularly vicious. Even without problems, most adolescents are unsure of themselves and are only too willing to exalt themselves by tearing down weaker peers. The young person with a difference of any kind becomes a perfect foil.

At this stage, too, boys and girls become more discriminating and selective about who becomes part of their social world. They derive a sense of status from those with whom they associate. Unfortunately, the teenager with learning differences is likely to be regarded as a low-status person, to be avoided. Several studies have also shown that adolescents with learning disabilities tend to be less involved in both school and extracurricular activities and derive less satisfaction from their involvement with peers. Therefore, it is particularly important to help them develop areas of competence. If a boy is a good soccer player, he probably will make the team, and if he is an artist, he may be asked to draw posters for school elections or paint sets for school plays. This will help others view him not primarily as LD but as someone with something to offer.

Jesse, a member of a minority group in a predominantly white community, was on the fringes of a rather rowdy group of eighth grade boys. He didn't actually start the fights or break the windows, but he was an observer at these events and the activists were his friends. Jesse had a long history of academic problems, but it was only in junior high school that he began to seek the excitement and notoriety that this group offered. A boy or girl who is afraid to compete in the world of achievers may find it easier to be the bad guy.

Luckily, Jesse was a soccer player and made the junior varsity team. That meant that he stayed for practice every day after school, and he gained some recognition. However, when his grades were poor or if he and his friends got into trouble, Jesse's parents grounded him, forbidding him to play in the next game. Fortunately, it was not hard for me to convince them that this was probably the single most important activity for him and keeping him from it should not be used as punishment. Not only did playing soccer keep Jesse busy after school and out of trouble, but it gave him status of the positive kind.

Young people whose peers reject them frequently express their hurt through a range of negative behaviors—from rowdiness to delinquency. Research in the field has reported the strong connection between undiagnosed, unremediated ADHD and learning differences and trouble with the law. Young people today have more freedom than children did a generation ago. As a result, a person who craves acceptance might, like Jesse, go along with the gang, suffering the consequences of its actions.

Craig, mild-mannered and conforming throughout elementary school, had an inordinate need to be part of the group. The only way the eighth grade boys would accept him was if he did their dirty work. If a pack of cigarettes was to be swiped from the local store, Craig was elected to do the job. He had two strikes against him from the beginning. He allowed himself to be exploited and, because of his naïveté, was always caught red-handed while the other boys walked away in the clear.

There is little doubt that life is easier for a teenager if he has even one good friend to help him feel important. But to become a true friend means to be caring and sensitive to another's needs and feelings. The required give-and-take is often hard for the adolescent with attention problems or learning disabilities. If he is still egocentric, his relationships may be one-way streets. He won't share much of himself with another but will tend to use the other person to fulfill his own self-centered needs. For many young adults, getting past their own immaturity and their narcissistic concerns can be a major stumbling block in the development of good mutual relationships, whether of the same or the opposite sex.

Parents frequently ask whether it is preferable for their LD adolescents to associate with LD peers rather than those in the "mainstream." Actually, the question may be academic, because, left to their own devices, many seem to gravitate to those with similar difficulties, even in college. If a person is reserved and awkward at a social gathering and has few friends, a supervised group of other learning-disabled young people might be necessary to fill the void. On the other hand, if one can manage to stay in the general population of peers, even with help, surely that should be encouraged.

I am reminded of Sara, who struggled with a lisp as well as learning problems all through school. With sheer determination not to appear different, she achieved amazing results. She refused to take slower courses in high school and made an equally strong effort to make friends. By her junior year, her grades were good and she had friends. She had also developed much of the social savvy that had been so obviously missing when she was younger.

Sara was the first to admit that her life was not easy. She studied hard and went to the math center almost daily throughout the year when she would rather have been socializing. However, she took pride in her success. Sara's parents had also rooted for her, never wavering in their support and delighting in her accomplishments. Only her SAT scores, the lowest in the school, reflected the residual effects of her learning problems.

As many parents do, Sara's mother asked me one day whether it was too late to make a difference in Sara's life, academically or socially. Far from being too late, I think parents have a second chance to rebuild and restructure relationships with their adolescents. Open communication within a family can be a significant part of the bridge between childhood and adulthood.

The following are a few suggestions you can use cautiously with your adolescent.

1. Encourage good self-care and hygiene. An adolescent may remember to comb his hair in the latest style but not to brush his teeth or use a deodorant. Be clear that your (unobtrusive) reminders are not intended to embarrass your budding adult child but merely to enhance his image with his peers.

2. Don't insist on a conservative haircut or button-down shirts if crew cuts and T-shirts are in vogue. Conforming to the peer group and looking like everyone else is all-important at this age. So save your confrontations for the more important issues.

3. Keep in mind that good manners and civility don't have to disappear in adolescence. You might devise a system of subtle clues that only your child will recognize, indicating that he needs to modulate his voice or give someone else a chance to speak.

4. Convey the idea that instant gratification isn't always possible. At times even he may have to postpone getting what he wants. If you are too busy to chauffeur him to his friend's and then to the movies, he may have to find another means of transportation or wait until you are available.

5. No teenager can afford to be ignorant about sex in these times. Although schools are introducing the topic earlier (to some parents' dismay), some young people still don't understand what to expect or how to handle it. There are major health concerns that parents cannot ignore, AIDS among them. Parents cannot pussyfoot around this difficult or even taboo topic, and they may need help with their own feelings about it. Then, too, with LD teenagers who seem so immature, parents may feel their child is not ready for a discussion about sex. As one father of a thirteen-year-old boy said, "I don't want to avoid talking about it; I just don't know how much to tell Sam." A clear, forthright discussion may clear up misconceptions and diminish any guilt. Remember, a teenager's curiosity and fantasies are normal, but they must also learn the facts from a reliable source.

6. Teach the adolescent how to be comfortable with pre-dating activities. Talking on the telephone or going to a party may seem overwhelming. An immature teenager may need very specific cues on how and when to act. I actually wrote out a script for a fifteen-year-old boy who wanted to telephone a girl but had no idea what to say.

We drew up a list of questions he could ask when there was dead silence on the other end of the line.

7. Encourage your adolescent to find a group to join. He may be devastated if he can't get in with the jocks at school, but there may be a group of aspiring musicians that would welcome him. Church groups, YMCAs, theater groups, or computer clinics may provide a place to meet peers. But his individuality must be respected, and parents cannot impose their own interests or values on him. On the other hand, if he is not morose about his lack of a social life, so be it—he just may be content to spend time alone at this point in his development.

8. Help and encourage your teenager to become independent. This necessitates taking some risks, such as letting him travel alone and leaving some important decisions to him.

If nothing seems to work and you continue to be concerned about signs of social trouble with your adolescent, seek professional help. There is little if any stigma today about seeing a therapist, counselor, or minister, and it may prevent future problems. The social aspects of a child's life are too important to ignore. Parents need to take a long-range view of children's social lives and plan their helping strategies as carefully as they do their education. If we neglect the social skills, all the academic teaching in the world won't prepare them for adulthood.

In fact, the social functioning of adults with ADHD is sometimes perceived by their families as their single most crucial area of need. Whereas school problems are finite, with an end point, social and interpersonal problems don't end with graduation or leaving school. Like their younger counterparts, adults with ADHD have been described as being more aggressive, domineering, noisy, hostile, and socially demanding (Barkley, 1995). Due in part to their impulsivity, forgetfulness, explosive temper, or mood swings, many have trouble keeping friends as well as jobs.

On the other hand, some children and adults with learning differences and ADHD seem particularly tuned in to what is going on around them. Their social skills may be a significant strength. They tend to be energetic (but not too much so), have solid verbal skills, and know intuitively when to leave a friend, parent, or boss alone. They also sense when it's appropriate to tell a joke and when not to. I've heard the expression "streetwise" used to describe this ability. Reading a book may be hard for them, but they know how to read people. It's a great trait to have, and some of our LD/ADHD young people seem to have it built in. They are the fortunate ones.

The following is a list of social skills you might try to help your child and adolescent develop. They are qualities that will enhance their social acceptance throughout the school years and beyond.

1. Actively listening to other people while they are talking
2. Maintaining eye contact while speaking or listening
3. Sustaining a conversation with "give-and-take" responses
4. Understanding nonverbal communication (facial expressions, body language)
5. Understanding and responding appropriately to another person's feelings
7. Being able to work and play in group settings
8. Awareness of how one's behavior affects others
9. Giving compliments when deserved
10. Negotiating appropriately for one's needs and wants
11. Being helpful to others without being intrusive
12. Being able to accept and respond to constructive criticism

Generally speaking, intervention for adults with ADHD and social problems centers around individual or group counseling, mediation, proper matching to jobs that "fit," and social skills education and training. For many, the combination of treatment and accommodation enables them to lead successful lives.

5

LIFE AT SCHOOL

When the school census taker came around counting prospective students for the new school in the area, Mrs. Brown laughed. Her only child, Teddy, was ten months old, and the thought of school was remote. Yet it seemed only a minute later that she was holding him by the hand as they entered the large brick building with the scrubbed desks and polished floors. It was a morning in early September, and Teddy was trying to act very grown up. He let go of his mother's hand and went into his classroom, choking back a tear. But what should have been his first successful experience away from home became a nightmare within the first few months. In retrospect, Teddy's parents said that he had been "a different—and much happier—child" before he started school.

When his parents and the school psychologist reviewed Teddy's early history, nothing seemed unusual. He had walked and talked when the other children in the neighborhood did and was a happy, cheerful toddler. He even played nicely with the kids in his play group. But all this changed in the first few months of kindergarten. What had happened to cause his bad moods, his frequent nightmares, and his reluctance to go to school? Although no one recognized his problems at the beginning, we now know that Teddy had learning disabilities.

Let's follow him for the next several years to see what children like Teddy typically experience in school and what their parents may have to deal with in the course of their children's education.

FIRST EXPERIENCES AT SCHOOL

Early in the kindergarten year when Teddy came home cranky from school, his mother was sympathetic but unconcerned. She assumed that he was irritable because of the long morning at school and the new group of children, and she was sure he would settle down in time. But when Teddy kept complaining about his " mean" teacher and the "hard work," Mrs. Brown became somewhat more concerned. When Teddy reverted to wetting his bed almost every night, she thought of talking to his teacher, but felt uncomfortable about doing so. Maybe Teddy's teacher would think she was blaming her or that, at the very least, she was an overanxious mother.

Many parents, particularly of first children, are reluctant to discuss a youngster's problems at school unless called in specifically to do so. They conform to an imagined rule of protocol: "Don't call us, we'll call you"—and that usually happens only when disciplinary measures are called for. Most adults of today grew up in awe of anyone in the role of pedagogue. Teachers and the school represented undisputed authority, to be feared by the young. Such a firmly entrenched image is not easily discarded. Thus, many parents refrain from contacting the school and are less involved in their children's education than current philosophy dictates. Several studies have shown that children do better when their parents take an interest in their schoolwork and have a vested interest in their success.

Most children adapt easily to school and have no difficulty learning. When the path is not so smooth, however, parents may need to take a more assertive stand for their children's sake. A child with problems in school needs an advocate, someone who can run interference for him. After all, he spends most of his day in school, and that is where he is most vulnerable. Most teachers today want to work in collaboration with parents and welcome as much information from home as they can get. In all likelihood, Teddy's teacher would have wanted to know right away that Teddy was so unhappy in school.

Finally, late in October, when Teddy's teacher called Mrs. Brown for a conference, both reported feeling nervous in anticipation of the meeting. The teacher didn't want to alarm Mrs. Brown, she said, but she knew something was "wrong," and conversely, Teddy's mother was afraid to hear the teacher's report. Her heart pounding, Mrs. Brown went to school. The conference went something like this: "Teddy's a darling little boy, but he seems quite immature for kindergarten. It's hard for him to listen, and he wanders aimlessly around the room much of the morning. He doesn't participate in the group activities, even briefly, and just seems young for the class. Some of the children are learning to read, but Teddy doesn't recognize many of the letters or numbers and won't let me try to teach him. He still can't write his name and says he doesn't want to learn. But he's a delight to have in the class!" (Teachers often make this last mollifying comment in a sincere attempt to add a positive note to the conference.)

For the next twenty minutes, Teddy's teacher and Mrs. Brown talked about things they could both do to help the boy. Teddy had once confided to his mother that "I need to sit on my teacher's lap more." The teacher suggested that Mrs. Brown read to Teddy at night, put magnetic letters on the refrigerator door for him, and practice counting objects around the house. In speaking to Mrs. Brown, I also mentioned that dice could be useful for recognizing "how many" and, later, for simple addition.

Mrs. Brown had mixed emotions when she left the school but was glad she had met with Teddy's teacher, who really did seem to know Teddy. After the meeting, Teddy's unhappiness at school was much easier to understand. Mrs. Brown felt a sense of relief in a way, now that she knew how to help her son. At the same time, she felt somewhat remiss in not having taught Teddy letters and numbers earlier, as the other mothers undoubtedly had. She had thought she might confuse him if she taught him "differently." Mrs. Brown also admitted to herself, though, that Teddy hadn't seemed the slightest bit interested in the books she had tried to read to him, and he couldn't seem to remember the names of the numbers even after she had repeated them many times. Parents often feel an unnecessary sense of guilt. It is hard to push learning when a child appears disinterested or reluctant.

When Mrs. Brown tried to work with Teddy at home, he was very resistant. He said he didn't like "work," which meant anything that he had to sit down for, except, of course, TV. He refused outright to work on letters, and even the sight of them brought on tears. The teaching sessions at home quickly deteriorated into temper tantrums and yelling, and little was accomplished. Teddy soon developed a full-fledged hatred of school, and his parents were anything but happy.

TO RETAIN OR NOT TO RETAIN?

In the spring, Teddy's teacher and the principal suggested to the Browns that perhaps Teddy should repeat kindergarten next year. Because he wasn't ready for the work of first grade, another year in kindergarten would give him the opportunity to "grow up" a little.

While Mr. and Mrs. Brown were not surprised to hear the recommendation that Teddy be retained, they didn't like the idea. They remembered that when they were in school only the "dummies" had been left back, and then these children were teased unmercifully. Besides, what would their friends and Teddy's grandparents say? The Browns lived in a community in which everyone would know. The stigma seemed more than they could handle.

Teddy's parents also thought that maybe the school was judging Teddy too soon. Perhaps he would mature over the summer. And even if he didn't, there was always time later on to consider repeating a grade. Schools usually honor parents' feelings in matters such as retention in a grade, so it was decided to let Teddy move on to first grade with his classmates in the fall, and the school would provide as much help as possible.

Whether or not to retain a child is never an easy decision—for parents or the school. A child's growth and development are not entirely predictable, and one must always weigh the benefits against the obvious disadvantages. Staying back can be a blow to a child's ego and other children may, indeed, ridicule him. Some schools today have a policy never to retain a child, whereas others advise retention frequently for children who don't seem prepared for the work of the next grade. This policy varies from district to district.

Criteria for Successful Retention

If the school does recommend retention for your child, you might want to consider several factors. Ask yourself the following questions.

1. *What will my child gain from repeating the year in school?* If your child seems capable but immature in some areas—social, academic, and emotional—an additional year might give him a chance to consolidate his skills and do the necessary growing. It can also give him an opportunity for leadership that he would otherwise lack. Also, I never fail to mention to parents that their child will be the first in the group to get a driver's license, an enviable status symbol.

   Perhaps because of the competitive nature of college and even nursery school admissions in some areas, many parents these days are asking their children's preschools to keep the child for an extra year, particularly if that child is a boy with a birthday late in the calendar year. Although girls are also being retained, boys are frequently less mature than girls in their young years and, therefore, less ready for the rigors of school.

The first criterion, then, is whether the child seems generally immature. We also have to consider his physical maturity. If a boy will be six feet tall at eleven years of age, as his father was, he may appear to be the grandfather of the third grade. On the other hand, if he was late in losing his baby teeth and is small, he might be an ideal candidate to repeat a grade.

2. *Where will my child stand in the grade that he or she repeats—top, bottom?* To justify retaining a child in a grade higher than kindergarten or first grade, one should be able to predict that the child will perform at least in the middle—or better yet, near the top—of the class, and stay there. If, on the other hand, his skills are so low that he will still be on the bottom academically, I would seriously question the advisability of such a move. He's being set up for another failure, this time with even younger children. There would be little ego boost and no academic advantage. For many children with learning differences, therefore, holding them back is not the answer. Retention, after all, does not make a learning disability go away.

3. *On what basis was the recommendation for retention made?* I have known school personnel who suggest retention for a child solely because of poor reading skills or low scores on standardized achievement tests. The earlier reason was the stated one for recommending retention for Daniel, a first grader in Teddy's school. (Unlike Teddy, though, he had seemed fine in kindergarten.) Daniel was a very bright, verbal child who couldn't read, it was true, but who excelled in all aspects of arithmetic. He was also a leader among his classmates. He was imaginative, and his artistic talent and fund of knowledge were amazing.

Daniel's parents didn't know what to do about Daniel's staying in first grade for another year, and they asked my advice. I was glad they had, for although I don't often disagree with school personnel, I felt that retention would have been wrong for Daniel. He was participating in every activity in the class, except reading, and he seemed to be learning. I felt it was important for him to continue to learn through every means possible until he learned to read. Reading, after all, is not an education in and of itself. It is an important skill, to be sure, but children can also learn by living and listening. Daniel would have been comfortable in first grade again only in reading. In every other area, he would have been out of step. For retention to be successful, the *whole* child has to benefit from the additional year.

4. *Does the school have the resources to help my child should he repeat?* There are several aspects to this question. First, will the child seem out of place, physically or socially, in the grade he'll repeat? Classes frequently have personalities of their own. One may seem particularly young, while another appears mature. And does the school have an appropriate support system for a child who may still have special needs, even if he does repeat a grade? Some teachers find it easier than others to make the necessary accommodations and curricular modifications.

5. *Can we as parents really accept the idea of retention?* Finally, for retention to be effective, there must be emotional acceptance on the part of the parents. This doesn't mean just verbal acknowledgment that another year would be helpful to the child. It means that you can honestly support the prospect of your child's spending another year in a grade. Only then can you help your child understand and accept the reasons for it and withstand the possible criticism and teasing of friends and neighbors. A parent's positive attitude can sometimes make an unpalatable idea acceptable to the child.

I know of one family whose three sons all repeated first grade very successfully. Two of the boys had November birthdays and were therefore young for the class, and the third son just seemed very immature. None of the boys had a particularly difficult time with the thought of retention. It became the accepted thing to do in their family, and all the children appeared to benefit significantly. The two older boys, who had not learned to read in first grade, went on to become excellent students by fifth grade. Perhaps they would have anyway, but undoubtedly with much more stress in the early years.

For another girl, a third grader in a competitive private school, the question of retention had been debated since she was in kindergarten. Finally, at the end of third grade, the headmaster said he didn't see how she would manage in fourth grade, when the curriculum "would take a giant leap forward." Jennifer was also physically small and shy, and she was unhappy in school. When the retention was discussed, Jennifer strenuously objected. She was afraid she would be teased and embarrassed in front of her peers—

and be "miserable." The headmaster made a bet with her. He understood her fears but promised that after two weeks of school, he would buy Jennifer an ice cream cone if she were still unhappy, but she would owe him one if she liked her new class. Of course, he won, but he didn't collect the bet. Jennifer's telling smile was reward enough for him. And after years of deferring the inevitable, Jennifer's parents were delighted as well.

On the other hand, if you cannot accept the idea of retaining your child, the likelihood of success is doubtful, and you and the school probably should not force the issue. Of course, you should discuss this with school personnel and let them make every effort to help you see the benefit to your child and support the recommendation, if it is valid. This may take several weeks, months, or even a year. But if, in the end, you and/or your child's other parent cannot come to terms with it, retention may not be best for your child and should not be implemented.

To sum up, repetition of a grade in school may be helpful when a child seems bright but young and ill-prepared for the next grade. The child's physical maturity and social adjustment may, in fact, be more significant than academic skills in making that determination. The other factors to consider are the composition of next year's class, where the child would place academically in that class, the help the school could provide, and most important, your approval and support. And if retention is to be implemented, the earlier it takes place in your child's schooling, the easier the adjustment is likely to be.

But let's return to Teddy's story. He did not repeat kindergarten but entered first grade. His parents waited anxiously to see what the year would bring. They didn't say anything to Teddy's new teacher about his problems in kindergarten, hoping that maybe Teddy's teacher of last year hadn't brought out the best in him. They also thought that perhaps he had matured over the summer. Then, too, if they told his teacher about his difficulties, they might be giving her too much food for thought. Perhaps Teddy had merely gotten off to a slow start and this year would be better.

At first Teddy went off to school each morning without complaint and brought home papers stamped with a smiley face. But soon that changed. He began to dawdle on school mornings, asking if he could stay home because he had a "stomachache." He often told his father he wished there were no such thing as school. It soon became apparent that things weren't going so well this year either. And on the days when a substitute was teaching the class, Teddy came home in tears. He spoke of having been asked to read aloud—when he couldn't—and was called on to answer a question he didn't know. Once the whole class was kept in from recess while Teddy finished copying a sentence from the blackboard. He was humiliated—and his classmates were angry.

One day in December, the school psychologist called Mrs. Brown, asking for permission to test Teddy. His teacher had made the referral because he didn't seem to be making much progress in reading and seemed so unhappy in school. The psychologist explained that he would try to determine the nature of Teddy's problems in the course of his evaluation.

Six weeks later, the Browns went to school to learn the results. The psychologist said that Teddy was of average intelligence, but that he probably had a "specific learning disability" (maybe dyslexia) that was making it hard for him to learn to read and write. Teddy was also easily distracted and was finding it difficult to learn in the casual, busy atmosphere of the classroom.

Teddy had been carefully placed in a class where there was less structure in the daily schedule than in a traditional self-contained class. Where he was, the children could select their own activities and lessons—up to a point—and they were free to move about the classroom during the school day. In these "open classrooms" children are not expected to remain seated at assigned desks, but may choose to work at designated areas—in the reading corner, at the science station, or at the math table. It was felt that Teddy could learn at his own pace in this kind of setting and not compare himself with his classmates, because there were so few competitive or group-centered activities.

However, after getting to know Teddy, the psychologist thought that the choice of class may have been inappropriate after all. The larger number of children and the extra movement in the room had proven difficult for Teddy. He never seemed to know where he should be or what he ought to be doing, which only contributed to his frustration. Rather than change the class at this point in the year, however, the psychologist suggested that Teddy's teacher try to structure his day and supervise him more closely. Henceforth, when Teddy arrived at school in the morning, a contract outlining the work plan for the day would be waiting for him. His teacher would also help him move from one learning area to another, since this seemed to be a problem for him. He had often gotten "lost" en route, taking walks down the hall to the bathroom.

For the first time, the Browns began to understand why Teddy couldn't concentrate on his work and why he seemed to be so forgetful. Then the psychologist said that Teddy eventually might need a special class for children with learning disabilities, where he could get more intensive help. However, no decision would be made until later on in the year and, in the interim, he should stay where he was. The school had the resources to help him, now that his learning problems had been recognized.

SPECIAL SERVICES IN SCHOOL

The following week, Teddy began going to the Resource Room in his school for forty minutes every day. There he worked with a learning disabilities specialist, either alone or in a small group of four or five children, on skills in which he was weak.

A *resource program* is only one of the possible services within a school designed to help children with learning differences and other handicapping conditions. Children are referred for specific help, with grouping usually based on educational needs.

Special education teachers trained in learning disabilities provide direct and indirect services to the children. The direct service is the individual teaching given to those children who come to the Resource Room, Learning Center, or simply "helping place," as it is sometimes called, for a specified time daily or several times weekly. This arrangement allows the children to be included in regular classes for most of the school day. An indirect service is one in which special education teachers consult with classroom teachers, giving them suggestions and strategies to help their students. This "teacher consultant model" is increasingly being used in schools around the country. In this model, in addition to indirect services, special educators also give direct services to children in their own classrooms, providing support in their areas of need. This provides somewhat less intensive help for children than a resource program, but has the advantage of being a "push in" rather than a "pull out" system. In other words, the children don't have to leave their classrooms to obtain the special help they need.

For Teddy, though, the Resource Room was a haven and a respite from the classroom. He felt secure there, knowing that the other children were in the same boat. It was the one place in school he didn't feel like a failure. In fact, he usually got 100s on his papers. Although some of his classmates objected to going for special help, he didn't mind at all. In his regular classroom, the teacher also helped him. Among other accommodations, she was able to shorten the required spelling list for the week and let him dictate rather than having to write the words. She knew what his learning needs were and planned his work accordingly.

Teddy's teacher made other modifications, too. In view of his short attention span, she made a deal with him. When he felt he had to move around, he could leave the room to get a drink at the water fountain, but only if he came right back. Teddy liked this responsibility and usually did not abuse the privilege, although he was tempted. As for most young people with learning problems these days, most of Teddy's needs were handled within the classroom by his regular teacher, supplemented by the special services available in school.

By April of that year, Teddy had begun to read a little and didn't seem quite so unhappy in school. He had made a few friends in the class, and they even included him in the games at recess. When the Browns met with Teddy's classroom teacher, resource teacher, school psychologist, and principal in May, the consensus was that Teddy should continue in a regular, but more traditional, classroom setting next year. The school would continue to provide the resource help that Teddy needed.

In September, at the very beginning of second grade, Teddy's parents made an appointment to meet with Teddy's teacher. They told her what Teddy could and couldn't do, and how he showed his frustration by resisting work and withdrawing into himself. It was decided that his teacher would send weekly progress reports home, and that neither Teddy's teacher nor his parents would wait until small problems became big ones before they communicated with each other. Teddy's parents also asked that the teacher read the psychologist's report from the previous year as well as the comments from the resource teacher.

The beginning of each year is the right time for parents to contact a child's classroom teacher. You may be reluctant to discuss your child's differences for fear of raising a red flag. And it is true that some teachers do discuss a child's difficulties too openly, embarrassing the child in front of his peers. But, barring an insensitive teacher, many months of bewilderment and frustration for both teacher and child can be avoided by an early meeting and an honest sharing of information.

The conference with the Browns helped Teddy's teacher know what to expect. She realized that his parents were willing to work with her, and she felt less isolated in the challenging task ahead. Learning more about a child can be a joint venture for parents and teachers. As they share information, they are better able to formulate realistic educational plans. In fact, federal law now mandates that every child with an identified learning disability *must* have an Individualized Educational Plan (known as an IEP), developed and approved by parents and educators together.

An IEP sets out, in some detail, the child's current level of instruction, his weakesses, and, most important, the goals that are to be met in school by the end of the year. These are supposed to include behavioral, cognitive, and affective or emotional goals and are subject to on-going reevaluation and revision every year. The IEP serves as a continuing diagnostic and teaching prescription for a child. In some districts, short-term IEPs are also required. These need not be shared with the parents, although parents may see them if they wish. Still, IEPs are valuable for teachers in writing the long-range goals.

Since 1986, when Congress passed Public Law #99-457, encouraging states to develop and implement early intervention services for infants and toddlers with handicapping conditions, children from birth to five years of age have also been entitled to special education services. (Prior to that, educational services were only guaranteed for students from five to twenty-one years of age.) For the youngest children, a Comprehensive Family Service Plan (CFSP) is written instead of the IEP. In the CFSP, the special needs of the family are specified and the appropriate help provided. The process for developing CFSPs is designed to be both flexible and functional and to be continuously responsive to the concerns and needs expressed by families. It is important to note that IEPs and CFSPs are written in specific behavioral terms rather than in broad generalities. A first grader's IEP might include such objectives as "John will recognize all capital letters of the alphabet and identify initial consonant sounds by June." IEPs vary greatly from district to district and even from school to school, but the intent is the same—to set goals and objectives for which the school will be accountable.

Throughout the fall, Teddy seemed to be progressing, and his parents breathed a sigh of relief over their decision to keep him in the regular school. Teddy's teacher even thought he might catch up with the class by the end of the year if he continued at his present pace. But he didn't. Maybe it was the bout with the flu, the long Christmas vacation, or just his learning problems. In any case, everyone got jittery again in March, when Teddy's achievement test results were in the lowest percentile. Then his teacher came up with the idea that perhaps Teddy should repeat second grade with her next year. But Teddy's parents argued that Teddy was a good athlete and popular with his classmates at last. It didn't seem fair to separate him from his friends. And, by April, he had started to move forward again. His reading improved and he even seemed somewhat more interested in school. In June, he was promoted to third grade.

As usual, Teddy loved the summer in day camp. He may have shied away from the challenge of a song fest or a camp play, but otherwise he was a great camper. He swam and played baseball, and his self-confidence grew. Reports from his counselors were glowing, and Teddy seemed relaxed and happy. His parents hated to see camp end almost as much as Teddy did.

In September, Teddy's third grade teacher called the Browns even before the Browns called her. She suggested a meeting with them, the principal, and the school psychologist. This time it was the teacher who wondered what Teddy was doing in third grade. His second grade teacher had spoken to her about Teddy, but she had no idea that he would be so low-functioning. "He must have forgotten a lot over the summer," she said (a problem typical of young people with learning difficulties). Now he was so far below the rest of the class that there was no group for him. He sat alone in class looking miserable. He was particularly unhappy about having to work in a first grade math book. He kept losing the book and telling everyone who would listen that he was sure he could do the work in the third grade math book, but his teacher wouldn't let him try. Everyone at the conference agreed that Teddy needed a cohesive, integrated program to help remediate his learning difference and boost his self-esteem.

For the time being, Teddy was assigned to an itinerant learning specialist who would work with him one hour a day on an individual basis. Many school systems employ teachers who travel from school to school, in lieu of, or in addition to, the resource teacher. Because Teddy needed all the help he could get, he was also assigned to the Resource Room for one period a day.

Teddy was lucky to have so many people attending to his educational needs, and his school was fortunate in having such a wealth of resources available. Many schools in the United States, particularly in large urban areas, have too few ancillary services—and too many children in need of them. Children with learning or attentional problems may flounder in school for years without benefit of diagnosis or treatment. Then parents and teachers wonder why the children act out their frustrations, getting into trouble and eventually dropping out of school. While it is true that supplementary educational services are expensive, so is caring for the educational misfits of society.

Although Teddy had the benefit of additional services at school, his parents were concerned that his day was so fragmented. Teddy was out of the classroom almost more than he was in it. So, once again his parents began to look for an appropriate special class for September. But in March, Teddy's teacher said she couldn't believe what she was seeing. Teddy was no longer at the very bottom of the class, and his attention span had improved. She felt he could stay where he was—with help. On again, off again. Is it any wonder parents are confused? They want to do the most they can for their child, but what *is* that? How will he be next year or even next month? Who knows?

Although Teddy's teacher enjoyed him and felt he probably could manage at least one more year in a regular class, his parents and the resource teacher didn't agree. They recognized the vast difference in academic performance between Teddy and his classmates and felt that he would suffer in the competitive atmosphere of fourth grade. And while Teddy was making good progress, he wasn't learning quickly enough to close the gap. In fact, in some areas, the gap seemed to be growing wider. Surprisingly, he was learning his multiplication tables along with the class, thanks to his good memory, but he still couldn't subtract and was totally confounded by word problems. He was not an abstract thinker, and many of the concepts of social studies eluded him. He also seemed very young and immature relative to his classmates.

A SELF-CONTAINED SPECIAL EDUCATION CLASS

In Teddy's community, two of the three elementary schools had classes for children with learning disabilities and other mild handicaps. Children who attended the school without these classes were bused from their homes to one of the other schools at no extra charge to the family. (Most states in the United States today provide free transportation when youngsters are identified as needing special education.) Teddy likewise attended the school without the special education class, so with the help of the person in charge of pupil personnel services in the district, Teddy's parents visited the two special classes that might have been right for Teddy. Typically, these classes are self-contained (students stay in one classroom with their teacher for most of the day), with no more than twelve to fifteen children in a class. There is one master teacher trained in special education and frequently a paraprofessional or volunteer in the class.

The kind of class Teddy's parents were looking at developed after World War II, primarily for those with mental retardation or severe emotional disturbance. Children were diagnosed and placed full time in an appropriate class for their category of disability. In recent years, there has been much controversy among psychologists and educators over the use of segregated classes, particularly for the mildly handicapped. Studies have shown that most children with learning differences who are kept in regular classes do better academically and socially than do children with similar problems in special education classes. Since 1975, when the U.S. government mandated "a free and appropriate" public education for all handicapped children "in the least restrictive environment," most children have been maintained in integrated, heterogeneous classes along with their peers.

But it is also recognized that some youngsters, such as Teddy, may benefit from a more comprehensive program than can be provided in a regular class, even with the services of an itinerant teacher and/or a teacher in a resource room. When children seem to be suffering emotionally and sinking academically, their educational needs may best be met in a small class with the full-time services of a teacher trained in special education.

Schools sometimes suggest special classes for more than just academic reasons alone. Often, it is the children's behavior and/or their sense of defeat in response to their learning problems that causes them to be referred for special education. At the point where special education was considered for Teddy, he was beginning to be boisterous and silly in class, presumably for attention. While his misbehaving was not serious, his parents felt he needed to get away from the pressures of his class and to be with other children who were also in need of prescriptive education.

A special education class can provide children with an atmosphere conducive to learning as well as a firm foundation in those basic skills that are essential building blocks to further learning. Knowing each child and his educational needs, a teacher can design a specialized curriculum. While children may remain in a special class for as long a time as needed, the goal is to move them back into the mainstream of education as soon as possible. For many students, two to three years usually is sufficient to give them the tools they need to learn and strengthen their self-esteem.

In thinking about sending Teddy to another school, the Browns had the expected qualms. Would he feel different, uprooted? How would his friends in the neighborhood react when they found out? Mr. Brown admitted that he even wondered whether Teddy would change if he attended a class in which some of the children had behavior problems. Would he copy them? Was this the right move for Teddy?

Teddy certainly didn't want to go to another school either. Even though the going had been rough, he didn't want to leave his friends and the school he knew. It's not easy to leave what is familiar, to change to an unknown, even for adults. Teddy's feelings made the decision regarding a new school placement even more stressful for everyone, but in the end, Mr. and Mrs. Brown decided that Teddy should transfer to the special class.

The wisdom of a child's being placed in a special class can long be debated, with few reliable guidelines to follow. There are always questions, but each child must be looked at individually. Then it is for school administrators, parents, teachers, and special educators to determine jointly whether a change is warranted and, if so, which program or combination of programs would be best. If I know the child or family, I am usually asked to attend meetings at which these issues are debated to share my observations, too. Even then, the most appropriate plan might be optimal only for a short time.

The Browns were fortunate in finding a suitable class for Teddy in a nearby school. Many communities have no special classes at all, however, and children might have to go to another district. Then, too, a school district or one nearby may not have an appropriate class for a particular child. In that case, parents may have to consider sending their child to a private school that provides special education services. While these schools do a fine job, they are very expensive. However, according to federal law, each school district is responsible for providing an "appropriate" education for every child. If appropriate classes are not available for a youngster, the school district may be obliged to foot the bill for private school.

In practice, however, schools will try hard to claim that their classes or resources are adequate. Like most individuals, they are not eager to incur the burden of another large bill—unless they have to. In some instances, you may have to become your child's advocate and insist on the most suitable program for the child. I'll discuss the procedures for achieving these goals at the end of this chapter.

Teddy was fortunate that he wouldn't have to travel too far to go to school. There would be twelve children in the class, ranging from eight to ten and a half years of age. Children in self-contained classes are usually grouped according to their achievement level and educational needs rather than according to their age or grade in school. So, strictly speaking, there are no grades. And it is not uncommon to find one child working in a fifth grade math book, a second grade reader, and a first grade spelling book.

As before, Teddy's parents spoke to his teachers at the beginning of each year, and they had frequent conferences at school throughout the year. The Browns were also called to school from time to time to participate in the planning and decision-making for Teddy. They were very much involved with Teddy's education—and they had to be. In the process, they became quite knowledgeable in the area of learning differences and thereby even more understanding of Teddy.

For Teddy, the next three years gave him the chance to have intensive, individualized instruction. He could learn at his own pace, and his teacher worked hard to teach him basic skills. His reading improved through a "word family" approach in which words that rhyme and are spelled similarly, such as "cat," "hat," and "sat," are taught together. This method worked best for Teddy because of his limited memory for sight words. When he was nine, he finally seemed to "break the code" of the English language, and by ten he became a relatively fluent reader. For the first time, he could pick up a book without feeling anxious. He even began to read a little for pleasure, but only when he could find a "super-good book," as he put it. He also learned to write a paragraph, using some semblance of correct spelling and capitalization. Math was still very difficult, though, and Teddy struggled long and hard to master the algorithms of subtraction and division.

The happiest outcome, however, was that Teddy seemed relaxed at school and he came home in a happier mood than he used to. During all this time, although he was obviously benefitting from the program, his primary goal, and perhaps greatest motivation, was to return to a regular class.

REENTRY INTO THE MAINSTREAM

After three years, the Browns and the team of specialists who had followed Teddy's progress thought he was ready to return to the educational mainstream. Had he continued in his original school, Teddy would have been a seventh grader by now, but upon his return, he entered the sixth grade, the beginning of the junior high school in his community. In effect, he had repeated a grade or lost one year. This is not unusual when youngsters return to a public school from special education. In Teddy's town, the junior high, or middle school as it is sometimes called, was in a different building from the elementary school, so Teddy was off to a new start, although many of his old pals were there ahead of him.

It is difficult to tell what Teddy would have experienced had he never left his old school. Several youngsters with problems similar to Teddy's had stayed, some quite happily, others in agony. In retrospect, the Browns were not sorry they had made the choice they did, but it was impossible to measure or quantify the results. They were glad, though, that Teddy would be returning to a more natural school environment.

For reentry to be successful, children need to be academically and socially prepared for the change. In his second year in special education, Teddy had begun to spend part of each day in regular classes in the school. At first these were nonacademic classes, such as music, art, and gym, but later he went into a regular social studies and science class as well.

When Teddy moved to the junior high school, he continued to receive some special services, though less intensively than in elementary school. The "Study Skills Center," a kind of resource room, was available to Teddy on an as-needed basis. There, the teacher, burdened with too many students to see, provided some help with difficult assignments, but she couldn't spend much time with Teddy. However, Teddy was able to take advantage of the audiotape library, which meant that he could listen to the books his classmates were reading. (Parent volunteers had taped some of the more difficult books that were required reading, such as *The Red Badge of Courage.*) In some classes, teachers permitted him to take tests orally if he couldn't write the answers quickly or legibly enough.

Nevertheless, the departmentalization, where students change classes for different subjects, demanded more of Teddy than ever before. He had to be more organized and work harder, and he frequently felt overwhelmed. No longer was he nurtured by a special education teacher from nine o'clock to three. He was now forced to respond to teachers who were specialists in their own subjects and did not necessarily make accommodations for students with learning differences. Here again Mr. and Mrs. Brown had to bring their knowledge and understanding of Teddy's needs to the school.

The Browns tried to interpret Teddy's difficulties to his various teachers, with varying degrees of success. Math still presented the greatest problem for Teddy, and his math teacher that year was not very flexible. Halfway through the school year, Teddy still had not managed to pass one quiz or chapter test, although his daily homework was usually correct and on time. Perhaps each test covered too much for Teddy to remember, and his anxiety probably got in the way. Finally, out of frustration, his parents came to school and asked if he could possibly be permitted to study from the math test itself (without the answers, of course), to have extra help from the teacher, or to use his calculator to avoid the computational errors he usually made.

Teddy's math teacher said she wanted to help Teddy, but she thought it would be "unfair" to the other students if she gave him special privileges. Although this attitude is understandable, more teachers today seem willing to make concessions to children with special needs. This is surely in the spirit of individualizing instruction, an approach that most teachers now approve. Perhaps teachers are discovering, as many parents have, that fair doesn't necessarily mean equal. After all, the goal of giving tests should be to see how much children have learned, not how badly they can fail.

By midyear, Mr. and Mrs. Brown found that Teddy was feeling burdened by his assignments and was leaning heavily on his parents to get them done. His organizational and study skills were still weak, and homework was a time of anguish and frustration. The school was just not able to provide enough reinforcement for Teddy. The Browns finally decided that the boy down the street, a quiet, well-organized high school junior, might help Teddy with his homework and set a good example. Teddy, though doubtful, agreed to give it a try.

The extra assistance for Teddy worked well for a while, until his "tutor" had to quit his job when he got too busy with varsity baseball. For Teddy and his parents, this was another jolt, just when things seemed to be going smoothly again. It seems that parents of children with special needs must always be ready to apply the Band-Aids to each new wound, but it hurts all over again when the Band-Aids are abruptly removed. It is not easy to go from crisis to crisis, but somehow many learning-disabled children and their parents manage to get through the difficult school years intact.

In eighth grade, the decision was made that Teddy would not begin a foreign language, even though it was part of the usual curriculum. Children with learning differences often find foreign languages extremely difficult, and it may be a good idea for them to avoid taking a language for as long as possible, or even forever. Although many colleges require a foreign language for admission, some will waive the requirement for students with documented learning disabilities. If a student does elect to take a language, Spanish or Latin is usually preferred. They are more regular in syntax than French or Russian, and the spelling is more predictable.

Interestingly, Teddy begged to take a foreign language in ninth grade. As important as it is to relieve youngsters of the burden of a language they are likely to fail, I believe in letting them try if they want to. Motivation can go a long way toward success, and, besides, there is always the fallibility of prediction. Children have been known to achieve amazing heights, despite all the evidence predicting failure. One young man who was getting failing grades in French refused to drop the subject "because I like it, even though I can't do it." If that was satisfaction enough for him, so be it. We arranged for him to take the course pass-fail rather than for a grade, and he was helped by his teacher and his parents until he finally learned enough to pass the second-year exam. Then he was content. Individual drive and determination must be admired and respected.

Teddy had entered the ninth grade in his local high school with more than his usual number of fears. He always had butterflies on the first day of school, but this year was the worst. As he said, "I sort of felt like the world was out there to torture me on the first day." The school seemed huge, teachers' reputations had preceded them, and Teddy was sure he wouldn't be able to handle the work. Never had he felt so small and alone. On the first day, he came home famished. He confessed to his mother that he hadn't had any lunch because he couldn't find his way back to his locker. His sandwich was safely inside it—somewhere in the school.

Halfway through the ninth grade, Teddy was struggling in Spanish, but he knew he had the option to drop it, with the school's blessing, if it proved to be too hard. He was also taking a modified algebra course, called "sequential math," that would take two years to complete rather than the usual one. Math continued to be his major stumbling block, and he was tutored once a week after school. His state required that he pass algebra to qualify for a high school diploma; otherwise, he would have eliminated math from his program long ago.

Teddy's English course that year was also a modified one, emphasizing the "survival" skills he would need after high school, such as reading for information and writing a business letter. The rest of his courses were in the regular track. Unexpectedly, he was doing well in social studies, with an understanding teacher and the help of a tape recorder. He taped most of his classes so he wouldn't have to struggle to read his own notes. Even his reports were given orally or on tape. Teddy was also beginning to use the computer for writing, which, with the spell check feature, became his best friend as his efficiency in word processing increased.

Teddy was determined to take a straight academic curriculum throughout high school, even though it was challenging—and he did have problems from time to time. However, there were some alternative educational programs in his district that might have served him well for his last two years of high school, had he chosen to go that route. One option would have been for him to attend his school in the morning and the vocational center in the afternoon. There he could have learned the skills needed for an occupation or trade. Carpentry, child care, horticulture, and auto mechanics were the choices available in his district.

Another possibility for Teddy might have been "distributive" education, where students work part-time in cooperating stores and businesses in the community. Students earn money as well as high school credits for their work. For many young people, these alternative high school programs may provide not only an introduction to a successful future, but a more relevant education than the college-oriented curriculum with which so many struggle. As the requirements for high school graduation become ever more stringent in the education race, young people with significant learning disabilities may not be able to qualify for the traditional diploma. To prevent their dropping out of school prematurely, creative planning and alternative education programs will be needed.

Regardless of the program selected to serve the student with learning differences, teaching approaches and materials must also be carefully chosen to meet individual needs. In addition to the basic considerations of age and severity of the problem, the teacher must also establish the specific environment, techniques, and strategies that will maximize each student's learning in both specialized and mainstreamed settings.

A few years ago, I read an article in an education newsletter, entitled "Schools Face a Crisis in Caring," in which the author spoke of young people who leave school prior to graduating from high school. The comment heard most frequently was, "My teachers wouldn't care." For young people to care about themselves, they must feel cared for as well. This is the challenge to our educational system: to provide an atmosphere of caring in our schools. As parents, you, too, have to care. But to be effective advocates for your children, you also need to know your rights according to the law.

PARENTS' RIGHTS AND RESPONSIBILITIES

You should know of the following safeguards provided in IDEA (Individuals with Disabilities Education Act), the federal law that protects the education of children with handicapping conditions. Under the regulations, you have the right to

1. Prior notice before a child is evaluated or placed in a special education program, and you must give written permission for the school to proceed
2. Read relevant school records
3. Obtain a private or independent evaluation of your child if you desire
4. Attend and participate in the meeting to determine whether an educational handicap exists and, if so, the appropriate services to help the child
5. An impartial due process hearing to challenge a decision thought to

be unfair or inappropriate regarding a child's educational place-ment

See Appendix A for more information.

I strongly suggest, however, that if at all possible parents avoid get-ting into an adversarial relationship with school or administrative per-sonnel. It usually doesn't help and can be destructive to all concerned. Wherever possible, it is best to work in collaboration with the school, negotiating for what you want. In my experience, public hearings and the court battles that follow are expensive and rarely productive. However, there are always exceptions to this, where parents may have no choice in deciding on a course of action.

The current education law also provides for the designation of a surrogate parent to be a child's advocate if the child is a ward of the state or if parents or guardians are unavailable. And, finally, the law provides for appropriate educational programs in the "least restrictive environment" for each child identified as having any kind of handicap-ping condition.

In the last several years, IDEA has been debated by congressional committees and its continuation threatened. It is up to the citizens of this country to see that this important law is maintained. What happens inside the schoolroom depends on the dedication and the efforts of par-ents as well as educators. Little that has happened thus far to protect children with learning differences would have occurred without parental pressure. Today, it is more important than ever that parents continue to be advocates for their own children and for young people everywhere.

6

THE HOMEWORK ISSUE

Mrs. Pratt, the mother of a nine-year-old, phoned early one morning to tell me of the terrible scene that had occurred the night before. Jimmy, a fourth grader, had finally decided to tackle the book report that was due the next day. True, it had been assigned three weeks earlier, but Jimmy had just finished reading the skinniest book he could find in the library. It was nine-thirty P.M. when he asked for his mother's help with his homework. She was annoyed that he had waited until the eleventh hour to tell her about the assignment, but seeing the panic in his eyes, she reluctantly agreed to help.

After five minutes of working with Jimmy, Mrs. Pratt realized how little he knew about writing a book report and, indeed, doubted that he had read the book at all. Jimmy was not just asking for help; he wanted her to do the assignment. It was at this point that she balked and refused to help at all. She told me of the anger she felt toward Jimmy. "It's your homework, not mine, and it's your fault that you waited until the last minute to do it. Besides, I'm exhausted and this is not the time for me to help you."

Jimmy yelled and screamed that he was "stuck" and couldn't go to school without the report or "the teacher will *kill* me!" For the next hour, the situation went from bad to worse. Mr. Pratt got into the act, telling Jimmy to stop crying and "get to work." Jimmy finally went to bed without having written a word. Guilty and upset, his mother couldn't wait to call me the next morning to ask how she and her husband could have handled the situation differently.

The first question that occurred to me was how much Jimmy had actually learned from the experience of the night before. Did he learn to write a report, or at least attempt it on his own? The obvious answer to both questions was no. He had learned nothing, except perhaps to be more afraid than ever of book reports. He also may have gotten the message that asking for help at home can start a world war. Jimmy had avoided doing the assignment, but he certainly had angered his parents—and disappointed himself.

Knowing that Jimmy's mother was usually very supportive and willing to help her sons with their schoolwork, I wondered aloud why this time had been so different. Perhaps the clues were at the beginning of our conversation. First, Mrs. Pratt was angry (justifiably so) at the lateness of the hour, Jimmy's disorganization, and his procrastination. Second, his inability to do the assignment highlighted once again the extent of his learning problems.

A parent can easily forget that a child has learning problems when they aren't displayed all through the day. But now, Jimmy's mother was angry that his disabilities were showing, and she realized that she was probably punishing him for his handicap. Maybe she was also angry with Jimmy's teacher for not structuring the assignment so that he didn't feel so lost. In effect, Mrs. Pratt was saying, "Let your teacher see how much you don't know." It also occurred to me that she probably found it easier to help her older son than to work with Jimmy, who relied on her more.

Most parents would agree that, in general, the emotional involvement with one's own child can make it difficult to help with homework. As one parent said, "Homework is an activity that involves reading, math, and parent testing." If a child does well in school, it is relatively easy to edit a composition or quiz him for a test. In fact, we even feel pleased and proud that he is learning so well. But when learning is a struggle and material acquired one minute is forgotten the next, it is frustrating for the parent as well as the child. This frustration is heightened when a tired parent is summoned at nine at night to help a youngster with homework that he has somehow managed to forget or put off until the last minute. A parent's natural instinct at that point may be a fight-or-flight response. To avoid a confrontation, parents may walk away from the child, who really does need support and encouragement.

HOW MUCH HELP IS ENOUGH?

How much should parents help children with homework? I think the answer becomes clearer if we ask ourselves what the purpose of homework is and what the educational goals are for a child. It's obvious that homework should be more than just busywork. As a colleague of mine said, tongue-in-check of course, "The two biggest time wasters for children are television and homework." If the idea of homework is to reinforce skills taught at school, parents may be needed at home as facilitators or adjunct teachers. Extra practice with addition or the week's spelling words is something most parents can do with relative ease. But for the child with a significant learning difference, and even more so for those with ADHD who can't sit still and concentrate, understanding, patience, and even *reteaching* may be needed at home. As the requirements of school become more challenging, it may be completely unrealistic to expect a child to do homework alone. Like it or not, a parent (or surrogate) will have to share the burden of homework if the child is to succeed in school.

Jimmy's teacher had probably taught the class how to organize and write a book report, but Jimmy had not mastered the technique. Perhaps he had been distracted by noise from the playground or the radiator in his classroom, or maybe his teacher talked too quickly or too softly. For Jimmy, who had an auditory processing problem, oral instructions alone were not sufficient. That meant that he missed much of what was said, particularly when there were distractions. He needed to be shown visually what to do in order to really understand the process. And with his poor memory, he would require more than one demonstration before he would even know how to begin. The reality was, then, that Jimmy really couldn't write his report by himself, but he might have come a step closer with his mother's help. Children like Jimmy learn more from a model than they do from their mistakes. I have seen it work. That might be considered *Homework Rule #1*: Showing a child how to do an assignment is usually more effective than letting him flounder alone.

Josh, in sixth grade, had a social studies assignment in which he had to outline a chapter of his textbook. He was at a loss, and in two sessions, I almost did the work for him, encouraging him to read aloud only the boldfaced headings to use for his outline. He did little of that first outline, but he was very proud that he could hand it in on time, along with the rest of the class. The next time he had to summarize a chapter, his mother called to say that although I had shown him how to do it the previous week, Josh still had no idea how to organize the material. I suggested that she or her husband help him as I had, encouraging him to identify some of the key words or salient points when he could find them. Unfortunately, they were looking for immediate results, and I explained that this wasn't realistic. By the sixth outline, which he brought to our session, I acted only as his secretary, writing down what he told me was important. He had finally gotten the idea of selecting the important facts, although it was still an effort for him to do the reading as well as the writing. As a bright seventh grader put it, "My brain doesn't function when I have to read and then write it down." *Homework Rule #2,* then, is this: One demonstration of a new process is rarely sufficient. Practice is the key.

Then I offered Josh another suggestion for his social studies homework. There were questions to answer at the end of each chapter. By the time he had struggled through the reading, he had usually forgotten the information or, more likely, had not understood the material in the first place. It may sound like advocating taking a shortcut, but I recommended that he read each question and find the answer in the text without reading the entire chapter first. Then, after answering the questions, he could read the chapter with greater understanding.

Josh looked surprised, as if I were suggesting that he cheat. When I assured him it was a legitimate strategy, he became more receptive to the idea. Then I went on to locate the appropriate paragraphs for him until he could find the information himself. (It makes sense to do this, particularly when chapters are long and replete with facts.) We found that Josh could absorb and retain more information this way, which pleased him. *Homework Rule #3*: Answering questions in a textbook needs to be broken down into smaller bites. Finding the answers in the text one at a time may be easier than prereading the entire chapter.

Some high school students prefer to write down or underline key words in the questions to look for in the text. Because social studies and science books tend to be literal, using the same words in the questions as in the text, they provide the student with a clue to the answers. The perceptive student might spot a key word, answer the question, and then continue with the reading.

For older, more advanced students, the SQ3R is a much-used technique for studying or preparing for a test. The acronym stands for "skim, question, read, recite, review." First, a student glances over the material to be read, getting the general idea of the selection. Then he asks himself some of the questions that might be asked in the reading. Reading the passage is next, followed by oral testing of his knowledge, either by himself, with a tape recorder, or with a surrogate teacher. A review of difficult concepts is the last step in this process. Sometimes the review can be enhanced by preparing a study sheet with key words or questions on the unit. Key words or questions are written on the left side of the page and the corresponding answers on the right. Then the student can test himself by folding the paper, keeping the answers hidden from view. And, incidentally, study sheets should be saved to prepare for final exams at the end of the term or year.

Another aid for the older student is for a parent to offer secretarial services. For many middle school or high school students, the mechanics of writing a paper is the hardest part. A parent's willingness to type a report can alleviate much of the anxiety associated with it. And I don't think it's a sin to correct spelling and punctuation errors as you go along. Making a list of spelling words written incorrectly, to be learned at a later time, might relieve you and the youngster of guilty feelings about the editing. *Homework Rule #4*: It's okay to be a child's secretary until he can combine the processes of thinking and writing into a legible product of which he can be proud.

WHEN HOMEWORK ISN'T DONE

The most obvious indication of trouble with a subject is when the books don't come home at all. "I forgot to bring my book home" or "I left my homework on the bus" are two of the common ways a child says "I can't do my homework" or "I don't want to do it." The youngster who denies having homework or who says he "did it in school" is probably avoiding the issue. "The dog ate it" or "It must have gone through the washing machine" may also sound familiar. When any or all of these become a pattern, a conference with the teacher clearly is warranted and the source of the problem should be investigated. A fourth grader I saw rarely brought books home, telling his mother, when she asked, that he had finished his homework. Then he'd go out to play or watch TV. Of course, his lies were always found out, with the predictable lecture, tears, and punishment that followed.

An assignment pad sent home to be checked or signed by parents may encourage a reluctant child do his homework. After protesting initially, one boy said he actually liked the "blue sheet" his school used for recalcitrant students. His teachers and one parent had to sign the sheet every day. As he told me, "It helps me remember even when my mind wants to forget." And for the child who can't remember to bring books home from school, an extra textbook kept at home eliminates one excuse for not doing assignments. Schools are usually willing to lend parents a needed book, unless, of course, they are in short supply. In that case, you might want to purchase a copy.

I've seen yet another interesting behavior—youngsters who do their homework but "forget" to hand it in. Translated, this usually means they are ashamed of the product, feel inadequate relative to their classmates, or want to "punish" themselves, their parents, or their teachers. That's what psychologists call being "passive-aggressive." It's not what the children do that is troubling; it's what they don't do that makes us angry.

I recently heard about a teacher who must have done something right with respect to homework. One morning a six-year-old girl with learning problems ran to the assistant teacher in the classroom, sobbing that she had not finished her homework the night before. The empathetic lady tried to soothe her, saying she was sure the teacher would understand. "No," the little girl tearfully went on, "Miss Stewart said if I didn't finish my homework, she wouldn't give me any more." That teacher obviously knew where her threat would be effective. Little children feel grown up when they have "real homework." Most little children, that is.

An exception is a first grader I'm currently seeing. He has ADHD-plus and is finding school a painful experience. He actually might be able to do the work but he simply cannot focus in class. His teacher's policy is to assign as homework any task not completed during the school day. He also had work assigned from his tutor and from the Learning Center in school. Consequently, he and his mother spend two or even three torturous hours nightly fighting over what should be a fifteen-minute assignment. When his mother told me of this, the boy looked so sad and said, "I hate homework. My brain just slows down after school. It could only speed up after I play." Needless to say, no first grader should spend more than half an hour on homework. Any work not completed in that time should be returned to school with a note to the effect that the allotted time had been spent (even if inefficiently). Also, I don't think classwork should be added to homework. It only creates a problem for the parents as well as for the tired and resistant child.

DIFFERENT SUBJECTS, DIFFERENT PROBLEMS

Each subject in school can present different kinds of homework problems. One boy made it a habit never to do his math homework. He claimed that he would not need math to be a baseball player. He and his teacher argued about his attitude for the better part of the year. He did his social studies and English assignments, but never his math. One day I suggested that he bring his math book to our next session. When I saw what he went through trying to copy down rows of addition and subtraction problems, I knew where he needed help—not with the work, but with copying the problems. For children with perceptual difficulties, transcribing from a math book onto paper can be a laborious and even dizzying experience. This young man's columns were askew, the plus and minus signs were mixed up, and he frequently copied the problems incorrectly onto the page. As soon as I wrote the problems for him, he could quickly compute the answers with few mistakes. For that child, either a workbook-text in which he could write or a willing transcriber at home would have helped. *Homework Rule #5*: Copying or reproducing math problems for a youngster is acceptable if that is where the difficulty lies.

For many LD youngsters, math is hard enough in school, but math homework can be their nemesis. First, they must be able to read and understand the directions, which may seem impossible to comprehend. Then, if they have ADHD as well, their impulsivity and frustration with the reading results in their plunging in before they know what to do. So reading and attention problems do affect a child's math. Many a child has been known to get an entire page wrong because he couldn't or wouldn't take the time to read the directions. And if he can't read the words "multiplication" or "product," no amount of knowledge of the times tables will help. He may be spared anger, tears, and the need to redo an entire assignment if a parent or other helper reads the directions to him. *Homework Rule #6*: Make sure the student understands the instructions before starting an assignment.

Another helpful strategy is to start the first few problems with the child. This will alleviate his anxiety and, at the same time, help him understand what to do. Then he can proceed on his own with more confidence. It's not unusual, though, for parents to say to a child who is reluctant to begin homework, "You start your math and if you have a problem, come to me for help." The difficulty with this approach is that the child may, in fact, do the math—but get every problem wrong. Then he has to relearn the process and redo the assignment. If he didn't hate math before, he does now, and he is probably angry with his parents for not helping him in the first place. *Homework Rule #7*: Start the problems or homework questions with a child who may feel insecure; then he can do the assignment independently with greater confidence.

Sometimes when I help a child with schoolwork, we do more than just the assigned lesson; I try to go a few pages ahead in the book. We read the directions together (usually twice) and talk about the task involved. That way, the material will be familiar when it's introduced in class. *Homework Rule #8*: Preteaching—going ahead—to introduce new vocabulary or concepts will help a child when the material is presented in class.

Parents sometimes feel insecure themselves about helping a child with homework, particularly with the new math in today's curriculum. Concepts and operations may be taught differently and are unfamiliar. An older sibling's explanation or a meeting with your child's teacher may help clear things up. A cautionary note: It's a good idea for the helping person to resist teaching a child more than he needs or wants to know. Some parents seem to have a special talent for trying to teach concepts and methods beyond the assignment. This can cause resentment and the refusal of help in the future.

Spelling is probably the least threatening subject for a parent-tutor, unless, of course, the child cannot remember a spelling even after many repetitions. There isn't much room to question how the subject is taught in school or to be confused by new methods. While children respond differently to various techniques of learning how to spell, I can suggest one way that seems to work for many. First, and most important, read the words to your child or have her read them if she can without error. If reading the words is hard, anticipate where she will get stuck and tell her the word first. Then have her read the list once more, giving the definition of each word. There is no point in a child's memorizing a series of letters without knowing what the word means. Besides, the spelling will be forgotten more easily if there is no comprehension.

A boy in eighth grade was trying to learn to spell the word "chaotic." He spelled it a few times, omitting or adding at least two letters each time. Finally, I asked him what the word meant. He said, "Honestly, I've never heard of the word 'chā-ō'tik.'" As soon as I pronounced it correctly for him, he knew what it meant and learned to spell it easily.

After the words on a list are read and defined, a child should point to each letter, saying the word as she traces it with her finger. Then, if she thinks she knows it, see if she can visualize it with her eyes closed, writing it in the air. It helps if she says the word again as she traces it with her finger. If she can see it in her mind, she should try to write it on paper, checking to see that she is right. She may need to repeat the process two or three times. Then do the same for the next word on the list. But don't try to teach more than five new words a day. Too much pushing to do "just a little more" can create overload and discourage a child, making her apprehensive about the next session.

Each night review the words learned before, so that by Friday all the words have been practiced and reviewed for the weekly test. Sometimes a child will say, "But I learn them by saying them out loud; I don't have to write them." While this does work for some, it usually is more effective to write the words and see them on paper. I tell youngsters that words have "faces." As you get to know them, they will look familiar and right. Incidentally, reviewing spelling or any subject just before bedtime is supposed to make it sink in while a person is sleeping. Maybe we do learn subliminally, after all.

Nothing stifles creativity like the pressure of an assignment to "be creative." Children will tell me the most original stories, fantastic or factual, but they freeze the minute they have to put their thoughts to paper. Sometimes brainstorming with someone before attempting to write is helpful, and organizing the thoughts to put down can be helpful to the reluctant writer.

A friend of mine told me about her son, who could never do his English homework because he couldn't come up with an idea he thought adequate. He'd sit for hours, tossing crumpled paper after crumpled paper into the wastebasket. His creativity seemed to vanish under pressure. Finally, his mother, sensing the extent of his torture, made a deal with him. She said she would suggest some ideas and even write the first sentence if he would then take over. Somehow this seemed to allay his anxiety, and he could then proceed on his own.

One girl's favorite subject was science, because "I don't have to be creative." When I asked her one day what her class was studying in science, she immediately replied, "Oh, we're not studying science, we're *doing* it!" Indeed, in many school systems, the science curriculum has been revised, making it more of a living experience for students. Nevertheless, writing up an experiment and drawing a paramecium that can be distinguished from an unintentional smudge on the page may be a real challenge for a student whose small motor coordination is not up to par.

It is when the science teacher takes off points for neatness and spelling, though, that many an enthusiastic student gives up. That's when a parent might have to intervene. One teacher added insult to injury by telling his class of fifth graders that they were responsible for the spelling of all the words in "dark print" in the chapter. Joe, one of the boys I worked with, couldn't find most of the words (he didn't know how to skim a passage), much less learn to spell them. If he had tried to copy the words on paper, they'd have been misspelled, anyway. I suggested that his teacher give him the list of words he would need to know for the test, so he could work on them for a week ahead of time.

Sometimes, however, it is the concepts of science that are difficult for students. They just can't envision the layers of the earth, for instance, and they try to learn the material by rote. But memorization is often hardest for those who don't understand the material. They may need an explanation with pictures as well as simpler words to really grasp the lesson.

It sounds as if the parents I know are very involved with their children's homework and, indeed, many are. Although some enjoy the role, others complain that their children are too dependent on them. One girl used to say, "Come on, Mom, let's do our homework." Her mother finally rebelled, telling her daughter that it wasn't *her* homework—she had already passed third grade. The mother was right, but where does a parent draw the line? We know that children do need help if the work is beyond them. However, if the assignment seems reasonable, a hands-off policy can foster independence and subsequently a feeling of competence.

RESPONSIBILITY FOR HOMEWORK

Too often, as the demands of school increase, the responsibility for initiating and doing homework shifts from the child to the parents. After a while, the child may try to avoid the task altogether. One mother challenged her son, accusing him of wanting her to do his work for him. This nine-year-old's response was an indignant "I do not, but who invented homework anyway? Whoever it was certainly didn't like children!" For children who don't like school, the complaint I hear most is about homework. As a frustrated second grader said tearfully, "It's not fair. I work in school all day and then have to do more at home, *and my teacher isn't even there!*" His neighbor, a hyperactive fourth grader for whom homework was also a daily battle, echoed this, claiming, "I hate homework. When I get home from school, I feel like a computer that's run out of memory. I need time to play and recharge." For him, it was the length of the homework, not the difficulty, that had to be modified.

Once the responsibility for homework shifts to parents, a power struggle with the child can ensue. If family expectations are too high, the child cannot afford to make mistakes. It may become easier to stop trying than to try to please his parents. Then only their nagging will bring him back to the homework table, and the work never gets done in a way that is gratifying, either for him or for his parents.

Johnny, a fifth grader, had a long history of learning problems and impulsiveness. Finally, his parents, tired of their son's reliance on them for daily work, tried to establish a new policy at home. Johnny was to do all his work on his own and then show it to them. Only then could he watch his favorite TV show.

On the first night of the new regime, Johnny went upstairs and dashed off his homework in five minutes flat. He hadn't read the instructions, though, and not understanding the work, wrote anything on the blank lines just to get it over with. He was devastated when his parents insisted that he do the assignment over again, this time properly. It took many weeks of no TV before Johnny could muster the self-control to do his homework calmly. His parents learned, too, to be somewhat less severe in their judgment and more appreciative of the effort he was making.

The goal of independence should remain a priority—for children's homework as well as for daily living. How much they can do on their own is a difficult but necessary question to ask yourself. Many parents and teachers are concerned that children rely so much on a homework helper as a crutch that they won't ever want to let go. On the contrary, when a sprained ankle feels better, I find that crutches are quickly discarded. If parents don't hold onto a child too tightly because of their own anxiety, boys and girls should let go as soon as they are able to "walk" alone.

Not surprisingly, children who feel inadequate all day long at school feel insecure when faced with a task they perceive as too challenging. The homework assigned may be appropriate and well within their grasp, but their fear alone makes the work seem insurmountable. They may not even need parental expertise, but merely the comfort of a parent's physical presence. I have suggested to some parents that they just stay in the same room as the child for at least part of the homework time. They can answer an occasional question or give an encouraging "That's good work" while reading the newspaper or paying bills.

WHERE HOMEWORK IS DONE

Most parents think the obvious place for homework is in a child's room, at his own desk, with as little noise or distraction as possible. Not necessarily. The correct answer is wherever a child feels he can work best. That may mean on the kitchen table, on the living room floor, or in the middle of family activities. Some children really dislike being alone in a quiet room, particularly when they're doing a job they don't like—and schoolwork usually fits that description. Nevertheless, there are others who need to be separated from sibling activity and other distractions in order to accomplish anything. Help your child find a private corner of his own. The father of a ten-year-old with learning differences, who also happens to be a school principal, told an audience that his son could read only to music, usually a favorite Beatles album. The boy's teacher had assigned reading for a half hour each night, and the tapes were played accordingly. His father added, "I never knew reading could be so loud!" But it seemed to work. The boy's parents assumed, probably correctly, that the noise of the tapes blocked out other stimuli or impinging thoughts, thereby improving the quality of his reading. As one ADHD adult expressed it, "When I'm working at my desk, I need the radio on to screen out my internal noises."

These stories also remind me of a boy who acted as if he'd been kicked in the solar plexus whenever he was asked to read aloud. Unable to catch his breath, he could scarcely get the words out. One day he asked if he could bring a favorite CD to show me the next time he came. Rather than "waste" time, I suggested that he read to me while listening to the music. It was amazing how much more easily he read with the music blaring (or perhaps I couldn't hear his errors?). For a long time thereafter we played music as we worked, and it definitely had a relaxing effect. Good pedagogy? In this field, whatever works is valid.

For some children, however, the distractions of rock-and-roll music or a busy kitchen can be disastrous. My only suggestion for parents of children who have trouble settling down to work is *not* to have a preconceived notion of where to do homework, but to know your child and set the scene accordingly. You might need to discuss this with his teacher or another professional. Whatever you decide, don't be rigid or rule out any possibilities for a happy homework place. *Homework Rule #9*: Allow a child to choose his or her favorite place to do homework as long as it's effective. Individual learning styles and preferences should be respected.

HOMEWORK TIME

When to do homework is no easier to answer than where. For some children, rising early in the morning to complete an unfinished assignment works well, while for others, the privilege of staying up for an extra half hour at night is better. For most children, though, the hours before and after dinner are best. That way, there are no midnight surprises and a child can have some time to play after school. One thing to keep in mind is your child's energy level. Coming home to a snack and a bike ride can renew his or her energy for homework later on. Being clear about when to come home is crucial in this kind of scheduling.

Short periods of concentrated work are usually more effective for learning than one long sitting. This is particularly important for the child who has a short attention span or difficulty concentrating. I have occasionally used a kitchen timer to encourage a student to work for fifteen uninterrupted minutes before the bell goes off. Then he can "unfasten his seat belt," walk around, raid the refrigerator, or make a phone call before returning to work. Psychologists call this the *Premack principle:* a unpleasant task is followed by a chosen reward. Return to work for another fifteen minutes, and the process is repeated. The goal, of course, is to stretch the work segments to longer and longer periods.

Every child reaches a point of saturation and diminishing returns. There's an old saying: "The brain can only absorb as much knowledge as the seat can endure." When a child has spent an hour on homework and is crying or looking bleary-eyed, it is probably time to stop and let his teacher know he did as much as he could. A teacher should also advise parents and children, early in the year, as to the expectations for the length of homework time. Children's individual differences also need to be considered. One second grader might do a good job in ten minutes while another struggles for an hour. I knew a boy who felt he *had* to finish the work assigned, no matter how long it took him or how late the hour. When I met him, he and his mother were working for three hours a night—painfully. The teacher and I put a stop to that very quickly. Most teachers would agree that thirty minutes should certainly be enough for a second grader, and anything more than that is excessive. If the child's response to homework is anger directed at parents, books, teachers, God, and the bedroom wall, someone had better check to see if the assignment is too difficult or too long.

WHO HELPS WITH HOMEWORK?

Most often, it's Mother who's elected to help with homework. The myth used to be that Father works hard all day and needs to relax when he comes home. But it may be Father, if he's not home during the day, who can more skillfully avoid a tantrum over a frustrating assignment. Today, with more mothers working, the father may also be called upon in the line of homework duty. Of course, if either parent has had a particularly hard day, he or she is probably not the parent of choice to help with a creative story or hard-to-teach fractions.

One word of caution about father-teachers. I have noticed that once fathers begin to teach, they sometimes become overzealous. One of my children used to say, "I don't like working with Dad because he tells me more than I ever want to know." By and large, children only want to be taught as much information as they'll need for school the next morning. Rarely is a young person so eager to learn that he is receptive to more knowledge than is required for class. It is usually wiser not to attempt to provide a whole encyclopedia of knowledge at one sitting. If handled well, the child will come back for more information as he needs it.

Then, too, a homework helper doesn't always have to be a parent at all. In fact, there used to be a credo in educational literature that a parent is not, and cannot be, his child's teacher or tutor. A child has many teachers, but only one set of parents. One respected authority in the field, Dr. Milton Brutten, wrote in his book, *Something's Wrong with My Child* (it's an old book, possibly out of print),

> There is rarely a parent, even one who is a good teacher of academic subjects . . . who can be effective tutoring his or her own

youngster. Parents are too emotionally involved with their children to be objective. When the mother-child relationship, or the father-child, is converted to that of teacher-child, the child in effect no longer has a mother, or a father, but only one more mediocre teacher.

For many families, the quote seems apt. As one mother said wistfully, "I wish there were no such thing as homework. I feel stupid when I don't know how to teach Janie math, and then I get angry at my own stupidity. Besides, I'm sending her to school to be taught by teachers who were *trained* to teach. Why does she bring it to me?"

Another parent described the sparks that fly every time he sits down to work with his son. "Homework is ruining our relationship! I don't want to lose my cool with him, but I can't help it. We always end up angry and screaming at each other." In these situations, parental help is obviously not the best idea.

I, too, once believed that parents should never work with their own children. It was only as I greeted parents in the waiting room of my office that I began to get a different perspective. I would find myself saying to a mother or father, "Harry and I have been working on learning to tell time. Perhaps you could continue it at home by having him count by fives and read the minutes on the clock." As long as my instructions were specific, most parents were very interested and eager to help. I noticed that their involvement helped them understand their child's learning problems. They were also able to appreciate their child's improvement and progress. In effect, parents became partners with their children in the learning experience.

In February of second grade, Eric was referred to me by a neurologist who was concerned about his learning and his self-esteem. The physician had recommended a special school for him, but Eric couldn't be admitted until the following September. I wanted to help him, but I only had one hour a week—a lunchtime at that—hardly sufficient to support him in his class, even for the balance of the year.

Eric's mother and I devised a plan. She would be included in our weekly sessions, after which she could follow through at home for twenty minutes on a daily basis. Sometimes we talked on the phone between sessions to assess the progress she was making with him. Eric did so well working with his mother that he never did attend a special school, and his mother, excited by his progress, found a career for herself in special education.

Since then, I have encouraged many parents to work with their own children at home. Occasionally I have even guided parents over the telephone without seeing the child every week. While this surely would not be appropriate for all families or even for most children, it is one of a variety of approaches that can be used when children need help.

In determining how to proceed, you must respect your own feelings and ability (or the lack of it) to work with your child at home and be guided accordingly. Of course, you should be a parent first, and then a teacher, but only if the role is mutually satisfying and not painful for either you or your child.

You should expect that children with learning differences and/or attention problems will require more assistance, more guidance, and more comforting with regard to homework than their siblings or classmates for whom learning is easier. If our goal, after all, is to help children compensate for their learning problems and become successful in life, they must gain as much as they possibly can from the educational system. If this requires the extra reinforcement called homework, let's try to keep it from becoming the most dreaded word of the day.

7

AFTER HIGH SCHOOL

In past years, graduation from high school was seen as the end of school for students with special needs. The majority of young people growing up with learning differences or ADHD were not expected or even encouraged to go to college. Their educational and vocational options were viewed as limited by their disabilities. If, somehow, they did manage to find their way to a university campus, they generally struggled alone, the nature of their problems unrecognized and their needs unsupported.

As recently as 1990, a journal article claimed that although LD students were being well served in public schools, the legal mandates and increased awareness had not significantly affected college enrollment among this population. The reasons given were (a) the hesitancy of high school counselors to advise LD students of postsecondary options and (b) the lack of specialized support programs offered by colleges and universities. This is changing, however, and there has been an increase in the number of special programs available on college campuses. Although services vary, most provide tutorial assistance, remediation, and counseling similar to that offered in elementary and high schools. As a result, the number of LD and ADHD students electing to go on with their education after high school has also increased incrementally.

OPTIONS AND TRANSITIONS

Today there are many one-, two-, and four-year college programs that admit students with disabilities who have earned a high school degree or General Education Diploma (GED). With the influx of students with special needs on college campuses, there is a need to facilitate and re-

129

fine the transition process. Making a smooth shift from a secondary to postsecondary setting is difficult for any student, but for students with learning disabilities, these changes can be particularly dramatic. The move from the protected and externally controlled environment of high school to an unstructured college setting can be overwhelming. Unlike high school, college requires that students function independently, managing their time, making their own decisions, and organizing their social lives. Because LD adolescents typically have not experienced this freedom, it is critical that you and your child plan and prepare carefully for this new challenge.

If your child will not attend college, it is still important that you prepare for life beyond high school. In this case, your transition planning must include vocational courses and community-based activities in preparation for a job. The goal of transition planning, then, is to help your child find appropriate postsecondary settings that best meet his academic and/or vocational interests and provide the needed support.

Since 1990, both state and federal laws have mandated planning for LD students. According to the Individuals with Disabilities Education Act (IDEA), a student's Individualized Education Plan (IEP) must include "a statement of the needed transition services . . . beginning no later than age sixteen and annually thereafter" to the age of twenty-one. (Some states, such as Minnesota, New Jersey, and Illinois, require that transition planning be initiated no later than age fourteen.) Federal law defines these services as:

> A coordinated set of activities for a student, which promotes movement from school to post-school activities, including post-secondary education, vocational training, integrated employment . . . continuing and adult education. . . .
>
> The coordinated set of activities shall be based upon the individual student's needs, taking into account student preferences and interests. . . . [Sec. 300.18]

In the past few years, materials designed to instruct younger students about possible career choices have appeared on the market. These games and kits provide the student with simulated work experience while they describe the skills and abilities necessary for success in each field. By exploring opportunities at a young age, LD children can gain an awareness of the world outside of school and what options the future can hold.

Individual planning for transition services as prescribed in the legislation includes three components: assessment, family participation, and procedures for the development of the IEP. This process begins long before the search for a specific college or job placement begins and is multifaceted, involving parents as well as the school.

ASSESSING YOUR CHILD'S NEEDS AND GOALS

Planning for the transition from high school to postsecondary programs should begin long before your child's last year of high school, probably no later than ninth grade. One issue to be decided early is the kind of high school diploma your LD child should seek and the graduation requirements for that diploma. There is growing concern among educators that the increasingly stringent requirements for high school graduation will reduce opportunities for students with special needs. Those who can't meet the new standards will be more likely to leave school without a diploma and without the incentive to pursue an education. In 1994, the Department of Education reported that 54 percent of LD students left school early, as compared with 32 percent of those without learning disabilities.

The options of reduced course loads, modification of foreign language requirements, and special testing conditions need to be arranged and implemented as early as possible—certainly before the question of untimed SATs arises in the junior year. Course waivers, typically for a foreign language or mathematics, may be necessary and appropriate, but they should be used only when based on valid diagnostic data, because there may be implications for postsecondary education. Although many colleges will admit students under special conditions, some still deny accommodations to those in need. In 1996, a discrimination suit was filed against a large university for changing its policy with regard to LD students. Under the new guidelines, the university reverted to stricter admission requirements and denied many students accommodations such as tape recorders and additional time on exams.

Whether a particular LD student can complete high school in an academic program depends on many factors, among them his aptitude, his motivation, and the severity of his problems. School doors should be kept open as long as possible, even when a young person tries to close them behind him in frustration. It is usually better for him to re-main in school than to attempt to enter the job market untrained and ill-prepared. Even though the law says a child may leave school at sixteen, the LD adolescent may need more time rather than less. The immature nineteen-year-old may still be adding to his maturity and to his core of skills as a senior in high school. Age alone should not be a reason to leave school.

Many young people with a history of learning problems—and even many without—give up on themselves during the high school years and expect their parents and teachers to do the same. They threaten to leave school, convinced that they cannot succeed in a system in which they feel so alone, so incompetent, and so miserable. Their parents may also encourage them to leave school when the cut slips and the failure no-tices come home. "After all," they say, "what is he really accomplish-ing in school?" Trying as it might be, it is critical that you continue to be caring and supportive of your LD adolescent. He needs other people to have faith in him even when he lacks faith in himself.

I recently met with Jack, a junior in a large public high school who is currently taking a history course for the third time. He failed it as a sophomore and again in summer school. Even if he passes it this year, he will still lack one credit to graduate. To say that he is frustrated and discouraged is an understatement. He is cutting classes and has threat-ened to run away from school and home. In a school conference, his guidance counselor apologized for not having had more contact with Jack during the past two years, but she had more than two hundred stu-dents assigned to her that year and was overwhelmed by her caseload.

During the meeting with the guidance counselor, I wondered about an alternative for Jack: whether he could take the history course pass/fail this time to avoid the frustration of a low grade. He still has trouble organizing his ideas and expressing himself on paper, not a good combination for passing written exams. Jack also complained that his teacher was "too vague. I need to know *exactly* what to study." So, the chances are good that he will fail the course again. Rather than an F, what Jack needs is the encouragement of an E for Effort and an A for Attendance. A pass/fail grade, therefore, was agreed upon.

Jack was more than pleased. And the best news was that he could earn an additional credit toward graduation by working. His school of-fers a work-study program that sounded ideal. Jack can work in a store after school and receive high school credit. He does want to finish high school, but is not yet certain of what will follow. At the moment, he thinks he might want to take a course in landscape gardening. While that could change, he *is* clear about what he doesn't want. "I know I don't want to go to college. I have to push myself just to finish this year and I don't want any more history or English courses, ever!"

Since the federal regulations went into effect in 1990, school districts throughout the country have addressed transition planning in a variety of ways. These range from comprehensive programming to minimal compliance. It seems reasonable to expect that students in transition will need help in meeting the challenges of everyday living, whether at home, in school, or in the community. To plan for this effectively requires a team effort, consisting of the student, family members, essential teachers, LD specialists, administrators or counselors, and others who know the student well. Creative options for the future and ways to achieve them will be more likely to emanate from a group than from one person's perspective.

YOUR CHILD'S ROLE IN PLANNING

Transition planning should be a student-centered activity that reflects your child's developmental and educational needs at any given time. The IDEA mandates that we consider students' interests and goals as primary factors in decision making. However, many young people who have grown up with learning disabilities have no idea who they are or what they can aspire to after high school. Their goals are undefined and the means of achieving them even less clear. Even if they do plan to go on to college, it is not uncommon for them to abdicate their role in decision making, relying on others to do their planning, complete their applications, and even, in some instances, make the school selection for them. In part, this emanates from their dependency, anxiety, and fear of rejection. I have known many who view themselves as lacking any learning strengths that would be attractive or even salable to a college. So they go through the process half-heartedly, claiming "I don't really want to go to college. . . . I'm only applying to satisfy my parents, but I probably won't get in anyway."

In reality, some of their concerns may be well founded: their academic skills may still lag, their organizational skills remain weak, and their goals are undefined. Many don't understand their disability, how it affects their learning, or how to interpret it to others. Little wonder they are ambivalent. When we discuss their reluctance to participate fully in the process, most can admit that they are, indeed, eager to attend college but are afraid no school will accept them. I usually can assure each student that there *is* an appropriate college, where others like them have been admitted. And I can always name at least one positive attribute that they offer a college, even if it is only their recently discovered motivation to continue their education. For those students interested in employment, career exploration that includes vocational classes, field trips to work sites, and volunteer work experience can help them identify their preferences and vocational interests.

Try to help your child see that individualized transition planning can be a golden opportunity for her to shape her own academic destiny by asking questions and participating actively in her IEP meetings. In the final analysis, your child has to become her own advocate, whether in college or employment. To do this, she needs to understand her learning differences, her learning style, and the kinds of courses or jobs to avoid. Even more important, she needs to recognize her strengths and be prepared to select programs in which she is likely to be successful, such as those providing a range of support services that will be compatible with her interests, abilities, and perceived needs. Until your child understands herself and her options, appropriate choices cannot be made. This, then, is the first goal in the transition process.

FAMILY INVOLVEMENT

Your expectations for your son or daughter as well as your own educational values will directly affect the goal setting and outcome of transition planning. Some parents insist on college for their children, even if inappropriate, and may have the unrealistic expectation that because their child is on a college campus, he will suddenly develop into an academic scholar. Many other parents are more than ambivalent about the prospect of college for their LD children who want to continue their education. "Why should we spend the money," the argument goes, "unless he is intellectually curious, willing to work hard, and will be successful?"

I have known families for whom the prospect of life after high school became World War III, lasting throughout high school. In addition to parental conflict, some adolescents want to attend college merely because their parents and siblings did; others feel they should attend because of the myth that success in life is only attainable with a college degree. Perhaps because of the overabundance of educated job seekers and the expense of higher education today, this is changing, giving young people more freedom of choice. As part of the transition process, then, any goals that you and your child disagree on may need to be resolved, compromised, or even mediated by a professional. However, be sure that person respectfully considers the interests of both parties.

Assuming that college is a realistic goal and financially possible for the family, I believe there are several valid reasons for LD students to consider college as an option. Not the least of these is the experience of independent living, possibly even away from home for the first time. Graduation from home is as important as graduation from high school, but that "diploma" may be even harder to earn. LD adolescents tend to be less mature and more dependent on you, their parents, than others of their age. At a time when most young people are striving for independence, those with learning disabilities may be reluctant to venture out on their own.

At the same time, you may have become accustomed to your child's dependency and find it hard to let go, particularly if his learning disabilities have been your primary mission and full-time job through the years. Many well-meaning parents try to protect their children from stress and disappointment by making transition decisions *for* them rather than with them. Remember that it is important for your child to be actively involved in the process, even though you may still have to be his "case manager," since he may not be prepared to predict the outcome of his choices.

You need to be realistic in your appraisal of your child's chance of success. I have known parents who cannot accept the compromise of a "second rate" college rather than the big-name school they had originally envisioned for their son or daughter. It may help to remember that your child will not be happy at a school for which he or she is not qualified. Several students have come to me for advice—and solace— after flunking out after the first year of college. Some lacked the requisite skills, but others, with their new-found freedom, devoted their energies to socializing rather than books. One young woman, deprived of TV in high school, spent her afternoons in her room watching soap operas. Even more typically, students today don't necessarily remain at one college for all four years. Many, with or without disabilities, transfer because they are ready for a greater challenge, their major interests have changed, or the social life did not live up to their expectations.

If your child should be denied admission to her school of choice, it's not necessarily the end of her education. It may simply mean that the college is in demand and space is limited or that your young adult is not ready right now. In such instances, it might be appropriate to consider a postgraduate high school year (generally offered at private schools) or even a year off before applying again. An academic program or work experience to strengthen learning strategies, promote study habits, and develop self-confidence will lead to success later on.

In sum, try to keep the following guidelines in mind throughout the transition process whether your child is in middle school, high school, or college.

1. *Student participation is crucial.* While it is an inherent right to be involved in one's own life planning, your child needs to be provided with the tools to be an effective contributor. Be sure he understands the nature of his disability, learns about his legal rights, explores career options, and develops greater independence in decision making.

2. *Transition planning should begin early.* It can start even at the elementary or middle school level. The teaching of life skills and learning strategies is as important as subject content. Resource or guidance personnel should help your child develop an understanding of the way she learns and how she might become a more efficient learner and self-advocate.

3. *Family involvement is primary.* Help identify your child's transition goals and support him in implementing them. Be sure that school personnel are sensitive to your family's values, needs, and cultural traditions.

4. *Transition planning must be comprehensive.* College and/or employment opportunities are only two of many options for which transition needs should be evaluated. Others include a postgraduate high school year, internships, and art or business schools. In considering any postsecondary program, the quality of life for the young

person is paramount. Work with teachers and school personnel to determine what academic and emotional supports your child will need in higher education or vocational placement.

EXPLORING POSTSECONDARY OPTIONS

Your child may need additional training after high school to be better prepared for adult life and employment. Today, there are several post-secondary options available to students with learning disabilities, ADHD, and other disabilities. For students considering careers in technical areas that don't emphasize reading and writing, vocational training may be most appropriate. Signed into law in 1994, the School-To-Work Opportunities Act is one program offering students with learning disabilities the opportunity to participate in vocational education. For other students, a technical college curriculum that emphasizes math, science, or engineering rather than language arts may be selected. Colleges with a "co-op" curriculum focusing on coursework as well as work experience also appeal to some students.

Community colleges, with their open admissions policies, low tuition fees, and less challenging curricula, may be the logical and advantageous first step for high school graduates who are unsure of their educational goals. The remedial services provided, as well as academic and vocational counseling, can help LD students decide whether to pursue higher education or seek employment after completing the two-year program. And if they do choose to transfer to a four-year college, the credits earned can usually be applied toward their degree.

SELECTING A COLLEGE

Anyone trying to select a college or university for a student with learning disabilities knows what a difficult process it is. Although almost all colleges are required by law to provide services for students with special needs, the programs offered vary both in commitment and implementation. The differences in available services reflect the philosophies of the institution as well as the obvious personnel and budgetary constraints. And these can change from year to year.

Many of the questions that you and your son or daughter have about potentially suitable colleges will be answered in the college catalogs, so call or write to have those sent. However, there are some additional factors that should also be considered. The following is a brief list of questions to ask.

1. Are there any special admission policies for students with learning disabilities?
2. Are there courses required for graduation that will be too difficult for my child?
3. Are students permitted to take reduced course loads on a continuing basis if needed?
4. What percentage of those who enter the college graduate?
5. Are support services provided by professionals or peers?
6. Are support services built into the student's schedule or voluntarily sought?
7. Are course substitutions allowed?
8. Is the LD support program at the college appropriate for my child?
9. Does the college provide for an associate degree (two-year program), with the option to continue toward a bachelor's degree?

Simply finding a good program or the one with the most services, then, is not necessarily the solution. A match must be made between your child's unique needs and the characteristics of the college and its LD program.

College entrance is usually possible even for high school graduates who have taken modified courses, no foreign language, and untimed SATs. Students with learning differences can be found on many campuses, ranging from local community colleges to Harvard. Indeed, some schools are particularly interested in educating students with learning disabilities, providing comprehensive programs and assistance. An extensive and current list may be obtained by writing to the Learning Disabilities Association of America (LDA), 4156 Library Road, Pittsburgh, PA 15234.

APPLYING TO COLLEGE

Once you have determined the characteristics of an appropriate setting, you can ask your child's guidance counselor to provide a list of institutions that meet those characteristics. Be sure the list includes a few that are "reach schools" and an equal number of "safeties." Then you can contact the colleges or programs and arrange interviews and visits. Although colleges don't always encourage interviews on campus, it can be especially important for LD students who may look marginal on paper but whose abilities and potential for success come across in an interview. Campus tours and the opportunity to sit in on classes may also help the LD student get a feel for the academic and social climate of the institution. For students who will require additional support, it's also a good idea to visit the facility where the special program is housed and talk to the support staff to get an overview of the services provided. After the visit, a brief thank-you note, written by your child, will be appreciated.

When students with learning differences apply to college, they are likely to have more than the usual number of questions and doubts. Understandably, your child (and you) will be concerned about her ability to meet the challenge of a college program in light of her academic and social difficulties. Here are my answers to some of the questions that students commonly ask:

Should I tell the colleges to which I apply that I have a learning disability? The answer depends on the degree of the disability. Now that there is greater acceptance of learning differences at both secondary and college levels, you can—and should—be honest with college admissions offices about your learning problems. After all, the college that would penalize a prospective student because of such disabilities ought not to be your first choice. According to Section 504 of the Rehabilitation Act, qualified persons with disabilities may not be denied admission or be subjected to discrimination.

What are my legal rights and how can I explain them to others? It is important for students with special needs to have a basic understanding of the laws that protect them in school and society. These provide the accommodations and modifications you will need, whether in college or the workplace. You should familiarize yourself with the basic tenets of IDEA, the Americans with Disabilities Act (ADA), and Section 504 of the Rehabilitation Act to know to what you are entitled under the law (see Appendix B).

How will I ever be accepted anywhere with my low SAT scores? A 320 may be a fine batting average, but it won't impress a college. Knowing that LD students may not test well, many schools will balance test results with grades and teacher recommendations. Some colleges today request an individually administered IQ test (usually the WAIS-R) and achievement results to assess the student's needs in college. The assumption behind this is that given native intelligence and the will to learn, the student will be able to succeed in college.

If I take SATs or ACTs, should I take them untimed? Students with identified learning disabilities and Attention-Deficit/Hyperactivity Disorders are permitted to take the Scholastic Assessment Test (SAT) and American College Testing (ACT) Program Test in special ways. Modifications for LD/ADHD students may include large type, a cassette, and/or extended time. Therefore, it is imperative that you be informed of your options in taking the tests under standardized and nonstandardized conditions. However, if the original diagnosis of your learning or attention problems was made prior to September 1993, there must be a reconfirmation within the last three years. (An IEP currently on file in the school will suffice.) Because any test modification is recorded on your school record, however, guidance counselors are divided about the wisdom of requesting special testing conditions. Some claim that the consequences don't warrant the accommodations, whereas others cite the positive gains in test results. It is my feeling that if you cannot read well under pressure, it is worth the price of the college knowing that you have a disability.

Will professors at college understand my learning problems? Again, it depends on the schools and the extent of the problem. In colleges that attract students with learning differences, accommodations are more likely to be made. In fact, some schools even make remedial courses available. However, unlike in the earlier grades when your parents could be your advocates, as a college student you will have to interpret your own problems to teachers and plan accordingly. I have known several college students who advised their professors that they work slowly and can't complete an exam during one class period. Although some teachers refuse to cooperate, most will make accommodations or some kind of compromise. I remember one professor, though, who told a student, "Bill, my boy, you don't need more time; what you need is self-confidence." It was apparent that what that professor needed was knowledge and understanding of learning disabilities.

Do I read well enough to keep up with the work at college? And if I do read slowly, can I manage to pass? A great deal of reading is required in most college programs, except in certain fields, but perseverance will help. Just as in elementary school and high school, a college student with a disability may have to work harder than other students do. You will have to select your courses carefully, eliminating some of the courses requiring heavier reading if that is your weakness or at least balancing them with easier ones.

THE APPLICATION

College applications come in various sizes and shapes, but almost always are intimidating to students with learning disabilities. Even before a prospective applicant thinks of putting pen to paper, she may have difficulty reading and interpreting the questions. Some LD students, ashamed of their handwriting and deficient spelling, simply can't face completing the application at all. They procrastinate, putting off the onerous task until the eleventh hour, when someone in the family begrudgingly does it for them. By that time, everyone is frustrated, with serious doubts about the wisdom of college at all. "If he can't even fill out the application, or ask teachers for references, how will he ever manage in college?"

The essays that are required frequently present a stumbling block for students who don't write well. Many whom I have helped initially claim that nothing of importance ever happened to them and they have "nothing to write about." I usually suggest that they write about something they know well rather than trying to sound erudite. Their own learning disabilities or lessons learned from a sport can be good topics if handled in a self-affirming manner. One boy wrote a touching essay about his struggles to survive in school with ADD. Another wrote, praising his baseball coach: "He noted my potential and gave me a chance to develop it. . . . He helped me achieve by helping me to believe in myself so that the next part of my dream can continue now."

For students who will continue to need support services in college, a current reevaluation is required within a year of applying to a college or postsecondary program. The purpose of this is to make realistic recommendations for an appropriate placement and services that the student will need. The testing can usually be done at the school, although some parents prefer to have a private practitioner do the evaluation. The college admissions office will advise you of the specific tests required.

Of course, if additional help in college will not be warranted, the learning disability need not be included on the application at all. In most instances, however, the student has learning accommodations still in place and will continue to need them. Extended time for tests, the use of tape recorders or laptop computers, and reduced course loads are some of the accommodations that can be requested in addition to academic and counseling services.

Given the cost of college today, you may need to file financial aid forms early in the process. The good news is that the federal government and state institutions are increasingly committed to making higher education accessible to students, regardless of financial status. Students with learning disabilities may also incur additional expenses, such as tape recorders and extra fees for tutoring and/or counseling. Be sure to factor these expenses into the financial aid request as well, or include them in your medical expenses when filing your tax return.

A COLLABORATIVE EFFORT

In the final analysis, transition planning must be tailored to fit the unique needs of each student. While college may be an appropriate goal for many LD and ADHD students, others will require a range of options. The choice of a college, vocational training program, or work experience is best arrived at through a collaborative effort. Although the key ingredient to success must lie in the choices young people make for themselves, parents, teachers, and guidance personnel can help them to develop and implement plans to attain their goals. As parents, you can support your child throughout his life in school by nurturing his development and validating his dreams.

8

RESOURCES AND TREATMENT APPROACHES

Y ou, the parents, are your child's greatest resource and most important advocates. You who know him best can provide him with the foundation for his future. And you are the people who will seek, and eventually find, professionals who can help him. The goal of finding help is clear, but the search for the right kind of help is a continual challenge. It is not surprising that parents are sometimes confused and imagine they are on a merry-go-round—moving, to be sure, but not reaching the objective—that of finding appropriate sources of help.

I once heard a speaker humorously liken the search process to a variation of the game of Monopoly. The goal of the game was to pass Go, having found suitable help with as few wasted motions and as little repetition of steps as possible. While most players could avoid landing on the trouble spots of Chance and Go To Jail, they frequently landed on squares marked "pediatrician," "school nurse," "psychologist," "social worker," "ophthalmologist," "optometrist," "pediatric neurologist," "allergist," "educational therapist," "remedial reading teacher," and "speech therapist." There was even a card reading, "Take a ride on the *Reading*." Perhaps the speaker was stretching an analogy, but to parents new to the game of finding help for their child through all of the professional services, it can seem like an endless maze with a no-win card in sight.

If you suspect that your child may have problems of any kind, here is what you should consider.

GETTING AN ACCURATE DIAGNOSIS

Identification of the nature of difficulty is clearly the essential first step. At the very least, an initial evaluation may be required, followed by periodic reassessment. When and how should this process start? You should seek professional advice as soon as you have questions about your child's development or ability to learn. The tension and anxiety created by parental concerns are likely to be conveyed to the child as well. Even very little children can be sensitive to parental stress. An early consultation may help relieve your anxiety, and if treatment should be indicated, the earlier it starts, the better.

First Stop—The Child's Doctor

Your pediatrician or family physician may be the first person you consult about your child's difficulties. Until recently, children's learning was considered to be solely an educational problem, to be dealt with later on in school. These issues were thought to be beyond the interest and purview of the physician. Parents were often put off with the familiar "Don't worry, he'll outgrow it," with the result that problems were not recognized until the child was suffering in school. In those days, there was little communication between home, school, and physician. Most often, a school crisis had to occur before forces were mobilized to diagnose and help the child—and the pediatrician remained in the dark.

Today, though, the pediatrician has become more involved with the special problems of physically healthy children and is the appropriate person to consult when learning or attentional difficulties are suspected. She should listen to your concerns, take a careful history of your child's development, and examine her patient thoroughly to eliminate the possibility of a physical basis for the problem. An informal checklist of behaviors frequently associated with learning differences or developmental lags is included here as a guide for physicians. If you and your doctor have not already discussed some of the behaviors on the list, perhaps you could go over them together. Although there are no quantitative norms, a thoughtful judgment can usually be made. If too many checks are in the questionable column, further evaluation may be needed. Your physician may recommend an ophthalmic evaluation, a speech and language exploration, psychiatric or psychological consultation, a neurological examination, and/or further diagnosis by a learning specialist. Most doctors can

A Physician's Checklist
for Identifying Children with Special Needs

Reported Behavior	Appropriate/ Questionable		Needs Further Investigation	
I. At Home Is child subject to				
1. poor sleep habits?	____	____	a. crying at bedtime b. restlessness at night c. nightmares	____ ____ ____
2. frequent, unpredictable temper tantrums?	____	____		
3. moodiness, irritability?	____	____	a. oppositional b. sad c. volatile	____ ____ ____
4. somatic symptoms?	____	____	a. stomachaches b. headaches c. on school days	____ ____ ____
5. dawdling in morning?	____	____	a. refuses to dress b. no breakfast c. late for school bus d. misses school bus	____ ____ ____ ____
6. complaints about school?	____	____	a. refuses to do homework b. procrastinates c. excessively dependent, relying on others	____ ____ ____
7. restlessness? Is he "always on the move"?	____	____	a. at meal time b. on trips c. on visits to friends and family	____ ____ ____
8. difficulty adjusting to new situations?	____	____	a. reluctant to leave home b. fearful of social situations c. excessive shyness	____ ____ ____
II. At School Is the child				
1. enjoying school?	____	____		
2. interested in learning activities?	____	____	a. rejecting "table" activities b. does not complete assigned work c. eager, then tunes out	 ____ ____
3. learning to read?	____	____		
4. able to follow directions?	____	____		
5. able to concentrate?	____	____	a. fidgety b. disruptive c. inattentive	____ ____ ____
6. relating to peers?	____	____		

Teachers' comments

STOP HERE IF ALL SEEMS WELL

A Physician's Checklist
for Identifying Children with Special Needs (cont.)

Reported Behavior	Appropriate/ Questionable		Needs Further Investigation	
III. Developmental Irregularities Is there evidence of				
1. delayed language or speech problems?	____	____	a. articulation b. syntax c. word finding	____ ____ ____
2. poor judgment and lack of common sense?	____	____	a. irresponsible b. accident prone c. in another world	____ ____ ____
3. impulsivity?	____	____		
4. poor motor coordination?	____	____	a. balance, hopping b. skipping c. catching ball	____ ____ ____
5. immature small muscle control?	____	____	a. cutting, coloring b. writing c. self-help	____ ____ ____
6. poor memory?	____	____		
7. lack of established handedness?	____	____		
IV. Family History Is there a history of				
1. learning or ADHD difficulties in the family?	____	____		
2. "retardation" in family?	____	____		
3. problems with siblings?	____	____		
4. problems in family?	____	____	a. illness b. divorce c. frequent moves d. marital stress	____ ____ ____ ____
V. Accomplishments				
1. What are the child's interests?	____	____		
2. What can he do well?	____	____		

recommend independent professionals in the area or a clinic where professionals in a variety of disciplines work together as a diagnostic team. If your pediatrician or family physician should simply dismiss your concerns with a wave of the hand, you may want to provide him or her with well-chosen reading material on the subject—or seek another, more supportive doctor.

FINDING A SPECIALIST

As parents, you might not flinch at a referral to an eye doctor or speech therapist, but the words "neurologist" or "psychiatrist" may be upsetting, particularly if these kinds of specialists have not been part of your experience. But be reassured, neither examination is uncomfortable or painful. The neurologist consulted for a child with learning problems is usually looking for signs of ADHD or developmental lags, unless, of course, the symptoms are indicative of something more serious (e.g., a seizure disorder or Tourette's). In some states, documentation of a visit to a neurologist may be required to qualify for special education programs.

A psychiatrist or other physician can also prescribe and monitor medication for children with ADHD. In addition, a psychiatrist or a psychologist can assess the emotional status of a child and help with problems of home management. A consultation does not necessarily mean that years of psychotherapy are in the offing. An objective assessment of the current situation might result in helpful suggestions for parents or the school. A therapist who had evaluated a ten-year-old and his mother, a friend of mine, came to the conclusion that mother and child were too dependent on one another, preventing the child from maturing. He suggested some strategies to work on at home to help them function more independently of each other. When he saw them six months later, many changes had been made, precluding the need for direct therapeutic intervention. Sometimes, as in this case, merely being helped to understand the problem is a big step toward ameliorating it.

A psychological assessment can also give you a picture of your child's current intellectual and perceptual functioning. A sensitive evaluation will help you become aware of your child's relative weaknesses as well as his strengths for learning. You should gain a clearer understanding of how your child views his world and the people in it.

If your pediatrician recommends an academic evaluation for a child of school age, you can turn to the child's school, a private learning disability specialist in the community, or one who is part of a clinic team. A "learning disability specialist" or "educational therapist," as it is frequently called, generally does the same kind of evaluation. Although the testing may overlap with that done by a psychologist, the learning specialist tends to place more emphasis on the educational and academic functioning of the child.

If you want the evaluation to be done in a school, you must put the request in writing. According to law, a public school (or one receiving federal funds) must honor the request and begin the process within thirty school days. The testing is free to any child in the school who is referred by a parent, caretaker, or even teacher. For children in private or parochial schools, however, a private evaluation may have to be sought. This would depend on the policy of the state and the local board of education.

In addition to the assessment, the evaluator can provide an important link to the classroom teacher and to the special services provided in the school. Typically it is the school psychologist or learning specialist who begins the diagnostic procedure. Speech therapists, occupational therapists, social workers, guidance personnel, and, of course, the child's teacher, may also be asked for their evaluations. At the end of the process, a meeting is held at which a committee decides whether, in fact, the child has an educationally handicapping condition and, if so, what services should be provided to meet the child's special needs (see Appendix A).

In the event that the school cannot offer special services and your pediatrician cannot suggest an appropriate resource in the area, there are several ways to locate one. The superintendent or principal of the school may know of resources or people in the area to call, or you may write to any of the following national organizations. They have printed material with useful information on where and how to obtain diagnosis and treatment for people of all ages with suspected learning disabilities and/or attention deficits. Descriptions of these organizations, along with the names and information about other organizations, can be found in Appendix E.

Learning Disabilities Association of America (LDA)
4156 Library Road
Pittsburgh, PA 15234
(412) 341–1515

The Orton Dyslexia Society (ODS)
The Chester Building
8600 La Salle Road, Suite 382
Baltimore, MD 21204
(410) 296–0232

National Center for Learning Disabilities (NCLD)
381 Park Avenue South, Suite 1401
New York, NY 10016
(212) 545–7510 or (800) 575–7373

Division for Learning Disabilities (DLD)
  of the Council for Exceptional Children (CEC)
1920 Association Drive
Reston, VA 22091–1589
(703) 620–3660 or (800) 328–0272

Council for Learning Disabilities (CLD)
P.O. Box 40303
Overland Park, KS 66204
(913) 492–8755

Children and Adults with Attention Deficit Disorders (Ch.A.D.D.)
499 NW 70th Avenue, Suite 101
Plantation, FL 33317
(954) 587–3700 or (800) 233–4050

Although most professionals and clinics tend to be located in or near large cities, you will probably be able to locate well-trained specialists within easy traveling distance if you search carefully. The state education department or a nearby college or university might be a useful resource as well.

EXPLAINING THE VISIT TO YOUR CHILD

Before visiting a specialist, you should explain to your child, as honestly as you can, what will happen. The professional with whom the appointment has been made should be able to guide you as to how to present it to your child. You might bring up the subject with such lines as, "We're going to see a woman who will help us find out just why school is so hard for you," or, "I spoke to a man who helps children find ways to learn more easily," or merely, "We think you're unhappy these days and we want to help you feel better." Parents frequently are surprised that I suggest that the truth be told as simply and honestly as possible. It is best to prepare your child in advance of the visit to give her adequate time to adjust to the idea, to ask questions, and to work through any fears or anxieties.

One mother, nervous about telling her child he was coming to my office for an evaluation, waited until the morning of the appointment. Then, just before she was ready to broach the subject, this perceptive six-year-old asked, "Mommy, isn't there someone who could help me learn to read?" He had helped his mother break the news, but he must have suspected where he was going, although the impending visit had not even been mentioned. As so often happens, some children seem almost psychic in their perceptiveness. You should tell your child in advance why he is being taken to a stranger's office and what he can expect to happen there, even if he is likely to balk. The same is true for medical or other appointments the child may find threatening. Some children, particularly those with ADHD, are prone to temper tantrums or flat refusals, so parents try to avoid this by keeping the appointment a surprise until the last moment. That is neither fair nor wise and can have repercussions. I have seen many angry, resistant children in my office whose parents were afraid of their reactions and, therefore, were not honest.

The objective and only worthwhile purpose for a diagnostic evaluation is a prescription for treatment. Pinpointing a problem is useless unless there is the likelihood of doing something about it. A detailed description of the child's abilities, learning style, strengths, and areas of difficulty should evolve from the diagnosis. Then you should receive a written report with recommendations for treatment; copies usually are sent to the physician and to the school as well. Of course, if you prefer to keep the report a private matter, that is your prerogative, but it does make it more difficult for the school to help your child.

DECIDING ON TREATMENT OPTIONS

Does your child need speech therapy, psychotherapy, remedial reading, assistance with math, or even special gym at the local Y? In many instances, the answer would be "all of the above," but that would be highly impractical. Priorities have to be determined and choices made. Does it seem more important for Johnny to learn to speak well, eliminating his lisp and "slushy *s*"? Perhaps so, if he is nine years old and self-conscious about it. Or should his reading improve before you worry about his coordination? Many times one area affects the other. To determine which treatment to choose, it may help to consult with the pediatrician and the school. It is probably worthwhile to formulate ideal plans, which may then be modified to coincide with reality—that is, available time, finances, and the emotional readiness of both your child and you.

Parents often ask when outside help should be considered in addition to the special services in school. I have met parents who are angry with the school's inability to handle every aspect of their child's difficulties. In reality, the school can do only so much—by law and in terms of budget—to meet the special needs of each and every child in the district. There may be times when outside help may be needed to supplement the assistance given at school. If family circumstances permit, it may be wise to seek private help when:

1. Your child requires a one-to-one relationship in order to learn. This may not be possible in school. For some children, a group of two is still a group, with built-in competition and distractions. With the financial pressures that exist in schools today, special groups most often are four or five children, as allowed by law.
2. School is stressful for your child. A child may need juice, crackers, and a "decompression chamber" in a cozy office rather than a classroom or cubicle visible to the school population.
3. Your child needs more time to learn and more reinforcement of skills than the school can provide in an existing program.
4. The programs in school simply do not meet your child's specific needs.

THE BEST TREATMENT IS A
COLLABORATIVE EFFORT

Every so often, I am asked what I do to help children in my private practice. I usually answer, somewhat facetiously, that most of my work is done with parents and teachers, and once in a while I might have to see the child. I realized long ago that I could not work with a child in a vacuum. No therapeutic intervention can be effective without support from family and teachers. Communication between parent, school, and outside therapists is vital and should be ongoing. You must feel free to communicate with professionals, asking questions, airing concerns, and conveying current information about your child. Telephone contacts, visits with your specialist, and conferences at school are always necessary.

Above all, you must feel at ease with the outside professionals you have chosen to work with your child. If you sense resistance or a lack of cooperation, the treatment cannot be successful. However, it is far better to try to remedy the situation by being honest with the professional you have engaged than to shop around from one professional to another, searching for an instant solution or cure. "Expert shopping" may be futile and only makes the child feel more anxious. When parents call me, expressing dissatisfaction with a helping person, I usually suggest that they discuss it with that person before making a change— particularly if the child is happy with the present situation. However, you do need reassurance that your child is progressing, and you should be able to air your concerns with the professional involved. If you feel uncomfortable, it might be helpful to get an outside consultation to relieve your mind that you are pursuing the best treatment. Then you can return to the therapist with greater confidence—or make a change, if that seems warranted.

When more than one professional is involved with your child, someone has to be captain of the team. You may have to be the self-appointed leader unless one of the professionals—pediatrician, educator, or psychologist—will assume the role of coordinator. Management is crucial to the success of any program, and periodic reevaluation, as well as collaboration, should keep everyone abreast of the progress being made, or the lack thereof.

DON'T FORGET THAT YOU NEED SUPPORT, TOO

Once your child's problems have been identified and are being addressed, you may want to turn to the resources most communities have available to parents. Frequently, when a child needs help, so do the parents. When William was a fifth grader (he is now in high school), he had a tutor who was helping him in school, but his parents felt incapable of handling him at home. He was provocative, constantly challenging their rules and decisions, with the result that they felt inept. It was clear that they needed help in parenting their willful son.

Late one evening, William's mother called me, saying that the situation at home was deteriorating rapidly. There were fights about everything, and they were becoming increasingly violent. To make matters worse, she and her husband disagreed about how to handle William. The situation at home hadn't been this bad since William's learning problems had first been diagnosed in first grade.

In a joint session, we talked about the parents' need to "be parents" and to assert their authority appropriately to protect their son. On the other hand, William, too, needed some autonomy and a sense of responsibility for his behavior.

William's father seemed particularly grateful for the counseling. He said he had originally reacted to his son's learning problems with "embarrassment, frustration, and anger." At the time the family sought counseling, he realized that he was "losing touch" with William, and he felt terrible. He believed that the counseling enabled him to have a more honest and closer relationship with his son.

William's parents were fortunate to have learned about their son's problems relatively early in his life and to have procured a good diagnosis and special education services for him. They also benefited from the special services offered in their community. After the psychoeducational evaluation, William saw a pediatric neurologist, who prescribed medication for his hyperactivity and answered many of the parents' questions. Later, William received speech therapy in school and tutoring in reading outside of school. Then came the family counseling. Expensive? Yes, but seeing the improvement in William and the burgeoning cohesiveness of the family made it seem a worthwhile investment to them. Although significant amounts of time and money were expended, the need for services didn't last forever. The parents also received a little help from the federal government in the form of tax benefits. According to an IRS ruling, if a child has been diagnosed as learning disabled or ADHD by a physician, the cost of the diagnosis, treatment, special education, and even books may be deducted as a medical expense (see the last section of this chapter for more information).

One additional community resource influenced William's parents. That was the parent support group they joined. There they received information about learning disabilities and ADHD, shared their concerns with other parents in the same situation, and learned about additional community resources available to them. There were special camp programs, discussion groups for siblings of children with handicapping conditions, and computer programs of interest. Perhaps most important, they also worked with other parents toward improving programs in the school for William and other children with similar problems.

Increasingly, parent groups have emerged as powerful advocates for children in the United States. They have been influential in writing and supporting legislation for the education of children with special needs in local communities as well as on the national level. Many of the innovative programs and services in schools today came from parental pressure at the grass-roots level. In many states, parents have expanded their local groups into statewide organizations. (Some of these organizations are listed in Appendix E.) Parent support groups have helped to create a positive public attitude toward children with a variety of disabilities while improving the education of all children.

In their enthusiasm to spread the gospel, parents and professionals, witnessing a successful treatment of a child's problems, may become quite insistent that their approach is the treatment of choice for other youngsters in need of help. They bombard friends, neighbors, and colleagues with advice that thoroughly confuses the uninitiated. While it is always a good idea to get referrals from a satisfied customer, I would suggest that you be wary when a parent or practitioner advocates a single technique as *the* solution. Some much-publicized and popular methodologies may help some children, but thus far research is inconclusive and, to my knowledge, there is no single best program for all children with either LD or ADHD, or both.

COUNSELING APPROACHES

In addition to remedial education, some children with disabilities need emotional support and strategies for behavioral change. It is not unusual that the family equilibrium can be so upset by problems associated with learning disabilities and ADHD that there is a need for intervention. Inappropriate behavior that may seem to reflect a primary emotional problem may, in fact, be secondary to the learning disability or hyperactivity. This is not necessarily so, but with appropriate interventions, family life can be significantly improved. Several possible approaches to addressing these problems are available. Two are described below.

Behavior Modification and
Cognitive-Behavioral Approaches

Behavior modification approaches to the education and management of children with learning differences came out of the research and theories of B. F. Skinner. Behavioral strategies aim to change and modify observable behaviors rather than to identify the psychological causes for a person's actions. Inappropriate or maladaptive behaviors are changed by manipulating a child's environment, with rewards ("reinforcers") for improvement and change. This approach is applied to educational and teaching situations as well as to social behaviors. For children who have not internalized or responded to the rewards of socially acceptable behavior, some kind of extrinsic reward system may be necessary until such time as good behavior becomes habitual. A teacher might give a child fifteen minutes of game time at the end of a day for completing an assignment on time or not shouting out in class. And a parent might reward a child by giving an extra half hour of play time or TV if morning chores are completed before leaving for school. Charts used at home may also be effective, with a small prize at the end of the week for success in achieving a goal. Since ADHD children have a bias toward novelty, the reinforcers may have to be changed after a time to be effective. Parents may have to be creative in this regard.

When applied to the treatment of discrete symptoms or problem behaviors, this approach is known as behavior therapy. It has been reported to be particularly successful for children with ADHD and for families who may be more concerned with improving behavior than understanding the underlying causes. Many of the principles, though, are effective for everyone.

In recent years, behavior therapy has relied increasingly on cognitive interventions to complement the more traditional methods. The central tenet of this approach is that thought mediates feelings and behavior. Changing maladaptive thinking and reinterpreting events, therefore, can help to ameliorate problems. For aggressive, impulsive children, for example, a therapist might teach self-instruction procedures in which the child learns to think about a problem, chooses a possible solution, and then evaluates the consequences of his actions.

Cognitive approaches with children are often used in group settings and may be used in combination with other techniques such as relaxation and social skills training. Family sessions in which goals and strategies for achieving them are focused on may also be important.

Psychotherapy

Dynamic or insight-oriented psychotherapy is an approach sometimes recommended for children with learning or attention problems when social problems or emotional concerns seem to interfere significantly with their lives. Children for whom learning is frustrating may develop negative feelings about themselves, making it hard for them to do well in any area. Some young people withdraw or stop trying, whereas others become overly aggressive or antagonistic. A better understanding of oneself and a positive self-concept are goals of this kind of psychotherapy, usually accomplished through therapeutic "play" or talking with a person trained in this technique.

Younger children, who find it difficult to express feelings and ideas in words, may use paint, crayons, puppets, toy soldiers, dolls, doll houses, doctor kits, and other toys to reveal their fantasies, wishes, fears, and worries. One boy of six even refers to me as his "worry doctor." He looks forward to coming to our sessions, using everything from the punching bag to the doll house, depending on his issues of the day.

Yesterday, Rob, age eleven, came home from school reciting his usual litany, "I hate everybody, I hate my life, and I hate me!" His mother, who had come to the door to greet him, was devastated. She was also angry that her efforts to help her son were not appreciated. She had quit her job to be with him after school, sent him to a special school, provided private tutoring, and chauffeured him anywhere he wanted to go. In other words, his wish was her command—and they both were miserable.

In therapy, Rob was able to talk about his anger. He was furious at himself for having a learning disability and at his mother, too. He blamed her for his parents' divorce, his poor grades, and his lack of friends. He also resented her overprotection of him. In therapy with the family, we tried to help his mother distance herself a little to allow Rob more freedom. At the same time, I was able to convince Rob that his anger, acted out at home, was not helping him; in fact, it was destructive to his relationship with his mother and his friends in the neighborhood. Rob was insightful enough to understand that there were other, more acceptable ways to express his feelings and that his anger sometimes was even aimed at the wrong target.

We also used some of the concepts of cognitive therapy, in which Rob's thoughts were reinterpreted to change his feelings. When Rob said he "never" won in a game, I questioned the "never," saying that it might feel that way, but actually he had won a game with me only last week. We talked about some of the other positive things he had accomplished, which, in the end, helped to change his outlook. Before too long, Rob was displaying less anger at home and seemed to feel better about himself.

Occasionally, a child's lack of achievement at school is erroneously attributed solely to emotional problems, and psychotherapy is initiated prior to testing for a learning disability or attention deficit. A tuned-in psychologist might refer the family for an in-depth psychoeducational evaluation to ascertain the primary source of the problems. And because children live with—and react to—parents and siblings, family therapy may be the treatment of choice. In some cases, a two-pronged approach—educational and psychological—can help a child more quickly and more effectively than one form of treatment alone. This is particularly true if the child is exceedingly anxious, fearful, impulsive, or unable to handle his feelings appropriately.

MEDICATION AS TREATMENT (PSYCHOPHARMACOLOGY)

In addition to behavioral strategies for ADHD youngsters, biochemical intervention or medication is frequently recommended, particularly for the hyperactive child. Dexedrine, Ritalin, and other amphetamine-related medications are usually prescribed, although antidepressants, such as desipramine or Prozac, have been used very successfully, depending on the child's symptoms. Recently, newer medications, including Effexor, have been touted as helping children with anxiety as well as ADHD. At this writing, some of the newer medications have not yet received FDA approval for children, but trials are being conducted that look promising. For some children who meet criteria for hyperactivity and are aggressive, clonidine, a drug for lowering blood pressure, is also used to help control their symptoms. It can also be used for children with tics.

It is currently estimated that 70 to 80 percent of children and adolescents with ADHD can be helped with appropriate use of medication. When drug therapy is effective, youngsters demonstrate diminished hyperactivity, improved powers of concentration, and increased ability to sit still long enough to learn. Sometimes even handwriting shows improvement. As one boy, age seven, said, "Ritalin is sort of like my remote control." He feels that it has helped him, and he even reminds his mother to give it to him before school. We have discussed the fact, though, that the medicine doesn't control him. Only he can do that, but with the aid of the medication, he can be more in charge of his own body.

Pharmacotherapy itself cannot produce learning—only time and teaching can do that—but the decrease in restlessness and distractibility and the increased attention span can facilitate the learning process. I know some ADHD adults who claim that a small amount of Ritalin enables them to be more organized and to function better in their lives.

Traditionally, physicians have assumed responsibility for the administration and monitoring of medical treatment, but it is important that you and the child's teacher assist the physician in judging the effectiveness of the therapy, because you see the child on a daily basis. Dosages and even the choice of medication may have to be adjusted, and someone who knows the child well should be aware of the effects of the medication. Regular examinations by a physician are also important to review the benefits of the treatment and to make sure that there are no negative side effects.

Parents frequently ask whether children on medication are at risk for becoming dependent on drugs when they are older. Actually, the evidence points to the opposite—that is, ADHD adolescents who have been treated with medication seem to have a lower rate of drug addiction than others. They reach an age, usually at twelve or thirteen, when they resist or even refuse to take their medication. However, those whose problems were not addressed prior to adolescence do appear to be at greater risk for abusing drugs as well as for mental health problems later on.

Another concern of parents has to do with the side effects of medication over time. It was reported that some children who are on medication for a long period of time may show a decrease in growth components—body structure and body weight. We know now that the growth process may be slowed somewhat while the child is taking medication, but it catches up quickly as soon as the medication is stopped. Since most children do not remain on the medication for several years, this usually is not a major issue.

No one would suggest that medication be prescribed unless absolutely necessary, but if a child cannot control his behavior and is receiving negative feedback on a daily basis from parents, peers, and teachers, the need is probably indicated. The pros and cons of medication should always be weighed against the amount of rejection and disapproval to which the child is subjected. Being deprived of medication may be even more detrimental to the child's sense of well-being than the negatives associated with medication.

If a trial of medication should be attempted, careful monitoring is crucial. You, your child's teachers, and your child's physician must communicate with each other to share observations and judge the effectiveness across settings and at different times during the day. I also like to see "drug holidays" given, usually during school vacations rather than weekends. Living with a child off medication can give you, the parents, an opportunity to determine whether the medication still seems to be warranted or if the child can maintain control without it. Of course, the school situation is likely to be the best testing ground in terms of the inherent stress for an LD/ADHD child. It's important to remember that medication is rarely necessary for life; it's usually a temporary support until the child is mature enough to go it alone.

ALTERNATIVE MEANS TO THE END

Some of the theories that have claimed to have *the* answer advocate visual training, colored lenses, special diets, or over-the-counter medications as a means of attaining a higher level of functioning. There may be validity to some aspects of these theories, but they are not the magic solution or panacea to all children's problems. On the other hand, although research may suggest that some of these methods are futile, nothing, in my opinion, should be categorically dismissed. Who knows? Perhaps faith in a treatment is enough to bring some positive results. Professionals should, however, know and report the evidence accurately to parents—without "selling" just one approach. At the same time, they must leave room for further investigation and study.

A few of the controversial treatments recommended for ADHD and/or learning differences are described below. Most are not used in isolation, but rather to supplement educational techniques that may be falling short of the goal.

Vision Training

Optometric training is a branch of optometry predicated on the acceptance of the relationship between visual abilities and school learning. Its practice is based on the assumption that visual perception is *learned* through developmental sequences of growth—physical, physiological, and psychological. Difficulties in learning can, therefore, be attributed to a dysfunction in visual efficiency and sensory-motor integration. Optometrists who work in this area believe that visual organization can be trained and will affect a child's academic performance. They prescribe stereoscopic and visual-motor exercises for youngsters to improve the areas of weakness and inefficiency.

One of the early leaders in this field was G. N. Getman, an optometrist and author of *How to Develop Your Child's Intelligence* (A Research Publication, 1962). This small book is basically a guide for parents and teachers of young children. It provides specific ideas for a readiness training program relying heavily on motor, sensory, and visual techniques. According to Getman, "Vision is involved in every meaningful learning activity. Thus vision training is intelligence training" (p. 106).

The response of other professionals to optometric training, especially developmental vision training, as a treatment for reading and learning problems, is not all positive. Some psychologists, ophthalmologists, neurologists, and educators have expressed serious doubts both as to the strength of the relationship between perceptual-motor skills and success in school and the efficacy of vision training for children with learning problems. Studies are conflicting, and the research reported is inconsistent. More controlled studies are needed.

Perception and Coordination

Perceptual-motor programs, such as those originally advocated by Kephart, Barsh, and Delacato, are based on the relationship between a child's motor development and academic learning. Although these programs are not as popular as they once were, proponents of them believe that motor skills form the basis for higher cognitive processing and, therefore, affect a child's ability to learn. Emphasis is on the natural order of development to avoid what is sometimes referred to as "splinter skills," those abilities that lack a basic foundation. These skills may not be permanent and will not generalize to other learning.

Materials such as those designed by Jean Ayres are based on the belief that motor difficulties such as uncoordination or poor balance will subsequently affect learning. Therefore, training in balance, muscular strength, spatial and body awareness, tactile receptivity, and coordination are thought to be important for a child's optimal functioning in school. Occupational therapists or physical therapists, who may be part of the diagnostic team, evaluate children's skills in this area and provide treatment where needed.

Whether perceptual-motor training has any effect on reading or academic skills has long been debated. This does not negate the value of perceptual programs for their own sake, however, particularly for young children. Improvement in motor coordination can help them feel better about themselves and more competent in the gym and on the playground.

EEG Biofeedback

Recent research in behavioral medicine has brought Biofeedback into use as a treatment for disorders that are mediated by physiological functioning. Learning disabilities and ADHD are two conditions for which that technique may be recommended. Proponents of this approach believe that ADHD children, in particular, can be trained to increase the type of brainwave activity associated with sustained attention and to decrease the activity associated with daydreaming and distractibility. The technique involves measuring levels of electrical activity in various regions of the brain and feeding the information into a computer. The results are transformed into a signal, giving the child feedback. With children, a reward system is usually used, indicating the success of the training.

Although some researchers have found this approach to be successful in reducing hyperactivity, methodological problems have limited generalization. Nonetheless, it may well be that biofeedback in conjunction with other techniques has promise for reducing some of the behavioral symptoms of the hyperactivity syndrome. More thorough, controlled studies clearly are needed to substantiate the claims made by proponents of EEG biofeedback.

Tinted Lenses

The use of tinted lenses as a method to improve reading skills in children with dyslexia has been a controversial issue in recent years. Syntotics, that is, colored light therapy, was first described in 1941 and was used by some practitioners to treat a variety of conditions, including reading problems. In 1983, Irlen reported successful treatment of reading disabilities with the use of tinted lenses. She asserted that 50 percent of dyslexic individuals are particularly sensitive to light—luminance, intensity, wavelength, and color contrast. By modifying light with colored filters, Irlen claimed, people with learning disabilities can read better, faster, and more comfortably. The lenses, prescribed specifically for each individual, have been reported to produce powerful results. However, to my knowledge, no details of Irlen's research have been published to support her hypotheses. Thus, although the efficacy of tinted lenses has not been completely disproved, neither has it been validated.

Anti–Motion Sickness Medication

Advocates of the theory advanced by Dr. Harold Levinson believe that ADHD and learning disabilities are caused by problems in the inner-ear system, which affects balance and coordination. To treat dyslexia, the symptoms of ADHD, and a variety of other problems, an array of medications and vitamins are prescribed. Although some individuals claim to have been helped by the medications and supplements, there is no scientific evidence to support this approach. Physicians generally are skeptical, citing the lack of anything more than anecdotal reports as evidence that the treatment is effective. They also claim that, anatomically and physiologically, there is no reason to believe that the inner ear is involved in learning or impulse control in other than marginal ways. However, as with all the controversial therapies, judgment must be deferred pending systematic research.

Nutritional Therapies

Megavitamin therapy is an approach advocated by those who believe that some people have a genetic abnormality that results in an increased need for vitamins and minerals. The treatment, therefore, consists of the administration of massive doses of vitamins and the maintenance of proper nutrition. Advocates of this theory claim that learning and behavior difficulties, as well as hyperactivity, can be improved with this regime. Allan Cott, M.D., an early proponent, found a significant decrease in hyperactivity, improved concentration, and an increased attention span in children treated with vitamins. Cott claimed that children who begin the treatment early and continue it over a long period of time generally make the greatest progress.

Because vitamins are almost synonymous with nutrition and

health, many parents find this approach appealing. However, to date there is a lack of supporting scientific evidence. Some critics attribute children's improvement in learning and/or attention to a placebo effect. Others have cautioned against the prolonged use of vitamins as detrimental to health. Everyone agrees that more research is indicated.

Homeopathic remedies, advocating small doses of vitamins, herbs, minerals, and other natural food supplements, have gained in popularity in recent years. One of my patients, diagnosed as having Pervasive Developmental Disabilities with a relatively poor prognosis, has exceeded everyone's expectations. In addition to an excellent special education program, play therapy, and parents dedicated to his progress, he is taking natural supplements that reportedly help him focus and learn.

Dietary Intervention

Special diets have also been championed for children with special needs. Dr. B. F. Feingold, former chief of the Department of Allergy at the Kaiser-Permanente Medical Center in San Francisco, attributed cases of increased learning and attention and fewer behavioral problems in children to the addition of chemicals in foods. Dr. Feingold found that ADHD children react adversely to synthetic food colorings and flavorings, which causes or contributes to their hyperactivity. He and his colleagues claim that an elimination diet free of such chemicals could significantly diminish the symptoms of learning problems and ADHD, that is, the aggressive, impulsive, hyperactive behavior.

A nutritionally balanced diet is advocated by the Feingold diet and others stressing natural products. Foods with synthetic additives as well as those fruits and vegetables containing salicylates (natural chemicals thought to produce similar adverse effects) are, therefore, prohibited. Although a cause-and-effect relationship between food additives and hyperactivity has not been established to the satisfaction of all researchers, many parents feel that the observed improvement for their children is too great to be disregarded. They are also likely to be the most aware when their child is misbehaving after eating a single piece of chocolate.

To date, there is little evidence that the intake of sugar significantly affects a child's learning or behavior. Controlled studies suggest that, for most children at least, the negative effects of sugar intake possibly have been exaggerated. Unquestionably, some youngsters do appear to be particularly sensitive to it, and parents' observations must be trusted.

Critics of a stringent diet for children hypothesize that any improvement noted may be the result of the additional attention paid to the child's physical well-being. While this may be questioned, there is little doubt that the diet involves a good deal of extra work for the family cook. I have also heard mothers complain that for the child with social problems, this regime may isolate him even more. He can't even enjoy the goodies at a birthday party! I can't help but feel that moderation is the best policy, whether in foods, vitamin supplements, or additives.

A connection between diet and behavior has also been made by those who identify food allergies as the most common cause of learning and behavior problems in children. Dr. Doris Rapp and others have complied an extensive list of behaviors that might indicate an allergic reaction, such as hyperactivity, aggression, temper tantrums, and sleep problems. They advocate dietary modification as the primary means of treating both learning disabilities and attentional problems. Although evidence linking food allergies to children's problems is still anecdotal rather than supported by controlled studies, it may be that allergies and sensitivities to foods contribute to behavior problems in a select group of children.

From these brief descriptions, it is clear that behavioral interventions for children with learning and attentional problems include a wide variety of techniques. Because of limitations in research thus far, the question of the effectiveness of a number of approaches remains largely unresolved.

BECOMING A WISE CONSUMER

How can you, the parents of a child with ADHD or learning disabilities, evaluate the best treatment methods or approaches for your child? First, by becoming an informed consumer, to the extent that you are able. An analysis of your family's resources—that is, time, money, energy, and proximity—is also important. A few additional tips follow.

1. Be wary of any treatment that claims to address a wide variety of ailments or disorders. Common sense tells us that the more grandiose the claim, the less likely it is to be true.
2. Don't rely only on the testimonials of parents who claim their child has been helped by the approach. An enthusiastic parent is worth

listening to, but should not be a substitute for substantiated evidence.

3. Be careful of an approach that claims to be a panacea for all children with ADHD, learning disabilities, social problems, or phobias. No method to date has been shown to be *the* cure for these disorders.

It may be reassuring to remember that, regardless of the treatment selected, a learning difference is usually not progressive—that is, it doesn't become worse over time. With appropriate diagnosis and well-researched intervention, the chances are good that there will be improvement. Moreover, even when parent and child are being helped and supported by a cooperative network of professionals and community resources, it is important for you to be aware that the natural growth of the child is perhaps your best ally.

TAX TIPS

Medical expenses can be itemized on your tax return if they exceed 7.5 percent of your total income. According to the *Tax Guide for Parents*, published by the Family Resource Center for Disabilities, as the parent of a child with a handicapping condition, including learning disabilities and ADD, you may include medical expenses as long as they are made "to alleviate your child's mental or physical condition." Medical deductions can include educational services, such as tuition costs for special education and tutoring, books and supplies, as well as a range of professional services, including testing and therapy.

It is important to document all your medical expenses by

- Keeping careful records of all expenses with receipts, dates of service, and expenses for at least three years, for possible auditing purposes
- Obtaining certification from your physician/mental health professional that the expense has been made for one or more of the following: diagnosis, prevention, treatment, or to alleviate your child's mental or physical condition

9

EMOTIONAL ISSUES

Although most children are resilient and grow into emotional health in the face of stressful life events, some children aren't so fortunate. It is not uncommon for a child with a learning disability to become discouraged and even pessimistic at times as a result of the problems he faces daily. That is to be expected when he compares himself to more successful age mates and fails to live up to his own aspirations. While it is heart wrenching for parents to see a child frustrated and unhappy, the child's feelings are not usually considered to be pathological and generally can be remedied with extra-large doses of understanding and support.

There are, however, some emotional difficulties to which children and adolescents with learning differences seem particularly vulnerable. Although not necessarily life threatening, they can affect the entire family and may even persist beyond adolescence unless they are addressed. They are

1. Learned helplessness
2. Anxiety disorders
3. Depression
4. Behavior disorders

Let's look at these within the context of learning and attentional problems to see how your child might demonstrate some of these symptoms at home and what you, as parents, can do to help.

LEARNED HELPLESSNESS

After repeated failures in school, real or imagined, children begin to feel a sense of helplessness, the "I can't" syndrome. They believe that they have no control over their lives and nothing they do makes a difference. Perhaps because of their fatalistic attitude, they assume little or no responsibility for their actions. If they do, it's generally only for their failures rather than their successes.

I remember Jan, a ninth grader, who told me with conviction that studying for exams doesn't help. The more she studies, she said, the lower her grades are. And she truly believed what she was saying. Whereas most students will attribute a high grade to studying efficiently and knowing the material, Jan was convinced that if she did well on a test, the reasons had nothing to do with her ability or preparation. The test was either "too easy," "the teacher made a mistake," or it was just "dumb luck." I don't remember that she ever took credit for a good grade. When Jan failed a test, however, she invariably attributed it to her being "stupid," incapable of doing well.

Jan had what psychologists call "an external locus of control." In other words, things just happened to her, and she had no responsibility for the outcome. In contrast to Jan's view, most students develop an internal locus of control as they mature. They know that they have a better chance of doing well on an exam if they study, and if they fail, they probably didn't apply themselves sufficiently to the task. In other words, they attribute the outcome to their own efforts. Studies have shown that children with an internal locus of control are relatively better able to withstand frustration, while those who don't take responsibility may not adapt to adversity as easily.

Learning to Take Responsibility

In my work with LD/ADHD children and adolescents, I try to help them realize that they can, indeed, make a difference and, to an extent, determine their own outcomes. They need to accept the idea that they must assume responsibility for their learning and even for their social relationships.

At seven years of age, Alex was unhappy in school, challenged by work he couldn't do. He was also small for his age, not athletic, and he used to complain, "The kids [at school] don't like me." When I asked him why that was, he replied, "Because I'm just not popular"—circuitous reasoning at its best. I tried to help Alex see that he might have a role in making enemies, since it seemed to happen everywhere, not only in school. In fact, Alex was always ready to fight.

When Alex told me of situations at school in which he was rejected or blamed, we discussed how he could have behaved differently. Sometimes we even turned the episode into a play. We were the only two actors, but we took different parts to show Alex his "starring role" in the conflicts. Gradually, he began to see that he wasn't unpopular just because of his "reputation" and that he could actually change his classmates' opinion of him.

As parents, you can also help your children learn that they can be effective agents of change. When you praise your child for calling a classmate for forgotten homework (even if it was your idea initially), you are acknowledging the value of his taking responsibility. And if he brings home a better-than-usual vocabulary test, it may be an indication that studying does pay. It is also important, though, to point out to your child that there are situations beyond his control. That will help him understand the difference. Although he cannot be responsible for what others do, he can be in charge of his own behavior.

Even when young people understand their problems and take responsibility for their own lives, they may still experience disappointment and self-doubt to the point where their sense of competence is seriously compromised. Low self-esteem, in fact, is almost always found in a child with a learning difference. If, as the analyst Erik Erikson said of the school-age child, "I am what I learn," how could a boy or girl feel capable when school is a struggle all day, every day? And if the home situation reinforces the child's feeling of not making it, his self-image will plummet even more.

To assess your child's self-concept, you might want to ask yourself a few questions. The following is a brief checklist designed to help you evaluate your child's self-esteem.

1. Does your child or adolescent avoid new situations?
2. Is your child very shy or awkward in social situations?
3. Does he avoid eye contact with people?
4. Does he deprecate himself frequently, saying he's "dumb," "bad," or "ugly"?
5. Is she unduly critical of other people?
6. Does she resist instruction in nonacademic activities and/or offers of help?

7. Is he excessively dependent on others for decisions?
8. Is your child too afraid of making a mistake or getting in trouble?

Children who have low self-esteem tend to be afraid of what the future will bring and, typically, confuse possibility with probability—if something *can* happen, it *will* happen. This, in turn, gives rise to anxiety, a vague, irrational fear or worry in excess of the reality of a situation.

ANXIETY DISORDERS

At certain developmental stages, almost all children have fears. Fears of the dark, monsters, and separation from parents are typical of the young child, but over time, these normal fears fade and children understand the difference between fantasy and reality. When learning is hard, though, the world seems unsteady and unpredictable. It's difficult for a child to know what she can depend on when she can't even rely on remembering information for tomorrow's exam. An unpredictable memory is only one cause for anxiety in the school-age child. Fear of failure, or even of success, can also create anxiety and worry. Many of the children I see look as if they are waiting for the other shoe to drop. Some have even told me that they always worry that "something bad is about to happen." That feeling of excessive dread or fear may signify an anxiety disorder.

Separation Anxiety

An anxious child's symptoms can range from mild restlessness and discomfort to absolute panic. Some children develop nervous habits or somatic symptoms and are overly concerned about bodily harm or injury. They may be subject to sleep disturbance and nightmares, or they may be afraid to separate from parents or caregivers. I see several children who don't like to go to unfamiliar places, even with their families. They feel safer at home and find every reason to stay there. Of course, once they do go out, they can have fun, but their parents have to force them to go. There are also children, usually in the early grades, who develop "school reluctance," or school phobia, that is, the inability to go to school. In addition to the fear of leaving their parents, they may also find the school environment frightening.

In the spring of second grade, Sara suddenly started crying every morning before school, complaining of stomachaches and "feeling sick." She begged to stay home and, at first, her mother let her. After a time, when her mother finally insisted that she had to go to school, Sara cried hysterically and refused to enter the building when brought there. It took the principal, the school psychologist, and Sara's mother to escort her to her classroom. Later, after Sara had calmed down, she was able to say that she missed her mother when she wasn't with her, and was afraid her mother would have an accident or get sick while she was at school.

In retrospect, the problem likely began the previous year, when Sara had a warm, gentle first grade teacher who didn't push her to learn to read—and Sara didn't disappoint her. In second grade, however, Sara's learning problems, as well as her "immaturity," had become more apparent. Her teacher was quite demanding, too, with the result that Sara became increasingly more anxious in the classroom. To keep Sara in school, her mother had to remain with her for several weeks, gradually moving from Sara's classroom to the library, and finally outside the building when Sara felt safer. In addition, her teacher encouraged her to carry her mother's photo in her lunchbox to look at when she felt lonely. Although Sara was not particularly happy in school, she eventually overcame her fear and was able to leave for school most mornings without tears or complaints of aches and pains.

At eight years of age, Anthony, a handsome, athletic boy who had been diagnosed as having "significant attentional problems without hyperactivity," was referred to me by his pediatrician. In addition to chewing on the collar and sleeves of his shirts, Anthony bit his nails until they bled. He rarely went to bed before midnight and then had problems sleeping through the night. Not surprisingly, he couldn't get up for school in the morning, and his teacher complained that he had trouble staying awake in class.

There are a number of strategies that can be used to treat children suffering with anxieties. For younger children, play therapy may be the first choice, since play is their primary medium of expression. Through guided play, the therapist can help a child reveal fears and work through them, setting limits on behavior when necessary. That was the primary approach I used with Sara and Anthony, with some behavior modification, role playing, and family discussions included as well.

Tessie, a curly-headed nine-year-old, refused to sleep in her own bed. She was afraid that someone would come into the house and kidnap her. She also wouldn't get out of her bed without her mother standing by for fear of "a monster waiting to grab me." While this kind of concern is expected of a five- or six-year-old, by the age of nine, rational thought usually takes over and the child is able to conquer these fears. Tessie even knew that her anxieties were strange as well as troublesome, but she couldn't get over them without help. In treatment, Tessie and I sometimes played, but she usually came into the office ready to sit down and talk, frequently with a handwritten list of issues she wanted to tell me about.

Obsessive-Compulsive Symptoms

Calvin, at fourteen, spent an inordinate number of hours each day on homework. He felt so pressured about school that he checked his book bag four times every night for fear that he had forgotten to do an assignment. Even when he was reassured that everything was finished, he had trouble putting his work aside to go to bed. He was so worried about what would happen the next day that he couldn't sleep. His anxieties were so severe that he insisted that his mother remain in the room with him at night until he fell asleep.

In sessions with Calvin, we talked about his worries and any incidents that had occurred during the week. We also discussed the basis of his fears and how to handle them. Favorite topics were classmates teasing, parents fighting, and conversations about him that were overheard. About six months after we began, Calvin was able to sleep alone in his room, without calling to his mother during the night.

Molly had full-blown panic attacks. Shortly after her sixteenth birthday, she suddenly felt so nauseous and faint one day in school that she had to go home. She told her mother she was sure she was having a heart attack. In the month prior to my seeing her, she had also been seen by four physicians, in response to her reports of blurry vision, an ulcer, appendicitis, and concern about a brain tumor. When nothing was found to be physically wrong, Molly was referred to me. She complained of waking in the morning feeling "scared" and unable to go to school almost every day. She was also subject to panic attacks when she was away from home, so that she had to give up her babysitting job and sleepovers with friends. Clearly, her anxieties were interfering significantly with the quality of her life.

The more anxious Molly became, the more she obsessed on

thoughts that, as she said, "stuck in my head and I couldn't stop them." For a month or two, she obsessed about getting sick; after that, it was her appearance. Molly was a beautiful girl who insisted that she "looked fat and ugly." She refused to go out socially until she could shop for the right clothes. Once in a store, however, she was unable to decide what she liked, so she'd come home empty-handed and more frustrated than ever. Molly also needed her homework to be perfect before leaving for school, even if it meant staying up well past midnight. If she didn't consider it just so, which was most of the time, she couldn't, or wouldn't, hand it in.

Molly's symptoms were typical of an obsessive-compulsive disorder (OCD), which often coexists with other anxieties, and sometimes with learning disabilities as well. Magical thinking (believing their fantasies will come true) and concern for conformity are characteristics frequently associated with children who are compulsive. A possible explanation for OCD is that it is the child or adolescent's way of avoiding underlying feelings that are too painful. Another theory is that it is the child's way of controlling not only her emotions but her world as well. When children have learning disabilities and/or ADHD, they frequently feel a lack of control over their lives. The rigidity associated with OCD gives them a sense of structure and boundaries within which to function. A biochemical and genetic component to these disorders is also likely.

At certain ages, compulsive actions are considered to be perfectly normal, part of a young child's development. Was there ever a child, for example, who didn't say "step on a crack and you break your mother's back"? Or a three-year-old who doesn't insist that her socks must be "even"? It's only when obsessional thinking or compulsive acts persist, creating problems for the child (and the family), that they are likely to be recognized as emotional disorders. Otherwise, a child's excessive neatness, cleanliness, and even fussiness about clothing might be interpreted as positive qualities or simply a personality quirk.

The young people whose problems I have described in this section reveal the power of anxiety and fear and the effect they can have on people's lives. All of them had learning disabilities and/or attention deficits that made them anxious in school, but each responded to their anxieties with qualitatively different symptoms. In thinking of approaches to help them, it was clear that their anxieties were so distressing that alleviating them had to be the priority in treatment, even more than their schoolwork.

In addition to seeing the children, I also worked with their families and their schools to alleviate whatever environmental stress we could. For Molly, medication was also prescribed that helped her feel less anxious and more able to cope with the demands of her life. Later that year, with the help of counseling and medication, she was no longer afraid that she would die; she was doing much better in school and was beginning to be socially active again. As a senior in high school, Molly was able to look forward to graduation and a year of business school before deciding her future goal—college or employment.

DEPRESSION

Depression is a mood disorder that has only recently been acknowledged to be a problem of childhood. It used to be thought that until adolescence, children couldn't be depressed; they could have sad moods, but these were considered to be transient, generally in response to a specific situation, frustration, or loss. We now know, however, that children as well as adults can, indeed, suffer from depression. Although a definitive cause has not yet been established, there are indications that depression may be biochemical and genetic in origin, rather than simply being a reaction to an event or environmental situation. Studies have shown that depression is three times more common in children whose biological parents suffer from depression, even if the children were adopted or lived with other families.

According to the current *Diagnostic and Statistical Manual,* the criteria for a diagnosis of depression are essentially the same for children and adults. Symptoms may cover a wide range of areas, including any or all of the following:

Physical
  Loss of appetite or overeating
  Sleep disturbance
  Lack of energy, lethargy
  Agitation
Emotional
  Pervasive sadness
  Self-deprecation

    Irritability
    Crying
Social
    Lack of pleasure in activities previously enjoyed
    Withdrawal from people
Cognitive
    Inability to concentrate
    Indecisiveness
    Preoccupation with morbid ideation
    Slowed thinking

The symptoms of depression in children undoubtedly vary as a function of their development, as well. Moreover, unlike adults, children may not have the vocabulary to accurately describe how they feel. Those with learning disabilities are likely to be even less able than others of their age to understand complex concepts such as guilt, self-esteem, and concentration. Rather than reflecting on their feelings and problems, then, they tend to act them out. In addition to the easily recognized crying, drop in school performance, unexplained irritability, and social isolation, I have found that children can also demonstrate a range of seemingly atypical behaviors in response to depression. Hyperactivity resembling ADHD, temper tantrums, volatile behavior, aggression, and even delinquency may be the prominent symptoms displayed, with no apparent despondency, lethargy, or withdrawal.

Learning Disabilities, ADHD, and Depression

In the last decade, a significant number of children with diagnosed learning disabilities have been found to be depressed, more than would be expected in the general population. Although an association between learning disabilities and depression has been demonstrated, the precise nature of the relationship has not been established. It seems evident, though, that it may be reciprocal. In other words, a child who is depressed is likely to find learning in school difficult. It's hard to concentrate when you're feeling burdened, sad, and lethargic. At the same time, a learning disability has also been found to put a child at risk for depression. Several authors have suggested that children with problems in school suffer from a chronic low level of depression known as dysthymia, rather than the more severe clinical depression. The disparity between their goals and their academic achievement may cause sadness and a feeling of worthlessness that is not easily dispelled.

Several factors associated with learning disabilities and other school-related problems may also account for a "reactive depression."

1. Low self-esteem, common in the LD population, has been found to contribute significantly to depression, as well as being a symptom of the disorder.
2. The anger and rage many children feel in response to their learning disabilities may also result in depression, particularly if the child blames himself for his failures. One six-year-old boy hits or bangs his own head when he is angry, rather than hurting others. Self-injurious behavior in young children is usually indicative of a significant problem that merits professional attention.
3. Social isolation has also been associated with depressive disorders. When children have difficulty learning in school and are also rejected on the playground, it is hard for them to feel happy.
4. Some types of learning disabilities seem to predispose children and adolescents to depression. Children with difficulties in math and spatial organization, even more than reading, seem most vulnerable. Byron Rourke has found those with "non-verbal learning disabilities" to be more at risk than others for depression and even suicide.

On the other hand, even young people without learning disabilities may become acutely depressed in response to their life situations. I'm thinking of Leah, whose adoptive parents separated when she was five years old. Because her father drank and abused her, he was only permitted occasional visits with supervision. After three years, however, he had remarried and was granted more frequent visits with his daughter. Leah was a pretty, vivacious girl who seemed to be doing well after her rocky start in life. Her mother was devoted to her and even gave up her job when Leah began to have problems in school. They were a twosome who did everything together.

When Leah was in sixth grade, she began to "forget" assignments, lose books, and fall asleep in class. She also ignored her friends and had no interest in going anywhere with her "overprotective" mother. In fact, she usually didn't want to leave her apartment. In talking to Leah, it became apparent that she was seriously depressed. She admitted that she couldn't concentrate in school, was "tired" all the time, and only felt good when she could sleep. Although Leah had seen a psychologist briefly when she was younger, she obviously was in need of help again. An updated diagnostic evaluation was done and treatment started. Leah responded well to the cognitive behavioral approach in therapy and soon was ready to "start living again," as she put it. Needless to say, her mother felt relieved—and grateful that she had been so responsive to help.

Differentiating Depression: The Evaluation Process

As I thought about Leah, I realized that it is not always as easy to identify a depressed child as it was with her. How do we know when a child who is experiencing difficulties in school might also be depressed? I recently saw Amy, a seven-year-old girl who had been diagnosed as having an Attention-Deficit/Hyperactivity Disorder, Inattentive type, as well as nonverbal learning disabilities. Her second grade teacher reported that she had trouble paying attention in class, tended to daydream, rarely completed assigned work, and was "restless in the squirmy sense." And, although she was beginning to read, she couldn't add 2 + 2 or copy a simple design on paper. She took forever to do her homework, claiming she was "too dumb" or "too tired," regardless of the hour. Then, when she finally went to bed, she couldn't sleep and wandered into her parents' room four or five times a night.

At first, it was unclear to what extent Amy's anxieties, her learning disabilities, and/or her depression were contributing to her attentional problems, or if the reverse were true. To treat her, I felt that an evaluation was needed to assess the relative roles of perceptual, educational, and emotional issues. In the past several years, major advances have been made in assessment techniques for children and adolescents. Although there is still the risk of perceiving only one part of the proverbial elephant, identification of depression as well as learning and attentional difficulties can generally be made on the basis of a comprehensive psychoeducational evaluation.

To initiate the process, I met with Amy's parents to get a developmental and social history. I learned that Amy had been an easy but placid infant, until her brother came along. She suddenly turned into an aggressive little girl, eager to hurt her little brother. Shortly thereafter, her parents separated and her mother went back to work. The family moved when her mother remarried, and Amy entered first grade in a new school. That was when her learning problems became apparent and, as the new kid on the block, she had no friends in school. Amy insisted that no one liked her, and she played alone at recess, claiming it was "more fun." One of the differences between children with learning disabilities and those who are depressed is the quality of their social interactions. Although depressed children may experience less rejection than those with learning disabilities, they also tend to interact less with peers—and tend to blame themselves for their isolation.

We talked some more about Amy's behavior, and then about other members of the family. I asked whether anyone had suffered from depression because, like many other illnesses, there seems to be a familial vulnerability. In fact, Amy's grandmother had a history of depression, for which she had been in treatment.

In the next session, Amy and I talked about her "sad feelings" and how she felt about school, her family, and her friends. I also asked her some of the questions I typically use in interviews with children to elicit pertinent information:

1. Do you like school?
2. What is your favorite subject or activity at school? What's the least favorite or the "worst"? (The answer to this frequently suggests a child's learning problems.)
3. Do you have friends at school? A best friend?
4. What do you like to do after school? Do you do it with friends or alone?
5. Describe your mother.
6. Describe your father.
7. Is there something about your family that you wish could be changed?
8. Is there anything about you that you would like to change?
9. Can you tell me about a particularly happy time in your life? A sad time?
10. Do you have any secret worries?
11. Have you ever been so unhappy that you wished you were dead? (This is a question usually reserved for children over the age of eight. Although younger children can be depressed and even express the wish to die, they don't usually view death as permanent or irrevocable.)
12. What do you think your problems are? Who or what could help solve them?

In conjunction with the interview, self-report inventories (forms children fill out themselves) are also useful because they tap the child's subjective feelings. The Children's Depression Rating Scale—Revised

(Poznanski and Mokros 1996) and the Reynolds Adolescent Depression Scale (RADS) (Reynolds 1987) are two of the measures that assess behavioral as well as cognitive signs of depression.

Direct observation, in the school as well as in my office, is an invaluable measure of a child's social interaction and behavior. How well does the child relate to me? Does she explore the office freely? Facial expressions can be at least as revealing as verbal expression. I recently saw a depressed child, for example, who sat passively on the chair, as if waiting for something to happen. There was little eye contact and no spontaneous conversation, which is unusual in young children. She also answered my questions succinctly in flat, colorless language with no enthusiasm.

I remember another boy of almost seven who was referred because of his lack of progress in first grade. He looked as though he wanted to smile at one point, but almost visibly restrained himself. When I told him it was okay to smile, he said, "I never smile, I don't like to." He said that both he and his mother felt sad "almost all the time," adding, "I'm the reason." When I asked him how that could be, he replied, "because I'm bad." He had a primary depression, and his mother did, too, as I learned.

On the other hand, a young child with a primary learning disability without depressive symptoms is more likely to look animated and explore the office physically, sometimes touching or handling everything in sight rather than merely looking with their eyes. And some children, with poor social perception, tend to stand too close to me or talk too loudly for my small office. In other words, many indications of depression and/or learning differences can be observed clinically with discerning eye plus experience with children.

Although no single measure can assess either learning disabilities or depression, the use of multiple sources of information can shed light on both disorders. It may be difficult at times to distinguish a primary depression from a situational one, but parents must know the signs of depression in children. To provide appropriate treatment we have to differentiate between depression and primary school-based problems.

In most instances, therapy is necessary for children struggling with depression so that they can be free to develop academic and social skills. Young people tend to respond well to treatment because they adapt readily, their symptoms are not yet firmly entrenched, and their personalities are still pliable. The effectiveness of medication for depression in children is also being explored, with the finding that some respond well.

BEHAVIOR DISORDERS

The essential feature of a behavior disorder, which, in today's vernacular, is referred to as a "conduct disorder," is a persistent pattern of antisocial actions by children and adolescents that violate the rights of others. Often beginning before the teen years, conduct disorders have been found to be four times as prevalent in boys as in girls. Fighting, lying, stealing, cruelty to animals, and fire-setting are common behaviors. Although the causes have not been established, psychologists have suggested that aggressive, antisocial behavior may be a defense against anxiety, a failure to internalize controls, or an attempt to gain social status among friends. There may also be a biological vulnerability, because children of antisocial parents are more likely to develop similar problems.

The symptoms associated with conduct disorders have frequently been associated with Attention Deficit/Hyperactivity Disorder, Predominantly Impulsive or Combined type, according to DSM IV. Children with learning disabilities have also been known to demonstrate disobedient, defiant, and attention-seeking behaviors, to the dismay of their parents and teachers.

Whatever the cause, these acting-out young people are the hardest to treat because they don't seem to care about others. The prognosis for aggressive, "acter-outers" with ADHD has been found to be less than optimistic without intervention, although, in fact, many do an unexplained quick turnabout in late adolescence. Most, however, need a combination of behavior therapy and someone who cares enough to persevere with them, no matter how long it takes. A savvy mentor can be a godsend for these troubled youngsters.

At seventeen, Pedro couldn't wait to leave school. He claimed he wanted to get a diploma, but he cut more classes than he attended and he rarely did homework, claiming he couldn't concentrate. From time to time, Pedro talked about getting a job, but he didn't seem to work at that either. Pedro's life at home was no better than his days in school. He lived with a cousin and an aunt who spoke little English and didn't understand, or particularly like, Pedro. He tried to avoid talking to them because every conversation ended in a fight, after which Pedro would storm out of the apartment and walk the streets most of the night.

Perhaps because he felt so deprived, clothes were very important to Pedro. He wore name-brand jeans, sneakers, and jackets that he clearly could not afford. Rumor had it that he was stealing, but for a long time there was no proof. Eventually, of course, he was caught and put on probation. He also got into trouble twice for fighting on school grounds, for which a three-day suspension was mandated. At that point, he wanted to be in school, and we were able to arrange for an in-school suspension for the last day. (He'd have less chance of getting into trouble that way.)

Although Pedro walked a tenuous line, his guidance counselor at school, his probation officer, and I as his therapist worked hard to support him. We communicated almost daily for a while. Knowing where Pedro was at any given moment was of utmost importance. In turn, Pedro responded well to the consistency and follow-through. To his credit, he managed to get to classes in his senior year, reported on time for his tutoring at school, and to my knowledge, stopped taking things he couldn't pay for.

PREVENTION—THE TREATMENT OF CHOICE

It may sound trite, but it seems to me that the prevention of emotional and behavioral disturbances in childhood should be the priority in mental health, rather than treatment for children after problems emerge. Why is it that our society is willing to allocate funds for treatment of the mentally ill adult while denying children the resources necessary for prevention? As the naturalist Luther Burbank wrote in the late nineteenth century, "If we paid no more attention to plants than we have to our children, we would now be living in a jungle of weeds."

Parents whose children suffer from emotional problems often ask themselves, "What did I do wrong?" Self-blame is not appropriate, because the causes are complex and rarely due to a single factor. Besides, guilt about a child's mental illness is usually as inappropriate as guilt about any other childhood illness, such as chicken pox. The key is to recognize the problem when one exists and seek appropriate treatment as soon as possible. The degree to which you, as parents, provide TLC, along with intelligent child-care practices, will help to build the foundation for your child's emotional life. You are your child's first advocate in finding solutions.

10

WHAT ABOUT THE FUTURE?

It is natural for parents of LD or ADHD children to ask, "What does the future hold? Will my child find a job? Will she find security and independence? What are the possibilities in terms of his potential?" And it may be just as natural for those of us who guide parents to want to give them something to count on. I have no statistics on the accuracy of predictions for children with learning problems, but I think it's safe to assume that forecasts for these children are no more reliable than long-range predictions about the weather. Perhaps in the future, with more refined techniques, our forecasting in both areas will improve but, for now, predictions for children's futures must be made with special care and revised frequently, if they are to be made at all.

THE DIFFICULTY IN MAKING PREDICTIONS

The most predictable quality about learning disabilities and ADHD is their unpredictability. In the course of living or working with these children and adolescents, parents and professionals learn to expect the unexpected, the good moments as well as disappointing ones. It is not easy to live with uncertainty, and the families of LD and ADHD young people seem to live with an almost continual stream of unanswerable questions and decisions—hence, the quest for predictions. Because families longing for answers will be guided by what they hear, professionals have to be cautious in their prognostications for the future. The repercussions may be too great if they are wrong.

Ginny, who is nineteen now, first saw a neurologist when she was not quite seven. He confirmed the diagnosis of "central nervous system dysfunction . . . with disabilities in both receptive and expressive language." He recommended that Ginny be taken out of public school and enrolled in an expensive private school where teachers would be understanding of her "severe learning problems." He shook his head gravely as he told the little girl's parents that they must be prepared for Ginny to be dependent on them for years to come. Chances were that Ginny would never go to college; indeed, she probably would not finish high school—at least not in public school.

This renowned physician was probably correct in his neurological assessment of Ginny. However, he neglected to take into account Ginny's fierce determination, her will to succeed, and the support of her parents. From second grade on, Ginny worked hard, with the help of an excellent tutor. She read with her parents every day at home and did her homework faithfully, with help, of course. Her teachers in the public school, impressed with her effort to succeed, helped her, too— before school, after school, even at lunchtime.

To everyone's surprise, Ginny graduated from her local high school on the honor roll and is now doing well as a sophomore in college. Her ambition is to become a teacher of students with learning disabilities, and I have no doubt that she will succeed. How many years of anxiety for Ginny's parents might have been saved had the physician only said, "The future doesn't look promising now, but I really don't know. The outcome of these problems tends to be difficult to predict." He might also have reassured Ginny's parents that, most often, learning problems are self-limiting. They usually don't get much worse than when they are first recognized, assuming there is proper intervention.

Judy, another young girl a few years older than Ginny, took matters into her own hands when her future looked bleak. She had always had an impossible time in school, even with help. She finally attended a special school, where she still struggled to learn. Her mother, who had been her only supporter, died when Judy was eleven, and she was left with almost no encouragement from her grieving father or her older siblings. In fact, no one expected very much of her.

Judy remembers, at fourteen, coming to the conclusion that she could never be a teacher with her problems with reading and spelling, so she decided to develop her modest skills in art. Perhaps because she started years ahead of her peers, these skills burgeoned into an impressive art portfolio while she was still in high school. Ultimately she was accepted into a school of fine arts, from which she recently graduated, with an offer of a job as a layout artist in an advertising agency. She still can't read very well and rarely chooses to do so for pleasure, but she has achieved her independence and feels good about her accomplishments.

While the predictions for Ginny and Judy were wrong, few would complain about the outcomes. Theirs were among the pleasant surprises. However, predictions can lead to terrible disappointment as well. Professionals may build parents' hopes when a child is young, only to leave them disheartened when the expected gains are not achieved.

As an infant, Brian was very slow in his development. He wasn't walking at two and a half, or even at three. The pediatrician, together with a consulting psychologist, assessed his problems and called them "developmental lags." "Brian will be fine," the doctors said. "He is just growing slowly."

Brian finally learned to walk, but his pace of learning other skills remained slow. He repeated kindergarten, but was still unable to recognize letters or write his name in first grade. When the school psychologist suggested a special class placement, Brian's parents objected, maintaining that the doctors had said Brian would eventually "catch up." It seemed logical for him to stay among normal children while he was closing the gap.

Brian's parents, I think, had visions of his suddenly making an academic leap, achieving at least an average level for his age. When he didn't, it was infinitely harder for them to accept his limitations, which would not go away, at least not in the foreseeable future. Their hopes had been raised by the experts, and in all probability they had desperately wanted to be convinced.

When I saw Brian in the tenth grade, he was sixteen and had dropped out of school. He said, "School was so hard for me; I always hated it. Everyone thought I was dumb and I did, too. And even if I could have finished high school, what would I do then? No one would have hired me. So what's the use?" Brian and his parents were disappointed and discouraged by the years of failure and the hopes that had not materialized. But what to do? Where to turn?

It probably would have been helpful for Brian and his parents to realize that the school years are often the hardest for those who struggle to learn. Once they are over, the differences among people are usually more easily accepted, and most adults seem to function in spite of their learning differences. They eventually find careers that minimize their disabilities and maximize their strengths, giving them a sense of accomplishment. While it is true that for many like Brian a learning disability becomes a living disability, affecting more than just school, those years eventually do come to an end. Brian actually found his niche in a job he obtained by himself in an ice cream store. He was so dedicated and reliable that he eventually became the manager, which gave him great satisfaction. And when last I heard, he had moved out of his parents' home and into a small apartment of his own.

In a recent clinical conference, a pediatric neurologist and I were telling parents the results of our evaluation of their ten-year-old son. Stan had major learning disabilities and an attention deficit disorder that made it hard for him to succeed in any area of school. It was likely that he would continue to struggle for some time to come. However, he was a good-looking boy and a competent athlete whom everyone liked. Even his teachers gave him the benefit of the doubt because he did try.

At the end of the meeting, the parents asked us to give our opinions as to the prospects for their son's future. We all agreed that while we couldn't predict with any degree of reliability, we could easily picture Stan as an independent, well-functioning adult. With his personality and charm, he would probably handle responsibility well. It was only the next eight years or so that concerned us. How could we preserve his personality and the will to learn?

Stan was one of seven children in his family. His mother, a vivacious lady with a good sense of humor, didn't seem to be getting gray hair from having three children with learning disabilities and many crises to handle. The professionals at that conference were, I think, as interested in her ability to manage her family with such equanimity as they were in her son's problems. I wondered aloud at her capacity to keep so cool and composed. She replied that she had developed her own philosophy. "I figure that anything my children will learn to do by the time they're twenty-one, I don't have to worry about now." That eliminated many concerns!

It is true that not all are so fortunate as Brian and Stan, however. Some young adults continue to be dependent on their families, emotionally and financially. They have difficulty in the workplace, as they did in school. They have trouble finding work, and even when they do, can't seem to keep the jobs, so they move from place to place in rapid succession. Although their deficiencies and lack of preparation may be partly responsible, more frequently it is their lack of social skills and inability to get along with others that contribute to their problems.

Lucille was a young woman who did manage to find work after

high school that wasn't too challenging for her and seemed appropriate. However, within a few days/weeks on the job, she either left without warning or was fired. When I discussed this with her, she'd say that she found the work "too hard," didn't like the boss or fellow workers, and/or anticipated being let go. First, I tried to teach her the wisdom of not leaving one job until she obtained another. Then we tried to figure out why she was having such interpersonal problems at work. In part, it appeared to reflect her feelings of inadequacy and incompetence. When she made an error and was corrected, she became defensive and angry, blaming someone else. Needless to say, she didn't ingratiate herself with her boss or her colleagues. Eventually she realized that she had to explain her learning problems and needs to an employer, even before starting the job. That did help and, for the first time, she finally found employment that she liked—and was able to keep.

YOUR JOB ISN'T OVER WHEN YOUR CHILD GROWS UP

Having provided early intervention, appropriate remediation, and even special programs during the school years, parents may be tempted to relax when their children reach adulthood, content that they have done everything possible. However, parents and professionals typically still have the responsibility of helping young adults plan and implement realistic goals. Only in this way can we ensure that fewer people than in the past will fall between the cracks.

Loretta couldn't wait to finish high school. She was still having a hard time settling down, even in tenth grade. When she was young, the doctors had said she would outgrow her hyperactivity by adolescence, but she really hadn't changed that much. At five, she raced nonstop through the supermarket; at fifteen, she had difficulty sitting through her classes. She no longer ran around the classroom, but she continually drummed her fingers on her desk or rhythmically kicked the seat in front of her. She was still impulsive, racing through homework assignments with little thought as to whether an answer was right. And she was disorganized, losing her books and forgetting where she left her belongings.

"She's too old for that," Loretta's parents complained to me. They realized that her behaviors were typical of those with attention deficit disorders, but that didn't make living with her any easier. Her mother once said in exasperation, "By the time she's thirty, we'll probably have a mature twelve-year-old. Some days I just don't have the energy to give what it takes to help her through the day." Her parents hoped she could finish high school, but they had no illusions about an academic future for her.

Loretta was fortunate in attending a high school that offered a vocational program as well as college-preparatory courses. In her junior and senior years, she was able to study hairdressing, which she loved. And she actually was able to focus in those classes. For the first time, she had a sense of purpose and a goal in life. Her parents, of course, were delighted.

BE REALISTIC ABOUT YOUR CHILD'S POTENTIAL

Some parents are overly ambitious for their children, deciding on high educational goals for them. They subject their children to years of remedial programs in hopes of ameliorating their learning or attention problems earlier and faster. I have known children who have little opportunity to develop any interests, have fun after school, or even make friends. All their energies are absorbed in their struggle to compensate for their difficulties. Goals can be set too high and achieved at too high a price.

I'm reminded of Raymond, whose parents were both in professional fields. They spared no expense to provide intellectual stimulation and specialized training for their son through the school years. Despite predictions to the contrary, Raymond did learn to read and write, and although he had no time to be with friends, he became a successful student in high school. Everyone was delighted when he was accepted at a fairly prestigious college following his graduation.

His father knew something was wrong, though, the next fall, when his son called home several times weekly "just to talk." Raymond's anxiety seemed to be building, his stuttering increased, and he didn't sound very happy. He complained that he was working very hard, but his grades weren't showing it. He was having the most trouble with an English literature course that required reading at least one book each week.

When Raymond's parents went to visit him for a weekend, they found that he was miserable. In addition to the academic stress he was under, he had not been accepted into a fraternity and had no social life. Raymond admitted that he felt like an outsider and confessed that, more than anything, he had hoped to make new friends and have fun at college.

One evening during the long weekend, Raymond invited the only two people he knew at school to join his family for dinner. The evening was a success, and his parents were pleased. They realized almost immediately, though, that both of the other boys also had obvious learning problems. Was this merely an accident or a matter of natural selection? We know how hard it is for some learning-disabled children to make friends. Perhaps Raymond's self-consciousness about his learning or his poor self-image led him to people with similar problems.

Eventually Raymond's parents and I wondered just why he was going to college. Was it his desire, his wish to please his parents, or his fear of disappointing them if he didn't? What was college going to prepare him for—and was it worth it? No one had yet tried to determine what Raymond really wanted or what he would be good at. A battery of vocational and interest tests might have been more worthwhile for him—and less expensive—than a B.A. in his pocket.

Some young people, as well as their parents, cling to unrealistic goals. Chris was sixteen, still in ninth grade, and his academic skills were extremely low. He'd had learning difficulties all through school. He never should have taken a foreign language, but he insisted on taking French. He was also in an algebra class, although math was one of his weak points. He still wasn't sure of his multiplication tables and couldn't remember the process of long division. As might be expected, Christopher was having a rough time, but he rationalized his F's by saying he was "too bored" in modified classes. He insisted on going into more advanced classes, convincing his teachers he could do better there. He also wanted to go to a large four-year college, but was unrealistic about his chances for admission.

There is an enormous difference between working hard to accomplish miracles and merely wishing for those miracles to happen. You owe it to your child to support her in her efforts to achieve her goals but, at the same time, to dispel the fantasies that are only that and nothing more. One young man whom I had helped to achieve small successes began to be more realistic in his goals and, even more important, perhaps, in his appraisal of himself. At the end of a session one day, he said with a smile, "I used to think I was Superman, but now I'm just Robert, and I like him." Needless to say, everyone enjoyed him more that way, too!

If a family is realistic, there usually are many options for children with learning differences. As I think about future prospects for boys and girls with difficulties, I'm struck by the fact that they have almost as many options as children without learning disabilities. It would be unrealistic for the child who cannot read to aspire to become an English teacher, but he might be successful as a draftsperson or an engineer. Kathy Peterson Rice, a dyslexic who struggled all through school because she could barely read, eventually graduated valedictorian of her class in Columbia's School of Engineering and Applied Sciences. She used ingenious ways to work around her disability and finally achieved what often must have seemed an impossible goal. Not everyone has the ability, the motivation, or the stamina to achieve what Kathy did, but there are many options and alternatives for young people with residual learning problems.

THE QUESTION OF INDEPENDENCE

While most young people with learning differences eventually do make it in society, some do not achieve independence. Even as adults, they may continue to require a sheltered environment. There are halfway houses, group homes, and special facilities where individuals can live, work, and find company among others with similar needs. For a few, the need for a protected environment after high school is only temporary, until they mature. Just as many of them didn't learn to read until two or three years after others of their age, so too, they may need more time to become adults able to live independently.

One young man, a handsome, strapping six-footer who made it through college with the help of tutors and tape recorders, became depressed in the last few weeks of college. He was worried about his future after graduation. He asked me, "How will I make a living if I can't read and write well? Who will hire me?" He said he had finally decided to apply to graduate school (he didn't even know in what field), admittedly to stay out of the job market for a while longer. While school was a terrible struggle for him, he felt too insecure to attempt to join the outside world. Actually, he might have been right in his self-assessment, although I doubt that graduate school was the answer to his problems. I, too, thought of him as much younger than his years. He seemed a typical sixteen-year-old in his thinking and in his emotional reactions. Perhaps he did need more time to grow up before assuming adult responsibilities. A volunteer job in the community with supervision or an apprenticeship might have bridged the gap between the protective atmosphere of school and the world at large—and certainly would have been less of a financial strain for his family.

ADULTS WITH LEARNING DIFFERENCES

So long as young people with learning differences are in school or are involved in special programs, they are relatively easy to observe. But what becomes of them when they go out into the adult world? No longer is their progress followed by teachers, guidance counselors, or researchers. Although we know more today about adults with learning disabilities, there are few precedents for others to follow. It is only in the last generation that children with identified learning differences have grown up. Indeed, many parents today only become aware of their own learning disabilities when their children's problems are identified. As adults, they have been actively employed as productive members of their communities, despite their inability to spell and their dependence on pocket calculators. Lagging academic skills don't necessarily interfere with daily living once out of school.

I have several friends who must have had learning problems as children. They still seem somewhat clumsy in their movements, forget names familiar to them, or cannot find words with which to communicate ideas. I merely regard them as awkward or inarticulate. I don't say to myself: "There's a person with a learning difference." Most of them are intelligent, responsive people who are interesting and fun to be with.

Perhaps my friends were the fortunate ones among the learning-disabled population. They may have been more able—or more determined—to succeed. And maybe their families somehow understood and supported them as children, even without much knowledge of their learning problems. We also hear of adults for whom life has not been so rewarding. Perhaps their frustrations with learning caused them to become angry, disillusioned people who act out against society. At least one recent study indicates that many adults for whom there was no intervention early in life still have traits characteristic of the learning-disabled child. They exhibit moodiness, restlessness, outbursts of temper, and difficulty sustaining relationships. All the adults in that study had a poor self-concept and most expressed a pervasive feeling of unhappiness, lack of fulfillment, and discontent.

Knowing an adult who is still suffering from the effects of a learning problem can make the problem loom larger than life. When Ronald's learning problems were recognized, his mother seemed overly upset and anxious. She finally admitted that she was afraid that he would follow in his father's footsteps. Her husband, a sensitive, caring father, had always had difficulty holding down a job. He and his wife felt that his learning disabilities were the cause. He had the usual difficulties with writing, spelling, and math, but he also found it hard to be organized at work and to learn new skills. He also acknowledged, when I asked, that he had trouble concentrating on a task and spent a great deal of time chatting near the coffee machine. He was anything but cheerful about his situation.

This man's learning disabilities also affected his family relationships. He depended on his wife to manage all the family funds and to make important decisions—and even to help him apply for jobs. He didn't trust his judgment or his ability to plan wisely for himself or his wife and children. What we are beginning to realize, perhaps, is that just as one child's learning difference affects the entire family, so may a parent with similar problems disturb the family system.

I recently attended a meeting at which the problems of the learning-disabled adult were considered. Two of the speakers addressing the meeting had learning problems. One of them admitted that he became angry and even jealous of his children when they received the remedial help that he never had. He had tended to blame others for his difficulties, absolving himself of any responsibility. However, he was currently in the process of getting help in order to be able to help his children.

I also read about a family in which the father was unable to read. He kept a veil of secrecy over his deficiency and, because of his fear of being discovered, was emotionally distant from his wife and children. His frustration and feeling of hopelessness pervaded the family, until his children responded with anger and detachment.

Knowing this, all of us who are involved with the development of children should try to aid future generations of adults with learning differences. Rather than placing all the emphasis on the education of the child, we would do well to focus on family involvement and treatment. Professionals in medical, educational, and psychological services must work together with you, the parents, to

1. Find appropriate health services when your children are young
2. Locate facilities for early identification and treatment of a child suspected of being at risk
3. Understand your own feelings and accept those of your LD child—and seek help if you can't
4. Be honest and forthright with your child about his problems and behavior
5. Recognize the possible effects of your child's learning difference on the entire family
6. Help your adolescent and young adult plan realistic goals and work toward implementing them

Most of all, you can help your child by accepting him for himself and seeing him as a person with good traits and bad, only one of which is his learning difference. He is, after all, just a child with a difference in the way he learns. He is not a learning disability with a child attached.

It may hurt to have a learning difference or ADD, but it shouldn't hurt to be a child.

APPENDIX A

THE EVALUATION
PROCESS

The process for determining whether a child has a learning difference and, if so, the course of action to be followed can be long and difficult for parents. Below is a step-by-step description of the process, which includes your options and rights along the way.

The Committee for Special Education

Called by different names in each state, a committee is established in each school district to coordinate the special education process. The committee determines whether or not a child has an educational handicap and, if so, what special education services are needed. As parents, you are entitled to actively participate in the planning process. You also have the legal right to agree or disgree with the recommended programs and the proposed goals and objectives for your child. The options and means for doing so are described in this section.

How Does the Process Work?
1. A referral is made by you, the parents, or school personnel to the chairperson of the committee or the principal of the school. The referral must be in writing, stating that the child is having difficulty in school and possibly has an educational handicap warranting attention.
2. Prior to taking any action, your child's school will arrange for a multidisciplinary evaluation, or you may choose to have a private evaluation at your expense. If you wish the school to do the evaluation, you will need to sign a consent form, giving permission. Thereafter, the evaluation process must be started within thirty school days, in accordance with federal law.
3. After the evaluation is completed, you will receive notice of the date and time of the scheduled meeting of the special education committee. You should also receive a copy of the results of the evaluation prior to the meeting. If the time given is inconvenient, you may request a change. (Wherever possible, both parents should plan to attend the meeting.)
4. At the meeting, the committee and other participants discuss the results of the evaluation and anecdotal material from parents, teachers, tutors, and other invited guests. The committee then decides whether the child is eligible for special education services and, if so, the appropriate services that are needed.

193

5. A projected IEP is drawn up informally at the meeting which will then be typed and sent to you for your approval and signature.
6. Should you disagree with the findings of the committee and/or the recommended IEP, you have recourse, called "due process" (see page 195).

Who Attends the Committee Meeting?
1. The student's parents, guardian, and/or foster parents
2. The student if high school age and he/she wishes to attend
3. Committee on special education members (mandated by law):
   a. Director of the special education committee or his/her designee
   b. School psychologist
   c. Teacher member (current teacher, a special education teacher, and/or speech/language teacher) who could provide services
   d. Parent member volunteer who lives in the district and has a child receiving special education services
   e. School physician or district psychiatrist (attends upon request)
4. Other school personnel who may provide additional information, for example, a social worker, reading specialist
5. Agency representatives who may have additional information to help in the planning
6. Persons invited by you for support and/or information (friend, relative, tutor)
7. Translator or sign language interpreter if needed

Timing of Committee Meetings
1. The committee must meet within thirty school days of receipt of consent or within forty days of receipt of a written referral.
2. An annual review is held once each year to review the child's progress and to plan for the next year.
3. You or your child's teachers may request a meeting at any time if you feel that changes in your child's services or program are warranted.

Note: The school cannot make decisions about a child without parental permission. Your permission must be obtained in writing before your child is initially evaluated to determine the child's special needs. Permission is also required before the child is placed in, transferred to or from, or denied placement in a special education program. For information on special education programs in the public schools of your state, contact your State Department of Education.

The IEP and Related Services

What Is an IEP?

An IEP, or Individualized Education Plan, is a written statement of special education and related services for a child. An IEP must include the following:

1. A statement of the child's present level of educational performance. This can include academic achievement, social adaptation, prevocational and vocational skills, motor skills, and speech and language skills resulting from the evaluation.
2. A statement of annual goals.
3. A statement of short-term instructional objectives.
4. A statement of specific special education and related services to be provided, and who will provide them.
5. A statement of the extent to which the child can participate in regular education programs.
6. A statement of the projected dates for the initiation of special services and the duration of special services.
7. A statement of the objective criteria and evaluation procedures that will be used to measure progress toward the goals. Progress must be evaluated at least annually.

How to Get a Due Process Hearing

As stated above, if you disagree with the committee's evaluation and/or proposed IEP, you have the right to a due process hearing. First, you should contact the school in writing to request a hearing with an impartial hearing officer, who will notify you of the date. The school has a responsibility to inform you of any free or low-cost legal services available in the area. As parents, you have the right to legal counsel and to present witnesses at the hearing. The hearing is closed and confidential unless you want it to be public. Throughout the process, the child must remain in his or her current school placement unless you and the school agree on a different temporary placement.

After the due process hearing, if you still disagree with the decision, you may appeal it to the state department of education. Following that, if the school or parents cannot resolve their differences, the case may be appealed in civil courts. While it is your right to request mediation or to formally appeal if you disagree with the recommendations of the committee, it is suggested that you request that the committee reconvene to discuss your concerns or review additional documentation. It is preferable to avoid formal due process proceedings if at all possible, as they can be expensive, time consuming, and unpleasant.

The Evaluation Process: A Summary of Parents' Rights

Active participation in the IEP. As the child's parents or guardian, you must give permission for release of records, preplacement evaluation, and documentation or justification for the child's initial educational placement.

Informed parents. You must be informed before any action regarding identification, evaluation, program, or placement is implemented.

Due process hearing. If you do not agree with the committee's recommendations or plans for your child and cannot resolve the disagreement informally, you are entitled to a free hearing with an impartial hearing officer.

Communication. All communication must be clear and in the parents' native language via a method they can understand.

Information. You may review all educational records, request copies of these records (there may be a fee), and request removal of information considered to be false or misleading.

Independent educational evaluation. You may obtain an independent educational evaluation at your own expense.

Confidentiality. All information on a child must be kept confidential.

Suggestions and Hints for Parents

Do . . . Find out about preschool services for handicapped children if you suspect that your young child has developmental delays or special needs of any kind. Federal law ensures a free evaluation and appropriate help for children from birth to twenty-one years of age.

Do . . . Make every effort to work with your child's teacher if your child is in school and is having problems. There may be some discoveries you and the teacher can make together—things that can be done *right now* to help your child. It may take thought, insight, and the willingness to try out suggested activities that can add up to a brighter outlook for you as well as for the child.

Do . . . Put your request for an evaluation in writing—to the principal of your school or the chairperson of the committee for special education services. Keep copies of the correspondence. If information is discussed on the telephone, write a letter confirming the gist of the conversation. Don't trust important matters to memory.

Do . . . Remember that you can ask for a reevaluation, even if your child is already placed in a special education program. This is especially important if you feel that the placement was based on old, inaccurate, or incomplete tests—or if you are dissatisfied with the program. It is important to keep track of your child's needs, to see whether the program is still appropriate or if a change is warranted.

Do . . . Give your *written* consent for the school to test your child, even if you have requested the evaluation. An explanation of your rights should be sent to you, including your right to inspect and review all relevant school records about your child.

Do . . . Keep your own file. Use it to document any steps you take to find appropriate education and related services for your child—from the "suspicion of need" stage on up. The file should include diagnostic test results and other professional reports, your notations of attempts to solve problems, reports from teachers about your child, and copies of letters to and from school officials.

Do . . . Attend all meetings about your child's IEP or educational plan. The law states clearly that an IEP team must include one or both parents, a guardian, or a surrogate parent.

Do . . . Prepare as well as you can for the school meeting that will design your child's educational program. Have your child's file ready, with information easily available on all testing and evaluations that have been done, by the school or privately. The meeting must be based on a recent and comprehensive evaluation, so check to be sure that this has happened.

Do . . . Be as clear as possible in your own mind as to the kind of help your child needs, for example, additional time, homework modifications, or social skills training. Does he need to have speech therapy for his lisp? Does your teenager need prevocational training or a work-study program?

Do . . . Bring along a helper to the meeting, if you will feel more secure. More and more people are being trained to act as advocates for parents in these new and unfamiliar circumstances. Ask members of your local parents organization for the names of advocates or ask another parent who has been through the process to help. Experience is a great teacher, and you can benefit from it.

Do . . . Back up your requests for services and accommodations with diagnostic reports and available information from professionals who know your child. You may want to ask that they accompany you to the meeting to support your point of view. This is your right according to law.

Do . . . Try to understand the issue of "inclusion" as fully as possible. The concept is based on the concept that handicapped children benefit, academically and socially, from being educated alongside their non-handicapped schoolmates. However, if a child needs a special class, he should be given the opportunity to join his peers in other school activities.

Do . . . Think about how to be assertive without antagonizing people. Meetings about a child's school needs are not intended to be hostile confrontations; they should provide the chance for an honest examination of alternatives. If everyone is truly concerned about giving the child the chance to grow and learn, it should be possible to iron out disagreements through persuasion and mutual understanding.

Do . . . Make sure that your child is not excluded from participating in a regular school program because of architectural barriers. This is against the law. The Americans with Disabilities Act (ADA) states clearly that school facilities must be made accessible and special adaptations made so that services are available to all students.

Do . . . Remember that diagnostic reports, important as they are, are not infallible. They don't say all there is to say about a child. Your job is to make sure that committee members know they are talking about a *real* child. Bring up all the real-life information you feel is relevant to your child's educational needs.

But Please . . .

Don't . . . Agree to an educational plan that you think is wrong. You don't have to sign anything at the meeting. You may want to "think it over" and consult with someone who could not attend the meeting.

Don't . . . Settle for poor or inadequate services. It you find that your child is deprived of assistance he needs, take action. As for changes in keeping with the promise of an appropriate program, if you feel that your questions or concerns are not being adequately addressed at the district level, you can and should contact the regional or State Education Department, whose responsibility it is to ensure compliance with state regulations.

Don't . . . Forget that your child is a young, responsive, growing, and developing individual, with human needs to laugh, play, and make friends. He is not merely a composite of his educational needs. The brightness of his social success may be as important in the total scheme of life as his academic progress.

Don't . . . Try to go through the process alone. Join with other parents in a support group or PTA to learn all you can about federal and state laws, the way your own school system works, and services available to help your child. You can add strength to a broader effort by educating school personnel and the community at large, and by creating public awareness of children's special educational needs.

APPENDIX B
LEGAL RIGHTS OF CHILDREN WITH DISABILITIES

Children with "handicapping conditions"—including children with LD—have a right to a free and appropriate public education. This right is guaranteed by federal law for children from birth to twenty-one years of age. The Education for All Handicapped Children Act of 1975 (Public Law 94–142) stipulates that

- All children have a right to receive a free, appropriate education at public expense.
- Every child with handicaps has a right to receive an education based on a full evaluation and assessment of individual needs.
- Every child who receives special education services must have an Individualized Education Plan (IEP). The IEP must state what special educational and related services the child will receive.
- Parents of children with handicaps will have a right to a due process hearing if they disagree with the identification, evaluation, or placement of their child.
- Every child with handicaps has a right to be educated with nonhandicapped children to the maximum extent appropriate.

In 1986, PL 99–457 amended the earlier law, mandating services for preschoolers with disabilities and calling for the development of statewide systems of early intervention services for infants and toddlers, from birth to age three.

The Individuals with Disabilities Education Act (IDEA) of 1991 also addressed the needs of children from birth to five years of age at risk for developmental delays. Under the law, funding was established for early intervention programs targeting low-income, minority, and other underserved populations.

The Rehabilitation Act of 1973 (PL 93–112) provided for comprehensive services to all individuals, regardless of the severity of their disability. It focused on adults and youth transitioning into employment settings. Section 504 of this act required that the needs of individuals with handicaps be addressed as adequately as those of nondisabled persons. As a civil rights provision (rather than a funding law), this act has been useful to parents seeking services

199

and accommodations for children who are not eligible or who are denied services under IDEA.

At the present time, children and adolescents with ADHD are not necessarily included under the Education for All Handicapped Children Act, unless their educational handicap meets criteria for a learning disability. Therefore, they are frequently given appropriate services under Section 504 of the Rehabilitation Act.

DIAGNOSTIC CRITERIA FOR ATTENTION-DEFICIT/HYPERACTIVITY DISORDER

ADD (or ADHD, as it is officially called today) is presumed to be a disorder of the central nervous system, characterized by problems in the areas of attention, impulsiveness, and sometimes hyperactivity. To be diagnosed as ADD, a child or adult must meet the criteria listed in the *Diagnostic and Statistical Manual of Mental Disorders,* 4th Ed. (DSM-IV), published by the American Psychiatric Association (1994). This manual contains the diagnostic codes currently in use throughout the United States. The following classifications and symptoms of the three types of ADHD have been adapted from that manual.

A. Either (1) or (2), or both:

(1) Six (or more) of the following symptoms of inattention have persisted for at least 6 months to a degree that is maladaptive and inconsistent with developmental level:

Inattention
(a) Often fails to give close attention to details or makes careless mistakes in schoolwork, chores, or other activities
(b) Often has difficulty sustaining attention in tasks or play activities
(c) Often does not seem to listen when spoken to directly
(d) Often does not follow through on instructions and fails to finish schoolwork, chores, or duties in the workplace (not due to oppositional behavior or failure to understand instructions)
(e) Often has difficulty organizing tasks or activities
(f) Often avoids, dislikes, or is reluctant too engage in tasks that require sustained mental effort (such as class work or homework)
(g) Often loses things necessary for tasks or activities (e.g., toys, school assignments, pencils, books, or tools)
(h) Is often easily distracted by extraneous stimuli
(i) Is often forgetful in daily activities

(2) Six (or more) of the following symptoms of hyperactivity-impulsivity have persisted for at least 6 months to a degree that is maladaptive and inconsistent with developmental level:

Hyperactivity
(a) Often fidgets with hands or feet or squirms in seat
(b) Often leaves seat in classroom or in other situations in which remaining seated is expected
(c) Often runs about or climbs excessively in situations in which remaining seated is expected
(d) Often has difficulty playing or engaging in leisure activities quietly
(e) Is often "on the go" or often acts as if "driven by a motor"
(f) Often talks excessively

Impulsivity
(g) Often blurts out answers before questions have been completed
(h) Often has difficulty awaiting turn
(i) Often interrupts or intrudes on others (e.g., interrupts conversations or games)

B. Some hyperactive-impulsive or inattentive symptoms that caused impairment were present before age 7 years.

C. Some impairment from the symptoms is present in two or more settings (e.g., at school (or work) and at home).

D. There must be clear evidence of clinically significant impairment in social, academic, or occupational functioning.

E. The symptoms do not occur exclusively during the course of a pervasive developmental disorder, schizophrenia, or other psychotic disorder and are not better accounted for by another mental disorder (e.g., mood disorder, anxiety, dissociative disorder, or a personality disorder).

Code (number) based on type:

314.01 Attention-Deficit/Hyperactivity Disorder, Combined Type: If both Criteria A1 and A2 are met for the past 6 months.

314.00 Attention-Deficit/Hyperactivity Disorder, Predominantly Inattentive Type: If Criterion A1 is met but Criterion A2 is not met for the past 6 months.

314.01 Attention-Deficit/Hyperactivity Disorder, Predominantly Hyperactive-Impulsive Type: If Criterion A2 is met but Criterion A1 is not met for the past 6 months.

Coding note: For individuals (especially adolescents and adults) who currently have symptoms that no longer meet full criteria, "In Partial Remission" should be specified.

—Adapted from *Diagnostic and Statistical Manual of Mental Disorders,* 4th Ed. (Washington, D.C.: American Psychiatric Association, 1994).

DIAGNOSTIC TESTS AND INSTRUMENTS

Some of the tests and instruments most frequently used by professionals in the course of a diagnostic evaluation for learning disabilities and ADD are described in this section. Although the specific materials selected may vary with the examiner and the presenting problem of the child or adolescent, an assessment will probably utilize at least some of the categories. While the list of instruments is far from complete, it represents a sampling of materials most frequently used. At best, though, results of testing must be considered tentative and reliable only in the hands of qualified and sensitive professionals.

Tests of Intelligence

Wechsler Intelligence Scale for Children-III (WISC-III) (ages 6–16)
The most widely used of the individual IQ tests for school-age children, this test consists of two parts: a Verbal Scale, tapping language and verbal abilities, and a Performance Scale, with subtests of perceptual and manipulative tasks. The WISC-III yields an IQ score for each scale as well as a total test score.

Wechsler Preschool and Primary Scale of Intelligence—Revised (WPPSI-R) (ages 3–7 yrs. 3 mos. of age)
An individually administered intelligence scale to appraise the abilities of the preschool child. The test yields an IQ similar to the WISC-III, based on subtests on the Verbal and Performance Scales.

Wechsler Adult Intelligence Scale—Revised (WAIS-R) (ages 16–75+)
An individual intelligence test to measure adult abilities. The WAIS is similar to the WISC in form and subtests.

Stamford Binet Intelligence Scale-IV (age 2–)
An individually administered intelligence test. It is used today primarily for younger children and people with lower abilities.

Woodcock-Johnson Tests of Cognitive Abilities—Revised (ages 2–95)
A comprehensive set of individually administered subtests for measuring cognitive abilities and scholastic aptitude.

Test of Visual Perception

Beery-Buktenica Developmental Test of Visual-Motor Integration (ages 2–15)
The child is asked to copy geometric forms in well-delineated spaces, which are then interpreted according to accuracy of reproduction.

Bender Visual Motor Gestalt Test (age 6–adult)
The subject is asked to reproduce designs on paper. How the forms are conceived and copied is interpreted in terms of perception, organization, and emotional indicators.

Wechsler Visual-Memory Scale (adolescents and adults)
An individually administered, clinical instrument for appraising major dimensions of memory functions in adolescents and adults, e.g. verbal stimuli and figures, meaningful and abstract material, and delayed as well as immediate recall.

Tests of Academic Achievement

The Wide Range Achievement Tests-3 (WRAT-3) (ages 5–75)
The three subtests in word reading, spelling from dictation, and arithmetic computation yield an overview of academic skills across subject areas. Norms are based on age, with grade equivalent scores and percentiles also given.

Wechsler Individual Achievement Test (WIAT) (ages 5–20)
A comprehensive individually administered battery for assessing the achievement of children in grades K–12. Age, grade equivalent scores, and percentile ranks are given. The tests are linked to the Wechsler Intelligence Scales.

Woodcock-Johnson Tests of Achievement—Revised (preschool–95 years of age)
A battery of tests of academic achievement covering the basic skill areas and content subjects.

Reading Tests

Woodcock Reading Mastery Tests—Revised (from age 5 on)
A comprehensive battery of tests measuring several aspects of reading ability.

Nelson-Denny Reading Test (Forms G and H) (high school and college level)
An assessment of students' ability in vocabulary, reading comprehension, and reading rate.

Gray Oral Reading Tests-R (GORT-R)
Assesses students' reading abilities for the purpose of identifying strengths and weaknesses in oral reading and to recognize those who may benefit from additional assistance.

Language Tests

Test of Written Language-2 (TOWL)
An instrument designed to identify students' proficiency in written expression and those who may need special help.

Rating Scales for ADD and Behavior Problems

Conners' Rating Scales—Revised (Parent, Teacher, Self-Report forms) (ages 3–17)
Evaluates problem behaviors in children and adolescents by obtaining and combining reports from teachers, parents, and adolescents.

ADD-H Comprehensive Teacher's Rating Scale (ACTeRs)
A rating scale of behaviors relevant to the classroom.

Projective Material

Thematic Apperception Test (TAT) (age 6–adult)
A projective measure of personality in which one is asked to tell stories in response to pictures, revealing drives, conflicts, and fantasies.

Children's Apperception Test (CAT)
Similar to the TAT, but for younger children. The pictures are of animals rather than humans to evoke children's fantasies. Children are asked to tell a story in response to the situations depicted.

Adolescent Apperception Cards (white and black versions)
Pictures portraying situations to which the adolescent is asked to respond with a story.

House-Tree-Person Drawings

The child is asked to draw a house, tree, and person, in turn, and the productions are interpreted in accordance with established clinical norms. Children's drawings have been found to reveal their self-perceptions and view of the world.

Rorschach Technique (preschool–adult)

A test of personality, using ink blots, in response to which the child tells what he/she sees.

APPENDIX E
RESOURCES

The author wishes to thank the National Center for Learning Disabilities for permission to reprint the following resource list, which first appeared in its publication *Their World*, 1996 edition.

National LD Organizations

National Center for Learning Disabilities (NCLD): 381 Park Avenue South, Suite 1401, New York, NY 10016. Telephone: (212) 545-7510. National Information and Referral number: (800) 575-7373.

A national nonprofit membership organization that offers a free information and referral service, conducts educational programs, raises public awareness of LD, and advocates improved legislation and services for those with learning disabilities.

Learning Disabilities Association of America (LDA): 4156 Library Road, Pittsburgh, PA 15234. Telephone: (412) 341-1515.

A national nonprofit membership organization, with state and local chapters, that conducts an annual conference and offers information and several publications.

Orton Dyslexia Society (ODS): The Chester Building, 8600 La Salle Road, Suite 382, Baltimore, MD 21204. Telephone: (410) 296-0232.

An international nonprofit membership organization that offers training in language programs and provides publications relating to dyslexia. Chapters are located in most states.

Division for Learning Disabilities (DLD) of the Council for Exceptional Children (CEC): 1920 Association Drive, Reston, VA 22091-1589. Telephone: (703) 620-3660 or (800) 328-0272.

CEC is a nonprofit membership organization that has seventeen specialized divisions. DLD is the division dedicated to LD. Both CEC and DLD provide free information and hold conferences.

Council for Learning Disabilities (CLD): P.O. Box 40303, Overland Park, KS 66204. Telephone: (913) 492-8755.

A national membership organization dedicated to assisting professionals who work in the field of learning disabilities. *The Journal of Learning Disabilities* is available through CLD.

Learning Disabilities Association of Canada (LDAC): 323 Chapel Street, Suite 200, Ottawa, Ontario K1N 7Z2, Canada. Telephone: (613) 238-5721.

A nonprofit membership organization with provincial and territorial offices that conducts programs and provides information for LD children and adults. Resources include books and pamphlets that may be useful to U.S. residents.

Parents' Educational Resource Center (PERC): 1660 South Amphlett Boulevard, Suite 200, San Mateo, CA 94402-2508. Telephone: (415) 655-2410.

A membership organization that conducts educational programs, publishes the quarterly *Parent Journal* newsletter, and offers information and referrals. PERC also maintains a library of books, articles, video and audio tapes, and recommended readings.

ADD/ADHD Organizations

Children and Adults with Attention Deficit Disorders (Ch.A.D.D.): 499 NW 70th Avenue, Suite 101, Plantation, FL 33317. Telephone: (954) 587-3700 or (800) 233-4050.

A national nonprofit membership organization that provides information, sponsors conferences, and holds regional meetings and support groups.

The National Attention Deficit Disorder Association (ADDA): National Headquarters: 1070 Rosewood, Suite A, Ann Arbor, MI 48104. Telephone: (313) 769-6690 or (800) 487-2282.

A national membership organization that provides referrals to local support groups, holds national conferences and symposiums, and offers materials on ADD and related issues.

The Attention Deficit Information Network, Inc. (AD-IN): 475 Hillside Avenue, Needham, MA 02194. Telephone: (617) 455-9895.

A nonprofit volunteer organization that offers information and holds support group meetings.

Note: Many organizations can be visited on the Internet. I recommend checking the World Wide Web for their sites and additional sources of information on these and related topics.

Local Advocacy and Support

Parent Training and Information Project (PTI): Federation for Children with Special Needs, 95 Berkeley Street, Suite 104, Boston, MA 02116. Telephone: (617) 482-2915.

A federally funded program that provides local resources and advocacy training for disability and special education issues.

Parent to Parent: National Parent-to-Parent Support and Information System: P.O. Box 907, Blue Ridge, GA 30513. Telephone: (706) 632-8822 or (800) 651-1151.

A program that matches parents with other parents based on the disabilities of their children.

Sibling Support Project: 4800 Sandpoint Way NE, P.O. Box 5371, CL-09, Seattle, WA 98105. Telephone: (206) 368-4911.

An organization for families that publishes a newsletter and holds support group meetings.

National Parent Network on Disabilities (NPND): 1600 Prince Street, Suite 115, Alexandria, VA 22314. Telephone: (703) 684-6763.

A membership organization open to all agencies, organizations, parent centers, parent groups, professionals, and individuals concerned with the quality of life for people with a variety of disabilities.

National Information Center for Children and Youth with Disabilities (NICHCY): 1875 Connecticut Avenue, 8th Floor, Washington, DC 20009. Telephone: (800) 695-0285.

An information clearinghouse that provides free information on disabilities and disability-related issues.

National Association for Gifted Children (NAGC): 1155 15th Street NW, Suite 1002, Washington, DC 20005. Telephone: (202) 785-4268.

An advocacy organization that ensures that gifted children (including gifted LD) receive the best possible education. Provides information to educators, administrators, and parents.

Books on Tape

Library of Congress—National Library Service for the Blind and Physically Handicapped (NSL-BPH): 1291 Taylor Street NW, Washington, DC 20542. Telephone: (800) 424-8567.

Provides books on tape, available to children and adults documented as learning disabled.

Recording for the Blind and Dyslexic (RFBD): 20 Roszel Road, Princeton, NJ 08540. Telephone: (609) 452-0606.

A national nonprofit organization that provides taped educational books free on loan, books on diskette, and library services. Most of their clients have learning disabilities.

Information Guides and Directories

The Complete Learning Disabilities Directory: Grey House Publishing, Inc., Pocket Knife Square, Lakeville, CT 06039. Telephone: (800) 562-2139.

Peterson's Private Secondary Schools: Peterson's, P.O. Box 2123, Princeton, NJ 08543–2123. Telephone: (800) 338-3282.

SchoolSearch Guide to Private Schools with Programs or Services for Students with Learning Disabilities: SchoolSearch Press, 127 Marsh Street, Belmont, MA 02178. Telephone: (617) 489-5785.

HEATH Resource Center (Higher Education and the Handicapped): 1 Dupont Circle, Suite 789, Washington, DC 20036-1193. Telephone: (800) 544-3284.

A national clearinghouse for information on colleges and other postsecondary education options for individuals with disabilities. Some of its publications offer college information specifically for people with learning disabilities.

College Resources: Books and Handbooks

Dispelling the Myths: College Students and Learning Disabilities (by Katherine Garnett and Sandra La Porta, 1990): A monograph for students and educators that explains what learning disabilities are and what faculty members can do to help students with learning disabilities succeed in college. Available from NCLD, (212) 545-7510.

Peterson's Colleges with Programs for Students with Learning Disabilities (4th edition, 1994): Peterson's Guides, Princeton, NJ. A state-by-state guide. Available from NCLD, (212) 545-7510.

The College Student with a Learning Disability: A Handbook (by Susan Vogel, 1985): An overview of college-related issues, including information on Section 504 as it pertains to students with learning disabilities and college personnel. Available from LDA, (412) 341-1515.

Unlocking Potential: College and Other Choices for Learning Disabled People: A Step-by-Step Guide (by Barbara Scheiber, 1992): Woodbine House, Bethesda, MD. A guide to postsecondary options.

Legal Resources

American Bar Association Center on Children and the Law: 541 North Fairbanks, Chicago, IL 60611. Telephone: (800) 285-2221.

This organization provides information on legal issues and referrals to local bar associations.

ADA Information Line (U.S. Department of Justice): Telephone: (202) 514-0301 or (800) 514-0301.

Answers questions about public services and accommodations in the Americans with Disabilities Act. Provides materials and technical assistance on the provisions of the ADA.

National Association of Protection and Advocacy Systems: 900 Second Street NE, Suite 211, Washington, DC 20002. Telephone: (202) 408-9514.

Provides literature on legal issues and referrals to federally mandated programs that advocate the rights of people with disabilities.

GLOSSARY

Due process rights Students with disabilities have rights protected by federal and state laws. If there is a disagreement regarding a student's program, formal and informal procedures are available to maintain a fair process for resolution, including the right to an impartial hearing to be arranged by the district Board of Education.

FAPE Free Appropriate Public Education as mandated by federal law.

IEP Individual Education Plan. The IEP constitutes the basis for instruction. It summarizes the child's current skills and abilities, establishes educational goals and objectives for the school year, describes programs designed to meet these goals, and enumerates ways to check the student's progress. The IEP also includes the student's classification of disability, the recommended class size, and the extent of participation in regular education.

Impartial hearing A formal procedure used to resolve disagreements between parents and school districts over the provision of special education services. The impartial hearing is a mechanism established to hear both sides of the issues and resolve the dispute in a fair manner through a third party.

LRE Least Restrictive Environment. The LRE means that children with disabilities are educated with children who are not handicapped, to the maximum extent appropriate. Removal from general education occurs only when the nature or severity of the disability is such that education in regular classes, with the use of supplementary aids and services, cannot be achieved satisfactorily.

RECOMMENDED READING

Books for Parents and Professionals

Alexander-Roberts, C. *ADHD and Teens: A Parent's Guide to Making it through the Teen Years.* Dallas, TX: Taylor Publishing Company, 1995.

Barkley, R. A. *Hyperactive Children: A Handbook for Diagnosis and Treatment.* New York: The Guilford Press, 1990.

Barkley, R. A. *Taking Charge of ADHD.* New York: Guilford Publications, Inc., 1995.

Bloom, J. *Help Me to Help My Child.* Waltham, MA: Little, Brown & Co., 1990.

Brooks, R. *The Self-Esteem Teacher.* Circle Pines, MN: American Guidance Service, 1991.

Brutten, M. *Something's Wrong with My child.* New York: Harcourt Brace Jovanovich, 1973.

Cordoni, B. *Living with a Learning Disability.* Carbondale, IL: Southern Illinois University Press, 1990.

Cramer, S. C. C., and W. Ellis, eds. *Learning Disabilities: Lifelong Issues.* Baltimore, MD: Paul H. Brooks, 1996.

Culter, B. C. *You, Your Child, and "Special Education": A Guide to Making the System Work.* Baltimore, MD: Paul H. Brooks, 1993.

Dendy, C. A. Z. *Teenagers with ADD: A Parents' Guide.* Bethesda, MD: Woodbine House, 1995.

Deshler, D., E. Ellis, and K. Lenz. *Teaching Adolescents with Learning Disabilities.* Denver: Love Publishing Co., 1996.

Fowler, M. C. *Maybe You Know My Kid: A Parents' Guide to Identifying, Understanding and Helping Your Child with Attention-Deficit Hyperactivity Disorder.* New York: Birch Lane Press, 1990.

Goldstein, S., and M. Goldstein. *Hyperactivity: Why Won't My Child Pay Attention?* New York: Wiley-Interscience Press, 1992.

Gordon, Michael. *ADHD/Hyperactivity: A Consumer's Guide.* New York: GSI Publications, 1991.

Greenberg, G. S., and W. F. Horn. *Attention Deficit Hyperactivity Disorder: Questions and Answers for Parents.* Champaign, IL: Research Press, 1991.

Greenhill, L., and B. Osman, eds. *Ritalin: Theory and Patient Management.* Mary Ann Liebert, Inc., 1991.

Hallowell, E. M., and J. J. Ratey. *Answers to Distraction.* New York: Pantheon Books, 1994.

Hallowell, E. M., and J. J. Ratey. *Driven to Distraction.* New York: Pantheon Books, 1994.

Hayes, M. L. *You Don't Outgrow It: Living with Learning Disabilities.* Novato, CA: Academic Therapy Publications, 1993.

Hughes, S. *Ryan—A Mother's Story of Her Hyperactive/Tourette Syndrome Child.* Duarte, CA: Hope Press, 1990.

Ingersoll, B. D., and S. Goldstein. *Attention Deficit Disorder and Learning Disabilities—Realities, Myths, and Controversies.* New York: Doubleday, 1993.

Kovacs, M. *Children's Depression Inventory—Revised.* North Tonawanda, NY: Multi-Health Systems, 1995.

Latham, P. S., and P. H. Latham. *Learning Disabilities and the Law.* Washington, DC: JKL Productions, 1993.

Levine, M. *Keeping Ahead in School: Student's Book about Learning Abilities and Learning Disorders.* Cambridge, MA: Educator's Publishing Service, Inc., 1990.

Levine, M. *All Kinds of Minds.* Cambridge, MA: Educator's Publishing Service, Inc., 1993.

Lobato, D. J. *Brothers, Sisters, and Special Needs.* Baltimore, MD: Paul H. Brookes Publishing Co., 1990.

Markoff, A. M. *Within Reach: Academic Achievement through Parent-Teacher Communication*. Novato, CA: Academic Therapy Publications, 1993.

Murphy, S. T. *On Being Learning Disabled: Perspectives and Strategies of Young Adults*. New York: Teachers College Press, 1992.

Nadeau, K. G., ed. *A Comprehensive Guide to Attention Deficit Disorder in Adults: Research, Diagnosis, Treatment*. New York: Brunner/Mazel, Inc., 1995.

Nosek, K. *The Dyslexic Scholar: Helping Your Child Succeed in the School System*. Dallas: Taylor Publishing, 1995.

Osman, B. B., and H. Blinder. *No One to Play with: The Social Problems of LD and ADD Children*. Novato, CA: Academic Therapy Publications, 1995.

Parker, H. C. *The ADD Hyperactivity Workbook for Parents, Teachers and Kids*. Plantation, FL: Impact Publications, 1990.

Poznanski, E. O., and H. B. Mokros. *Children's Depression Rating Scale, Revised CCDNS-R)*. Los Angeles: Western Psychological Services, 1996.

Quinn, P. O. *Adolescents and ADD: Gaining the Advantage*. New York: Magination Press, 1995.

Reynolds, W. M. *Reynolds Adolescent Depression Scale*. Odessa, FL: Psychological Assessment Resources, Inc., 1987.

Rief, S. F. *How to Reach and Teach ADD/ADHD Children*. West Nyack, NY: The Center for Applied Research in Education, 1993.

Silver, L. *The Misunderstood Child,* second edition. New York: McGraw-Hill Book Co., 1992.

Smith, S. L. *No Easy Answers: The Learning Disabled Child at Home and at School*. New York: Bantam Books, 1995.

Smith, S. L. *Succeeding against the Odds: Strategies and Insights from the Learning-Disabled*. Los Angeles: Jeremy Tarcher, Inc., 1992.

Taylor, J. F. *Helping Your Hyperactive Child*. Rocklin, CA: Prima Publishing & Communications, 1990.

Trapani, C. *Transition Goals for Adolescents with Learning Disabilities.* Austin, TX: PRO-ED, 1990.

Turecki, S., and L. Tonner. *The Difficult Child.* New York: Bantam Books, 1985.

Tuttle, C., and G. A. Tuttle. *Challenging Voices: Writings by, for, and about People with Learning Disabilities.* Los Angeles: Lowell House, 1995.

Vail, P. L. *Emotion: The On Off Switch for Learning.* Rosemont, NJ: Modern Press, 1994.

Vogel, S. A., and P. B. Adelman. *Success for College Students with Learning Disabilities.* New York: Springer-Verlag, 1993.

Weiss, L. *Attention Deficit Disorder in Adults: Practical Help for Sufferers and Their Spouses.* Dallas: Taylor Publishing Co., 1992.

Wender, P. H. *The Hyperactive Child, Adolescent and Adult.* New York: Oxford University Press, 1987.

Videos

Barkley, R. *ADHD—What Can We Do?* New York: Guilford Press, 1992.

Barkley, R. *ADHD—What Do We Know?* New York: Guilford Press, 1992.

Levoie, R. *How Difficult Can This Be? Understanding Learning Disabilities through the F.A.T. City Workshop.* East Norwalk, CT: CALLD, 1990.

Phelan, T. *Attention Deficit Hyperactivity Disorder* [two-part video and book]. Glen Ellyn, IL: Child Management, Inc., 1990.

Books for Young People

Betancourt, J. *My Name Is Brain—Brian.* New York: Scholastic, Inc., 1993.

Blume, Judy. *Tales of a Fourth-Grade Nothing.* South Holland, IL: Yearling, 1972, 1991.

Cummings, R., and G. Fisher. *The Survival Guide for Teenagers with LD (Learning Differences).* Minneapolis: Free Spirit Publishing, Inc., 1993.

De Clements, B. *Sixth Grade Can Really Kill You.* New York: Scholastic, Inc., 1985.

Dunn, K. B., and A. B. Dunn. *Trouble with School: A Family Story with Learning Disabilities.* Minneapolis: Free Spirit Publishing, Inc., 1993.

Fisher, G. L., and R. W. Cummings. *The Survival Guide for Kids with LD.* Minneapolis: Free Spirit Publishing, Inc., 1990.

Fisher, G. L., and R. W. Cummings. *The Survival Guide for Teenagers with LD.* Minneapolis: Free Spirit Publishing, Inc., 1990.

Galvin, M. *Otto Learns about His Medicine.* New York: Magination Press, 1995.

Gehret, J. *Eagle Eyes: A Child's Guide to Paying Attention.* Fairport, NY: Verbal Images Press, 1991.

Gehret, J. *The Don't Give-Up Kid and Learning Differences.* Fairport, NY: Verbal Images Press, 1996.

Getman, G. N. *How to Develop Your Child's Intelligence.* Luverne, MN: G. N. Getman, O. D., 1962.

Gilson, J. *Do Bananas Chew Gum?* New York: Lothrop, Lee and Shepherd, 1980.

Gordon, M. *Jumpin' Johnny Get Back to Work! A Child's Guide to ADHD.* Dewitt, NY: GSI, 1993.

Hayes, M. L. *The Tuned-In, Turned-On Book about Learning Problems,* revised. Novato, CA: Academic Therapy Publications, 1994.

Janover, C. *Josh: A Boy with Dyslexia.* Burlington, VT: Waterfront Books, 1988.

Krauss, R. *Leo, the Late Bloomer.* New York: Windmill, 1971.

Levinson, M. *And Don't Bring Jeremy.* Austin, TX: Holt, Rinehart and Winston, 1985.

Meyer, D. J., P. F. Vadasy, and R. R. Fewell. *Living with a Brother or Sister with Special Needs: A Book for Sibs.* Seattle: University of Washington Press, 1985.

Moser, A. *Don't Pop Your Cork on Mondays.* Kansas City, MO: Landmark Editions, 1988.

Moser, A. *Don't Feed the Monster on Tuesdays.* Kansas City, MO: Landmark Editions, 1994.

Moss, D. *Shelley, the Hyperactive Turtle.* Kensington, MD: Woodbine House, 1991.

Moss, R. A., and H. H. Dunlap. *Why Johnny Can't Concentrate: Coping with Attention Deficit Problems.* New York: Bantam Books, 1990.

Nadeau, K. G., and E. B. Dixon. *Learning to Slow Down and Pay Attention.* Annandale, VA: Chesapeake Psychological Publications, 1993.

Quinn, P. O., and J. Stern. *Putting on the Brakes: Activity Book for Young People with ADHD.* New York: Magination Press, 1993.

Roby, C. *When Learning Is Tough: Kids Talk about Their Learning Disabilities.* Grove, IL: Albert Whitman & Company, 1994.

Rodgers, Mary. *Freaky Friday.* New York: Harper & Row, 1972.

Shreve, S. *The Flunking of Joshua Bates.* New York: Scholastic, Inc., 1984.

Smith, S. L. *Different Is Not Bad, Different Is the World.* Longmont, CO: Sopris West, 1994.

Viorst, Judith. *Alexander and the Terrible, Horrible, No Good, Very Bad Day.* New York: Aladdin Books, 1987.

INDEX

219